WHAT DOES JUDAISM SAY ABOUT...?

LIBRARY OF JEWISH KNOWLEDGE
Geoffrey Wigoder, General Editor of the Series

The Jews of the United States
What Does Judaism Say About . . . ?
Bible and Civilization
Biblical Archaeology
Kabbalah

𝕿𝖍𝖊 𝕹𝖊𝖜 𝖄𝖔𝖗𝖐 𝕿𝖎𝖒𝖊𝖘

Library of Jewish Knowledge

WHAT DOES JUDAISM SAY ABOUT...?

by LOUIS JACOBS

QUADRANGLE / THE NEW YORK TIMES BOOK CO.

Published in the Western Hemisphere by
QUADRANGLE/THE NEW YORK TIMES BOOK CO.
10 East 53 Street, New York, N.Y. 10022.
Distributed in Canada by Fitzhenry & Whiteside, Ltd., Toronto.

ISBN 0-8129-0349-8
Library of Congress Catalog Card Number 73-77032

Manufactured in the United States of America

Contents

Introduction

Although the topics in this book are arranged for convenience in alphabetical order, it is neither an encyclopedia nor a dictionary of the Jewish religion. The aim of this book is limited to the consideration of themes widely discussed in the contemporary world in their relationship to Judaism. Consequently, the subjects are not examined primarily from the point of view of Jewish history. The purpose is rather to see what Judaism has to say now about these issues. With this aim in mind it has been difficult to avoid entirely a somewhat didactic, though it is hoped not a sermonic, form. Most of the topics discussed are also not those one would normally find in a Jewish encyclopedia.

The major obstacle to any endeavor of the kind attempted here is the difficulty in pinning down the entity called "Judaism." It is acknowledged that the title: *What does Judaism say about . . . ?* begs the question in that it assumes that the answer is there to be found. The truth is, of course, that Judaism is not monolithic, with entirely consistent views on all topics. One can only think in terms of a consensus of opinion among the great teachers of Judaism and frequently even that cannot be discovered. Whether any writer on religion can be entirely objective is a moot point. In a book of this nature he would be wise not even to try. Subjectivity is here a virtue in that it calls attention to the complexity of the ideas found in Judaism so that one man's conclusions, influenced by his personal predilections, are bound to be different from the conclusions drawn by others. Without this kind of reservation, the exponent of Jewish attitudes toward complicated moral and religious problems soon finds himself speaking of *the* Jewish view when what he is really putting forward is *a* Jewish view—his own.

There are many positions about which it can be stated with considerable ease and clarity that Judaism is either for or against them. Judaism is for justice and compassion and it is opposed to idolatry, oppression, and hatred. On such themes as ambition, happiness, infallibility, optimism,

1

and stoicism the answers are bound to be far more elusive. The method adopted here is first to discover whether a given topic has been discussed directly in the classical sources of Judaism or, if not, whether an attitude can be inferred from statements in these sources. The sources may display a variety of opinions on the matter and it is then necessary to try to discover which is the more authoritative. With regard to some problems there are fresh insights arrived at only in more recent times, which render precarious a direct application of the ancient teachings to the new situation. The only approach is to note tendencies and suggestions, avoiding dogmatism as far as possible, and to resist the temptation to write a collection of Responsa.

Some topics have been treated in greater length than others, either because of their importance or because there is more material on them in the Jewish sources. For most of the topics comprehensive bibliographies are not available, but the attention of the reader is called to books and articles, especially in English, in which relevant discussions are to be found.

Most of the topics examined are controversial. Their consideration may stimulate further controversy. If it does, so much the better. Easy answers to questions on which men of goodwill are divided are generally bogus solutions. There is much warrant in the Jewish tradition for the view, in the words of Maharal of Prague, that the search for the Torah is itself Torah.

Abortion

The main Rabbinic statement regarding abortion occurs in the Mishnah (*Oholot* 7:6). The date of the passage is uncertain but is not later than the end of the second century C.E. The passage reads:

> *If a woman is in hard travail (she finds it extremely hard to give birth to her child and there is consequently danger to her life) her child must be cut up while it is in her womb and brought out limb by limb, since the life of the mother has priority over the life of the child. But if the greater part of it has already emerged (from the womb) it may not be touched, since the claim of one life cannot override the claim of another life.*

The meaning of this is clear. It is not permitted to murder one person in order to save the life of another. Consequently, once the greater part of the child has emerged from the womb it is considered as if the child had been born and the child is then a person in Jewish law. The life of the mother must not be saved by destroying that of her child. But while the child is still in the womb it is not a person in law. To destroy a fetus is not to commit an act of murder, so that when the fetus is destroyed in order to save the mother's life it is not comparable to the case of murdering one *person* in order to save the life of another.

The Babylonian Talmud (*Sanhedrin* 72b) takes up the matter further. Although it is not permitted to murder one person in order to save the life of another in normal circumstances, it is permitted to kill a potential murderer if this is the only way in which the life of his intended victim can be saved. The technical term for a potential murderer is *rodef*, "a pursuer," i.e., one who pursues another in order to kill him. Why, then, asks the Talmud, does the Mishnah make a distinction between the fetus and the child the greater part of which has emerged? True, in the

3

latter case the child is a *person* (the term for this is *nefesh*, "a life") but i.
he not a *rodef*? That is to say, it is the child which threatens the life of the
mother and the law is that a *rodef* must be killed in order to save the life
of his intended victim, and this applies even if the *rodef* is a minor and so
not responsible for his actions. The answer given in the Talmud is that
the mother is not "pursued" by the child but by "Heaven," i.e., it is the
result of natural causes and hence the child's life cannot be made forfeit
on the grounds that he is a *rodef*.

The famous French commentator Rashi summarizes the Talmudic
argument as follows: The question of *rodef* can be disregarded since it is
all due to natural causes. Therefore the principle applies that it is forbidden to murder one person in order to save the life of another so that
once the child has acquired the status of a person (*nefesh*), i.e., when the
greater part has emerged, it is forbidden to destroy him even to save the
mother's life. But a fetus is not a person (*nefesh*) and its destruction is
not an act of murder. Consequently, the fetus must be destroyed if this
is the only way in which the mother's life can be saved. Other commentators interpret the Talmudic passage differently from Rashi but Rashi's
interpretation seems the most plausible and is generally followed.

Nowadays, the problem of whether or not an abortion is permitted in
Jewish law depends, then, on the question of whether the destruction of
a fetus is considered to be homicide. If it were, no abortion would ever
be permitted. But since the fetus is not a person in law its destruction
is not an act of homicide. All the codifiers agree, therefore, as the Mishnah
rules, that where the life of the mother is at stake an abortion is not only
permitted in Jewish law but must be performed.

However, cases of abortion in order to save the life of the mother
(as in the Mishnah) are, nowadays, extremely rare, if they occur at all.
When abortion is discussed it is in the context of terminating an unwanted
pregnancy. Although feticide is not homicide, the whole tenor of the
Talmudic discussions on the subject suggests that it is, nonetheless, a
serious offense and it follows, therefore, that it is only to be undertaken
for the weightiest reasons. The codifiers are divided on what would be
considered weighty reasons for terminating a pregnancy. Many of them
permit abortion when the birth of the child would cause the mother to
lose her sanity. Many of them would permit it if the doctors are of the
opinion that the child would be born seriously deformed or as an
imbecile. (The case of the thalidomide babies is one instance of this.)
Others would permit it in cases where the pregnancy is the result of rape,

especially the rape of a married woman. None would permit abortion for economic reasons or where the child is simply unwanted.

An excellent summary of all these views is given in English by David M. Feldman: *Birth Control in Jewish Law*, New York, 1968, part 5, pp. 251–294.

Adoption

In ancient Near Eastern civilizations, legal adoption was recognized. There are references to it, for example, in the Code of Hammurabi, which dates from around 1700 B.C.E. Yet there are no laws regarding adoption in the Bible. We read in the Book of Genesis (15:2–3):

> And Abram said: "O Lord God, what wilt Thou give me, seeing I go hence childless, and he that shall be possessor of my house is Eliezer of Damascus?" And Abram said: "Behold, to me Thou has given no seed, and, lo, one born in my house is to be mine heir."

But it is not stated that Abram adopted Eliezer as his son and that he would inherit as a son. It would seem from the verse in Exodus (2:10) that Moses was adopted by Pharaoh's daughter.

> And the child grew, and she brought him unto Pharaoh's daughter, and he became her son.

This presumably refers to the situation in Egyptian and not in Israelite law. In the Book of Ruth (4:16–17) we read that Naomi took Ruth's child and became nurse to it and her neighbors declared that Naomi had given birth to a son but this hardly refers to legal adoption. The closest we come to legal adoption in the Bible is the verse in Esther (2:7):

> And he brought up Hadassah, that is Esther, his uncle's daughter: for she had neither father nor mother and the maiden was of beautiful form and fair to look on; and when her father and mother were dead, Mordecai took her for his own daughter.

The background, however, is that of the Persian Empire in which legal adoption may have been recognized. It is interesting that, according to some of the Rabbis, Mordecai did not adopt Esther as his daughter but

6

married her. In all events there is no definite evidence that Biblical law knew of legal adoption and the evidence points, in fact, the other way.

In Rabbinic times, although Roman law does know of legal adoption, no provisions are made for it in Rabbinic law. In Rabbinic literature the case of Pharaoh's daughter (*Megillah* 13a) and that of Naomi (*Sanhedrin* 19b) are quoted in support of the view that one who brings up an orphan in his household is considered by Scripture as if he were the father of the child. But it should be noted that those passages are non-legal. They do convey the Rabbinic view that it is exceedingly meritorious to look after orphaned children but the references are to foster parentage, not to legal adoption. The closest Rabbinic law comes to adoption is the institution of the *apotropos,* "legal guardian." (It is significant that a Greek word is used.) Trustworthy men would themselves undertake, or be appointed by the Court, to look after the estate of orphans and there are detailed instructions in the Talmud as to how they were to carry out their duties. The orphans are not, however, the legal heirs of their guardian so that it remains true to say that Rabbinic law does not know of legal adoption. There is nothing, however, to prevent foster parents from making a will in favor of the children they bring up.

In such matters Jewish courts have the power to introduce new legislation. Thus in the State of Israel the Adoption of Children Law of 1960 empowers a court to grant an adoption order for children under the age of 18, and this applies not only to orphans but to children whose natural parents wish them to be adopted. Outside Israel Jews are, of course, governed in these matters by the laws of the country in which they reside.

For all that, an adopted child is not treated as a natural child in every respect. If, for example, Jewish parents adopt a non-Jewish child the child does not become Jewish automatically but requires to be converted formally to the Jewish faith. The laws of consanguinity would not apply to the child in respect of the near relatives of his adopted parents. He may marry, for instance, the natural daughter of his adopted parents. Strictly speaking, the laws of mourning to be observed after the death of a parent do not apply to a child in respect of his adopted parents, but there is no reason why he should not observe them and the general practice is for him to do so. There is some debate as to whether the child should be called to the Torah by the name of his adopted father: "A son of B." Whether the child is a Kohen, Levite, or Israelite depends on the status of his natural, not his adopted, father.

Advertising

Advertising on the vast scale in which it is now practiced in the mass media is a modern phenomenon. Particularly in the United States, Jews have been prominent in this important branch of commercial activity. The ethics of advertising have been widely discussed. When considering the views of Judaism on this subject, it must be appreciated that since advertising in the modern sense could not have been noted in the classical sources of the Jewish faith, it is basically a matter of applying the ethical principles that are found there to the new situation.

Let us first mention the few references to any kind of advertising in the Bible and Talmud. Sellers of goods must have had some methods of bringing the attention of prospective customers to their wares but there are very few indications of how this was done in practice. No doubt the most usual method was for people with goods to sell to proclaim the excellence of their wares in the market place. Perhaps the prophet's admonition (Isaiah 55:1–2) is based on such proclamations by the merchants:

> Ho, every one that thirsteth,
> come ye for water.
> And he that hath no money;
> Come ye, buy and eat;
> Yea, come, buy wine and milk
> Without money and without price.
> Wherefore do ye spend money for
> that which is not bread?
> And your gain for that which
> satisfiest not?
> Hearken diligently unto Me, and
> eat ye that which is good.
> And let your soul delight itself in fatness!

Similarly, there are references in the Talmudic literature to peddlers hawking their goods. A well-known Talmudic passage (*Avodah Zarah* 19b) tells of the third-century Palestinian teacher, R. Alexandri, that he once entered the market place and called out: "Who wants life?" Naturally, all the folk there came to buy the elixir of life he was offering for sale, whereupon he quoted the verses: "Who is the man that desireth life . . . ? Keep thy tongue from evil, and thy lips from speaking guile" (Psalms 34:13–14).

One of the greatest of the Jewish moralists, R. Moses Ḥayyim Luzzatto (b. Padua, 1707, d. Ereẓ Israel, 1747), was the author of *Mesillat Yesharim* ("Path of the Upright") in which the road to saintly living is marked out. The 11th chapter of this frequently studied book describes in detail the sins to which most men are prone. Luzzatto first quotes the Rabbinic saying that the energetic will succeed (*Pesaḥim* 50b) and the verse in the Book of Proverbs (10:4): "The hand of the diligent makes rich." These sayings demonstrate, says Luzzatto, that it is quite worthy and even admirable for a man to praise his wares in order to persuade others to buy them. But, Luzzatto goes on to say, there is a stern admonition in the Torah: "You shall not wrong one another" (Leviticus 25:17) which, according to the Rabbis, applies to every form of deceitful dealing and to all men (*Ḥullin* 94a). Consequently, a man must always be on his guard not to be led on from legitimate praise of his wares to the exaggerated extolling that amounts to deceit. Luzzatto quotes in this connection the verse: "The remnant of Israel shall not do iniquity, nor speak lies; neither shall a deceitful tongue be found in their mouth" (Zephaniah 3:13).

Luzzatto refers to the Talmudic discussion in tractate *Bava Meẓia* 60a–b. Here it is stated that it is not permitted to paint old goods so that they appear to be new for this is to mislead the customers. Furthermore, while there is strong objection to painting old goods so that they appear to be new, there is no objection to painting designs on new goods in order to render them more attractive. The principle which emerges clearly from this and from similar passages is that it is perfectly in order to improve goods and to sing their praises provided there is no misrepresentation. Luzzatto (in Mordecai Kaplan's translation, Philadelphia, 1936, p. 77) puts it in this way:

> *"But," you will say, "how, in the course of bargaining, can we avoid trying to convince our neighbor that the article*

we want to sell him is worth the price we are asking?" There is an unmistakable distinction between fraudulent and honest persuasion. It is perfectly proper to point out to the buyer any good quality which the thing for sale really possesses. Fraud consists in hiding the defects in one's wares and is forbidden. This is an important principle in the matter of business honesty.

On the basis of these principles of strict honesty and integrity, combined with the right of a seller to urge his customers to buy, it is possible to appreciate how the Jewish teachers would view modern advertising. The manufacturer or seller of a product is entitled to engage experts in communication techniques so that what he has to sell will be presented in a way that will attract customers. Advertising has become an industry in its own right and is a legitimate pursuit. What the advertiser must not do is to describe his products as having virtues they do not actually possess. To do this is fraudulent and is strictly forbidden. The problem today is further complicated by the use of exaggerated language. If everyone knows that the claims made for certain products have to be taken with a grain of salt, it can perhaps be argued that no misrepresentation is involved when superlatives are used that are not strictly applicable to the products in question. Matters of this nature can only be left to individual standards of fairness and integrity. The Jew should always seek to be guided by the highest standards of commercial integrity.

Aged, Care of

The Jewish people from its outset has paid particular attention to the welfare of the aged. In many passages in the Bible the "elders" are the wise men, the judges of the people. We read in the Book of Leviticus (19:32):

> *Thou shalt rise up before the hoary head, and honor the face*
> *of the old man, and thou shalt fear thy God: I am the Lord.*

The Rabbis understood this literally, that whenever an old man passes by one should rise to one's feet as a token of respect. The Talmud (*Kiddushin* 33a) states that the third-century Palestinian teacher, R. Johanan, would rise to his feet even when heathens who were old passed by because, he said, they have had so many troubles in their long life, i.e., respect for the aged is based on the many experiences they have had. The whole philosophy of care for the aged is expressed in the Psalmist's poignant cry (Psalms 71:9):

> *Cast me not off in the time of old age;*
> *When my strength faileth, forsake me not!*

When the Book of Deuteronomy speaks of the sufferings of Israel as the result of being conquered by a barbaric nation, it describes (28:50) that nation as "of fierce countenance, that shall not regard the person of the old, nor show favor to the young." Similarly, the prophet Isaiah, speaking of a corrupt generation, describes it (3:5):

> *And the people shall oppress one another,*
> *Every man his fellow, and every man his neighbor;*
> *The child shall behave insolently against the aged,*
> *And the base against the honorable.*

Respect for the aged became a dominant idea and was expressed in daily Jewish life. The standard Code of Jewish Law, the *Shulḥan Arukh,*

In modern times stress is laid on keeping the aged occupied. These two octo-genarians are working at bookbinding in one of the "Lifeline for the Old" workshops in Jerusalem.

states the rules about rising before the aged and gives the definition of old age as 70 years (*Yoreh Deah* 244:1). It is interesting that while the Levites serving in the Temple were retired at the age of 50 (Numbers 8:25–26), because the work was demanding, it was not customary for Rabbis to retire if they could still carry out their tasks adequately. There are a number of instances in Jewish history of Rabbis serving until their death at a very advanced age. R. Hai Gaon, head of the great Babylonian academy in Pumbedita, was 99 years of age when he died in the year 1038 and he was active in his office to the very end. R. David Ibn Abi Zimra, after 40 years of leadership of the Jewish community in Egypt, settled in

Erez Israel where he was active until his death at the age of 94 in 1573. The famous Talmudic scholar R. Aryeh Leib b. Asher became Rabbi of Metz at the age of 70 and served in that capacity until his death in 1785 at the age of 90. Legend has it that the community leaders, though impressed by his learning, were reluctant to appoint him because they wanted a Rabbi who would serve a lengthy term of office; he assured them that they would have at least 20 years of service from him.

The aged were, then, to be highly respected and regarded. Care for the aged who were poor or infirm and unable to look after themselves was, in Jewish life, a special instance of the general obligation of charity. But during the past 200 years or so most Jewish communities have made special arrangements for the care of the aged. In comparatively modern times each Jewish community of any size has established an old-age home (*moshav zekenim*).

As a result of improved methods of healing and environmental factors, the expectancy of life has been greatly increased in our day and the need to care for the aged is becoming more pressing. Some thinkers have even dared to suggest that the time might come when the extremely aged will be painlessly removed, following the example of some primitive societies in which old people quietly leave the tribal home to die away from the haunts of men so as not to be a burden to the young. Needless to say such an attitude is utterly abhorrent to Judaism. There is much wisdom in the comment of Baḥya Ibn Asher (13th century) on the Fifth Commandment (Exodus 20:12):

> *Honor thy father and thy mother, that thy days may be long upon the land which the Lord thy God giveth thee.*

Baḥya remarks that it is undoubtedly true that care of aged parents can be a severe burden but in return God promises longevity to those who shoulder the burden.

Alcohol

Religious people have entertained two opposing views on the use of alcohol. Some, aware of the evils of drunkenness, have banned all strong drinks. Others have not only permitted the use of alcohol but have advocated it as a religious duty. It is not surprising, therefore, that in the classical sources of Judaism there are to be found many differing attitudes. In some of these sources the danger to morals of wine-drinking is stressed while in others wine-drinking is strongly advocated. It might be mentioned, incidentally, that wine was the intoxicating beverage in ancient Erez Israel because grapes were plentiful. In ancient Babylon wine was more scarce and here the usual intoxicant was beer made from dates, which were plentiful in Babylon. In the Babylonian Talmud (*Pesaḥim* 107a) this beer made from dates was called "the wine of the country," i.e., the national drink.

In ancient Israel there were men who took a Nazirite vow. A whole chapter in the Book of Numbers (Chapter 6) deals with the laws governing the Nazirite. Among the rules he took upon himself to observe were to let his hair grow long, to avoid having any contact with a corpse, and to drink no wine. The later Jewish teachers were divided on the interpretation of the Nazirite laws. Do they mean that to avoid wine in this way is an ideal? Some of the Rabbis said, indeed, that the Nazirite is a holy man but others said, on the contrary, he is a sinner because he denies himself the wine that is God's gift to man (*Ta'anit* 11a). There is also a Biblical reference to a family which abstained from wine as well as from building houses and cultivating the soil. These men, the Rechabites (the descendants of Jonadab son of Rechab), were held up as an example of loyalty and obedience by the Prophet Jeremiah (Jeremiah 35), but there is no suggestion in that chapter that it was advisable for others to follow the way of the Rechabites. (Various non-Jewish temperance groups call themselves Rechabites.) The priests in the Temple were not allowed to drink wine immediately before they performed their service. In the Book of Leviticus (10:8–11) we read:

The drunken Noah being covered by his two sons Shem and Japheth (Genesis 9:20–24). Detail from the *Golden Haggadah*, Barcelona c. 1320.

> *And the Lord spoke unto Aaron, saying: "Drink no wine*
> *nor strong drink, then, nor thy sons with thee, when ye go*
> *into the tent of meeting, that ye die not: it shall be a statute*
> *for ever throughout your generations. And that ye may put*
> *difference between the holy and the common, and between*
> *the unclean and the clean; and that ye may teach the children*
> *of Israel all the statutes which the Lord has spoken unto him*
> *by the hands of Moses."*

On the basis of the last verse—"that ye may teach . . ."—the Rabbis (*Ketubbot* 10b) rule that a teacher who drinks even a small quantity of wine must not give decisions in Jewish law because he lacks the clarity of mind required for a balanced judgment.

The misfortunes which result from drunkenness are pointed out in the stories of Noah (Genesis 9:20–24) and Lot (Genesis 19:30–38). The fruit eaten by Adam when he sinned (Genesis 3) is not, in the Jewish tradition, an apple; one of the Rabbis (Midrash, *Genesis Rabbah* 15:7) argues that it was the grape, thus making it responsible for bringing sin into the world. The Prophet Isaiah, speaking of drunken orgies, says (Isaiah 28:7–8):

> *But these also reel through wine,*
> *And stagger through strong drink;*
> *The priest and the prophet reel*
> *through strong drink,*
> *They are confused because of wine,*
> *They stagger because of strong drink,*
> *They reel in vision, they totter in judgment.*
> *For all tables are full of filthy vomit,*
> *And no place is clean.*

The stubborn and rebellious son in the Book of Deuteronomy (21:18–21) is described (in verse 20) as "a glutton and a drunkard."

But all this must certainly not be understood as a blanket disapproval of imbibing strong drink. On the contrary, the Psalmist (Psalms 104:15) praises God for "wine to gladden the heart of man, oil to make his face shine." The Book of Proverbs (31:4–7) says:

> *It is not for kings, O Lemuel, it is not for kings to drink*
> *wine;*
> *Nor for princes to say: "Where is strong drink?"*

Lest they drink, and forget that which is decreed,
And pervert the justice due to any that is afflicted.
Give strong drink unto him that is ready to perish,
And wine unto the bitter in soul;
Let him drink, and forget his poverty.
And remember his misery no more.

On the basis of this it was the custom in Rabbinic times to bring wine as a gift when visiting mourners. In one passage in the Babylonian Talmud (*Eruvin* 65a) it is said that wine was only created for the purpose of comforting mourners. In the same passage, in hyperbolic vein, it is said that when wine is poured out like water in a house there is blessing in that house. In the same passage again (65b) it is said in punning fashion that a man's character can be discerned by his *kos* ("cup"), his *kis* ("money-bag"), and his *ka'as* ("anger"), i.e., by how he conducts himself when he has partaken of wine, with his wealth, and when he loses his temper.

On the verse in the Book of Judges (9:13) in which it is said that wine "cheers God and man" the Rabbis (*Berakhot* 35a) comment that wine "cheers" God because the Levites in the Temple only sang at the time when the libations of wine were poured out on the altar. This idea of using wine in God's service was extended by the Rabbis to the use of wine for *kiddush* and *havdalah*, on Sabbaths and festivals. At the *seder* on Passover every Jew was expected to drink four cups of wine. It has been argued that the reason Jews on the whole stay sober and inebriation is rare among them is that Jewish children are accustomed from their infancy to partake of wine in small quantities when *kiddush* is recited. Especially on the festival of Purim it was held to be a religious obligation to drink wine. In a well-known passage in the Babylonian Talmud (*Megillah* 7b) the rule is recorded that a man is obliged to become so intoxicated on Purim that he is unaware whether he is blessing Mordecai or cursing Haman. This is the only instance of an injunction to get drunk in the whole of Jewish literature, and most of the commentators argue that it was not, in fact, to be taken literally. But some pious Jews, in their anxiety to obey Rabbinic teaching, did take it literally. It is reliably reported of the founder of the Lithuanian Musar movement, R. Israel Salanter (d. 1883), a man noted for his austere, puritanical way of life, that on Purim he would imbibe piously until he really became drunk.

In the Ḥasidic movement alcohol was partaken of in order to dispel feelings of sadness—a cardinal sin for the Ḥasidim—and to awaken enthusiasm in God's service. The opponents of the movement ridiculed the Ḥasidim for their addiction to the bottle. A popular Ḥasidic saying is that it is a great thing to drink a glass of brandy (or vodka) because drinking it the Jew says: "Blessed art Thou, O Lord our God, King of the universe, by whose word all things come into being." It became a custom among Hasidim for a member of the group celebrating a happy event in his family circle to provide alcohol and cakes for all the congregants after the synagogue service. This Ḥasidic practice has now been adopted by many non-Ḥasidic Jews. The Ḥasidim did not believe in private drinking. Even when indulged in, drinking was to be a group activity with the aim of strengthening feelings of friendship and companionship. Drunkenness was severely frowned upon and the Ḥasid who could not hold his liquor was despised. The probably unfair Yiddish saying: *shikker iz a goy* ("only a gentile gets drunk") is indicative of the way in which the Jews of Eastern Europe looked upon unbridled indulgence in alcohol.

On the whole, it is true to say, Judaism urges its adherents to steer a middle course. Drunkenness is held to be wrong and un-Jewish but complete rejection of alcohol is not advocated. A man may drink but how many drinks he should have is left to him to decide as a free human being aware of the perils of alcoholism. According to the great Jewish teacher Naḥmanides (1195–1270) in his commentary to the Torah, this is implied in the verse: "Speak unto all the congregation of the children of Israel, and say unto them: Ye shall be holy; for I the Lord your God am holy" (Leviticus 19:2). Naḥmanides points out that certain things are categorically forbidden by the Torah but the command to be holy implies that a man must not overindulge even in those things that are permitted. Among other examples Naḥmanides mentions is indulgence in alcohol. He uses in this connection the remarkable expression "a scoundrel with the permission of the Torah," i.e., it is possible for a man to commit no formal wrong and yet so indulge himself in permitted things that he frustrates the whole purpose of Judaism.

Alienation

Alienation, in the sense in which this term is frequently used nowadays especially by existentialist thinkers, refers to the feeling of estrangement modern man is said to experience. Man finds himself in a hostile world which seems to have no purpose. Not only are his desires frustrated but the "guarantee" of a meaningful world that medieval man is said to have had is no longer available. The only incontrovertible fact confronting man is the consciousness of his death. Because he cannot give meaning to his life it is modern man's situation to be estranged from his being. He is in a perpetual state of anxiety (*Angst*). He knows that there are other beings in the world but these make demands on him that he cannot satisfy so that he is haunted by feelings of guilt. Sartre has said that "the other is Hell." The only hope that is held out by the purveyors of this stark philosophy is for man to recognize his situation and live with it, acknowledging that he cannot do anything about it. The alien can only find cold comfort in the thought that his dream of finding a home will never be realized.

Basically, the philosophy of alienation is atheistic. Judaism teaches that there is a God who has a purpose for man, even though, some Jewish thinkers have held, we cannot fully fathom that purpose. Judaism, too, knows of a kind of alienation, of a divine dissatisfaction with things as they are. The Psalmist (Psalms 119:19) cries out: "I am a sojourner on earth." The Midrash (*Ecclesiastes Rabbah*) comments on the verse: "Neither is the soul satisfied" (Ecclesiastes 6:7) that the soul is like a princess who is married to a commoner. The most precious gifts her husband gives her fail to satisfy her. In the same way, the soul is dissatisfied with all the pleasures of the world because it comes from God and belongs to a higher order of existence. But for Judaism man's case is not hopeless. True he is estranged from God by the mere fact of his finite existence but he has been given the *mitzvot*, the precepts of the Torah, to bring him nearer to God, the source of his being.

19

R. Moses Ḥayyim Luzzatto's *The Path of the Upright* has been mentioned earlier in this book. In his introduction Luzzatto asserts (ed. Kaplan, p. 15):

> *No reasonable person can believe that the purpose for which man was created is attainable in this world. For what is man's life in this world? Who is really happy here, and who content? "The number of our years is threescore and ten, or even by reason of strength fourscore years; yet is their pride but travail and vanity" (Psalms 90:20), because of the suffering, the sickness, the pain and vexations which man has to endure, and finally death. Hardly one in a thousand finds that the world yields him true pleasure and contentment. And even that one, though he live a thousand years, passes away and is as though he had never been.*

Luzzatto's conclusion is that man's true home is not here at all but in the Hereafter where he can enjoy God's presence for all eternity. But this world is nonetheless highly significant, for it is by his deeds here that man makes the good his own and so comes near to God that he might merit the glory of His presence in the Hereafter.

For many today this statement of Luzzatto's is too otherworldly. But it is a classical Jewish approach to the problem of alienation and provides an insight into how even those of us who are not prepared to go the whole way with Luzzatto might come to grips with the problem.

Ambition

There are various types of ambition. It would be unnatural if the young did not dream of getting on. Most people want to carve out a better life for themselves and their families. Parents like to see their children successful. "That is my son the doctor" is more than a stale Jewish joke. Yet on the debit side there are the frustrations which stem from unrealized ambition, the rat race, the ceaseless effort to keep up with the Joneses. In this and in other matters balance and proportion are everything. That is why, in the Jewish tradition, one finds teachings which accept and even advocate ambition and others which deprecate it.

In praise of ambition are many of the maxims in the Book of Proverbs. Typical is the verse (22:29):

> *Seest thou a man diligent in his work? He shall stand before*
> *kings: He shall not stand before mean men.*

The Midrash (*Canticles Rabbah* 1:1) applies the verse to Joseph's rise to fame from a poor slave boy to ruler of Egypt. On the verse: "The Lord thy God will bless thee *in all that thou doest*" (Deuteronomy 15:18) the Rabbis (*Yalkut* to the verse) observe that God's blessing does not come automatically but only after man's own efforts to earn a living. The man who is quick to take advantage of a situation and profit by it is called by the Rabbis (*Pesaḥim* 50b) "one who is energetic and gains thereby." As for spiritual ambition, there is the saying of a late Midrash (*Tanna de-Vei Eliyahu* 25) that every Jew should say: "When will my deeds approach those of my forebears" (in the context, Abraham, Isaac, and Jacob).

The perils of ambition are, on the other hand, pointed out in a number of sayings. The second-century Palestinian teacher R. Eleazar Ha-Kappar said (*Avot* 4:21): "Jealousy, lust, and ambition put a man out of the world" (i.e., destroy him). The meaning is evidently that once a man becomes a slave to these traits his life is not his own. A well-known

Rabbinic saying (*Eruvin* 13b) has it that a heavenly voice proclaimed that the teachings of the School of Hillel were to be preferred to those of the School of Shammai because the Hillelites were more modest and less inclined to claim honors for themselves than were the Shammaites. "To teach you that whoever seeks fame finds fame eluding him while whoever runs away from fame finds that fame runs after him." In another passage (*Avot* 5:19) it is said: "He in whom are these three things is of the disciples of Abraham our father; but he in whom are three other things is of the disciples of Balaam the wicked. A good eye, a humble spirit, and a lowly soul—they in whom are these are of the disciples of Abraham our father. An evil eye, a haughty spirit, and a proud soul—they in whom are these are of the disciples of Balaam the wicked." Abraham is the prototype of the completely unselfish person. He refuses the gifts of the king of Sodom (Genesis 14:22–24) and magnanimously gives Lot the choice of territory (Genesis 13:7–9). Balaam represents the greedy and the grasping, his eye only on personal gain (Numbers 22:2–22). Another second-century Palestinian teacher, Ben Zoma, said (*Avot* 4:1): "Who is rich? He that rejoices in his portion." Some of the Hasidic teachers apply this even to spiritual ambition. While a man must aim high he must be aware of his spiritual and intellectual limitations. He must "rejoice in his portion," even in his spiritual portion. While Maimonides (*Yad, Teshuvah* 5:2) states that since there is freedom of the will every man can become as great as Moses, a famous Hasidic anecdote describes the Hasidic master, R. Zusya of Hanipoli, as saying that on judgment day he will not be asked why he was not Moses but why he was not Zusya! This maxim also occurs in a sermon on the wisdom of contentment by Jacob Anatoli (d. 1256), author of *Malmad ha-Talmidim* ("Goad of the Disciples") (sermon to *Mattot*, p. 152b): "If a man cannot get what he wants he should want what he can get."

Maimonides is aware of the tensions in this matter of ambition when he writes (*Yad, Deot* 3:1):

> *A man may say that since jealousy, lust, ambition, and so forth belong to the evil way and they put a man out of the world, "I shall reject them entirely and go to the opposite extreme," to the extent that he will not eat meat, nor drink wine, nor marry, nor live in a fine house, nor will he wear good clothes, only such garments as sackcloth or coarse wool as do the gentile priests. This, too, belongs to an evil way in which*

it is forbidden to go and one who walks in this way is called a sinner.

Maimonides' advocacy of the "middle way" in all things has been severely criticized. He believes, for example, that excessive generosity should also be avoided and here, it has been argued, Judaism would advocate the extreme. But on ambition Maimonides is surely speaking out of the best traditions of Judaism. A life without any ambition would be deprived of its driving power. God has given mankind the good things of life for man to win and to enjoy. But unbridled ambition is soul-destroying so that the good Jew will not allow himself to become prey to it. He will do his best to achieve whatever he is capable of achieving but proceed always in a spirit of unselfishness and quiet trust in God.

Animals

With Judaism's strong emphasis on the significance of man it is not surprising that many Jewish thinkers have a completely man-centered philosophy according to which animals were created for man's purposes. The Book of Genesis does not state explicitly that animals were created solely for man's benefit, but in the Creation narrative in Genesis man is described as the culmination of God's creative activity, with the corollary that all creatures are subordinate to him (Genesis 1:26–28):

> *And God said: "Let us make man in our image, after our likeness; and let him have dominion over the fish of the sea, and over the fowl of the air, and over the cattle, and over all the earth, and over every creeping thing that creepeth upon the earth." And God created man in his own image, in the image of God created He him; male and female created He them. And God blessed them; and God said unto them: "Be fruitful, and multiply, and replenish the earth, and subdue it; and have dominion over the fish of the sea, and over the fowl of the air, and over every living thing that creepeth upon the earth."*

Saadiah Gaon in his book *Emunot ve-Deot* ("Beliefs and Opinions") (I, 4) gives three possible answers to the question why God created animals and other creatures other than man. The first answer is that God simply willed it so. The second is in order to reveal His wisdom to mankind, and the third that it is to benefit mankind. Maimonides, on the other hand, in his *Guide for the Perplexed* (III, 13) does not consider the question why God created the animals a significant one. God willed it so and it is incorrect to understand the Genesis narrative as implying that animals, sun, moon, and stars were created solely for man.

Another debate between Saadiah and Maimonides is whether animals go to Heaven. Saadiah[1] argues that God does compensate animals with a share in Heavenly bliss for the suffering they undergo when they are slaughtered by man for his food. Maimonides[2] considers the view that animals are recompensed in Heaven to be an alien and un-Jewish one. Judah Halevi in his *Kuzari* (III, 11) discusses the problem of animal suffering, of why nature is "red in tooth and claw." He frankly states that we do not know the answer to this terrible problem but since the wisdom of the Creator is evidenced in the astonishing skill with which the animals are endowed we can only bow in submission. As Judah Halevi puts it:

> *When an evil thought suggests that there is injustice in the circumstance that the hare falls a prey to the lion or wolf, and the fly to the spider, Reason steps in warning him as follows: How can I charge the All-wise with injustice when I am convinced of this justice, and that injustice is out of the question? If the lion's pursuit of the hare and the spider's of the fly were mere accidents, I should assert the necessity of accident. I see, however, that this wise and just Manager of the World equipped the lion with the means for hunting, with ferocity, strength, teeth, and claws, but He furnished the spider with cunning and taught it to weave a net which it constructs without having learnt to do so; how He equipped it with the instruments required, and appointed the fly as its food just as many fishes serve other fishes for food. Can I say aught but that this is the fruit of a wisdom which I am unable to grasp, and that I must submit to Him who is called: "The Rock!—His deeds are perfect" (Deuteronomy 32:4).*

In poetic passages in the Rabbinic literature, however, it is suggested that animals exist solely for man. Thus the Midrash (*Genesis Rabbah* 8:6) remarks that animals, birds, and fishes were created on the analogy of a king who had a tower stocked with all good things. If he receives no guests what pleasure does he derive from so stocking it? Men are God's "guests" and the animals are "stocked" for his benefit. In the Babylonian Talmud (*Shabbat* 77b) it is said in similar vein that God created nothing that is useless, the snail as a cure for scab, the fly as a cure for the sting of a wasp, etc.

A rather different Rabbinic conception is that each species of animal

[1] Saadiah, *Beliefs and Opinions*, III, 17,

[2] Maimonides, *Guide for the Perplexed*, III, 17.

Many medieval illustrations show that pets were a familiar part of the Jewish household. In this Italian *Haggadah* from the 16th century, a cat and a dog are happily consuming the leftovers under the *seder* table.

sings its own particular hymn of glory to its Creator. There is, in fact, an ancient compilation known as *Perek Shirah* ("The Chapter of Song") in which there are listed the particular scriptural verses used by God's creatures as their song of praise to Him[1]—each song appropriate to its speaker. Thus the cattle sing: "Who is like unto Thee, O Lord, among the mighty?" (Exodus 15:11). Birds sing: "Even the sparrow hath found a house, and the swallow a nest for herself, where she may lay her young" (Psalms 84:4). The dog sings: "O come, let us bow down and bend the knee; let us kneel before the Lord our Maker!" (Psalms 95:6).

Judaism teaches that cruelty to animals is strictly forbidden. The Rabbinic name for this offense is *tza'ar ba'ale hayyim* ("pain to living creatures"). A man must look after the animals in his care. He should not eat his own meals before he sees that his animals are fed (*Berakhot* 40a). One of the "seven laws of the sons of Noah" (i.e., laws binding, according to Judaism, on all men, non-Jews as well as Jews) is the prohibition of eating meat from a living animal. The slaughter of animals for food (*shehitah*) must be carried out with a knife free from any notch, there must be no pause while cutting, no pressing of the knife, the knife must

[1] *Jewish Encyclopaedia*, "Shirah, Perek," Vol. XI, pp. 294–296.

not be inserted under the animal's skin, and the knife must be inserted at the right spot, neither too low nor too high. Some authorities have made the plausible suggestion that these laws are intended to avoid unnecessary pain to the animal. It is true that there is a tendency in Rabbinic thought to observe these and similar rules without looking for "reasons" but simply because they are in the Torah, yet this did not prevent some of the medieval commentators from advancing avoidance of cruelty to animals as the motive behind a number of the Biblical laws.[1] Thus the rule that the mother bird be sent away before taking the young (Deuteronomy 22:6–7); the prohibition of slaughtering an animal and its young on the same day (Leviticus 22:28); and of plowing with an ox and an ass together (Deuteronomy 2:10) have all been explained on the grounds that to do those things is to be cruel to animals. This would certainly seem to be the reason for the prohibition of muzzling an ox when it treads out the corn (Deuteronomy 25:4).

The Book of Jonah concludes with the words "and also much cattle" (Jonah 4:11). God wishes to spare not only the human inhabitants of Nineveh but the beasts as well. The Psalmist (Psalms 147:9) praises God who "gives to the beasts their food, and to the young ravens which cry." In a remarkable passage in the Babylonian Talmud (*Bava Meẓia* 85a) it is told how R. Judah the Prince ordered a calf being led to the slaughter to go to its death because "For this thou wast created." He was afflicted with sufferings which did not leave him until he showed compassion to some weasels that were in danger of extinction, saying: "His tender mercies are over all His works" (Psalms 145:9). The point of the story is that while it is permitted to kill animals for food this should be seen as a necessary evil. It was wrong for the great teacher to order the calf to go to the slaughter in order to fulfill its destiny, as it were, since this is a callous attitude. The famous mystic R. Moses Cordovero (1522–70) writes in his little ethical treatise *The Palm Tree of Deborah* (Chapter 3 end):

> *Furthermore, his mercy should extend to all creatures,*
> *neither destroying nor despising any of them. For the Supernal*
> *Wisdom is extended to all created things—minerals, plants,*
> *animals, and humans. This is the reason for the Rabbis*
> *warning us against despising food. In this way man's pity*

[1] Maimonides, *Guide for the Perplexed*, III, 48.

should be extended to all the works of the Blessed One, just as the Supernal Wisdom despises no created thing . . . He should not uproot anything which grows, unless it is necessary, nor kill any living thing unless it is necessary. And he should choose a good death for them, with a knife that has been carefully examined, to have pity on them as far as possible. To sum up, to have pity on all things and not to hurt them depends on wisdom, unless it be to elevate them higher and higher, from plant to animal and from animal to human. In turn it is permitted to uproot the plant and to kill the beast, to bring merit out of demerit.

The general principle which emerges from all these teachings is that animals may be used for man's benefit (otherwise, the Jew would have to be a vegetarian and refuse to wear leather shoes), but the pain caused to the animals should be reduced to the minimum. Also if the pain is excessive and the benefit to man is one he can well do without, it is better not to use animals even when man does benefit. That is why many Jewish teachers refused to countenance the forcible feeding of geese in order to fatten them up for the market and the plucking of feathers from live geese. R. Moses Isserles in his notes to the *Shulḥan Arukh (Even ha-Ezer* 5:14) writes:

Wherever it is for the purpose of healing or for some other purpose there is no prohibition against cruelty to animals. It is consequently permitted to pluck feathers from living geese and there is no objection on the grounds of cruelty to animals. Nevertheless, the [Jewish] world avoids this because this is cruel.

In other words things that are permitted according to the strict letter of the law should be avoided if cruelty is excessive. This means that to some extent the law has to be interpreted in such a way that men must decide for themselves to what extent practices involving cruelty to animals should be accepted or rejected, the test being always whether the cruelty is excessive and whether the benefit to man justifies the act.

On the basis of this a very good case can be made out for vivisection of animals provided safeguards are taken to reduce the pain to a minimum. Here the benefits to medical progress are considerable and the price worth paying. More questionable would be the slaughter of animals in an extremely painful way for their skins and furs, as well as cruel methods used to obtain perfume from animals. There cannot be any decisive ruling on these matters, but well-intentioned Jews will be guided by the principles to which we have referred.

Architecture

There is neither a special Jewish attitude toward architecture nor any specially Jewish architectural style. But Jewish teaching is in favor of sound building and adequate planning. Very revealing is the Rabbinic comparison (*Genesis Rabbah* 1:1) of the Torah to an architect's blueprint. Before God created the world, it is said, He "looked into the Torah" like an architect who first consults his plans before beginning to build. There are many references in both the Bible and the Talmud to building. Especially in tractate *Eruvin* in the Talmud there are numerous accounts of how houses were grouped around a central courtyard. If one opens a copy of this tractate one discovers elaborate diagrams drawn by a medieval commentator to illustrate the details given on these matters.

The second half of the Book of Exodus is devoted largely to a detailed description of the Tabernacle the people erected in the wilderness as a house of God. From the measurements given of the various parts it is clear that the Tabernacle was highly symmetrical. In fact some scholars have tried to construct models of the Tabernacle on the basis of these measurements, while a more modern view is to treat the account as academic with the measurements those of an ideal structure. Ten cubits appear to be the standard, ten being both a natural number (the ten fingers and toes) and a sacred number (the Ten Commandments). In the first book of Kings (Chapters 5–8) there occurs the account of how Solomon built his Temple. From the measurements given it appears that the Temple was a comparatively small building but one of great splendor and magnificence.

The main communal building activity engaged in by Jews throughout the ages was synagogue construction. The architectural styles used for synagogues were generally those of the peoples among whom the Jews resided. In the 19th century many synagogues were built in a Moorish or Oriental style in the belief that this was appropriate to the home of a religion which comes from the East. In modern times there has been

The Nuremberg Reform Synagogue, dating from the late 19th century, is a striking example of the Moorish influence popular in the period.

The interior of the Florence synagogue, built in 1882 and regarded as one of the most beautiful in Europe.

considerable experimentation in synagogue building. The Talmudic rules that the synagogue should be built in the highest part of the town and that it should be higher than all the other buildings in the town, although recorded in the *Shulḥan Arukh* (*Oraḥ Ḥayyim* 150), could obviously not be adhered to in towns where the majority of inhabitants were not Jews and these rules have consequently become a dead letter. Based on the Kabbalah is the rule, also recorded in the *Shulḥan Arukh* (*Oraḥ Ḥayyim* 90:4), that a synagogue should have twelve windows, corresponding to the twelve tribes of Israel, because each tribe has its own window to Heaven. But while some synagogues still follow this rule others do not.

Apart from these few details considerable license is given to the synagogue architect. Relevant in this connection is the Responsum of the outstanding legal authority R. Ezekiel Landau of Prague (d. 1793). The old synagogue in Trieste was destroyed by fire and a magnificent new synagogue was erected in 1787. A scholar in Trieste consulted Rabbi

B'nai Israel Synagogue in Millburn, N.J. in which the Magen David is prominently featured, as is a sculpture by Herbert Ferber.

Landau for his ruling since it was intended to build the new synagogue with an octagonal shape. The question was whether a synagogue has to have any particular form or style. Rabbi Landau's reply was published in his Responsa collections, *Noda Bi-Yhudah* ("Second Series," *Orah Hayyim*, No. 18). The learned Rabbi argues that since there are no rules in the Talmud or the Codes as to the shape of the synagogue, it is safe to assume that the normal oblong shape has no special sanctity and an octagonal or, for that matter, any other shape is perfectly in order. However, Rabbi Landau lived at a time when the winds of change were blowing in the Jewish world. He, like many of the Rabbis of his day, was suspicious of innovations which threatened the traditional pattern of Jewish life. Consequently, he concludes:

> *All this I said in accordance with the strict letter of the law. But I wonder why they should want to do this and I thought that perhaps they saw something like this in the palaces of princes or in some other houses and they wanted to copy it. But the truth is that it is not proper for us in our exile to copy princes and to be envious of them. If this was the reason, I recite for it the verse: "For Israel has forgotten his Maker, and built palaces" (Hosea 8:14). It is better, therefore, not to change any of the old customs, especially in this generation. But if their*

reason was that there would be more room if the synagogue is built according to these specifications there is not the slightest fear of anything being wrong.

This Responsum became the official ruling on the question and has made possible the richest variety of architectural styles for synagogue building. It might be mentioned that the practice of using the Shield of David (*Magen David*) as a feature of synagogue decoration or of building the synagogue in the shape of a *Magen David* finds no support at all in the Jewish traditions. Professor G. Scholem in his essay on the Shield of David[1] has demonstrated that the *Magen David* is not a specifically Jewish symbol at all and that its use in synagogue buildings dates from the beginning of the 19th century when Jews who observed crosses on church buildings wished to have a symbol of their own.

[1] *The Messianic Idea in Judaism,* pp. 257–281, New York, 1971; see *Encyclopaedia Judaica,* Vol. 11, cols. 687ff.

Art

The ancient Hebrews clearly had a deep appreciation of beauty and a fondness for beautiful things. The chapters of the Book of Exodus (25 to end) dealing with the Tabernacle and its furnishings are a typical example of the use of aesthetically satisfying objects for the adornment of God's house. Gold, silver, brass, and wood, fine yarns and decorated cloths, as well as various precious stones, were used for the purpose of building and decorating the Tabernacle. A key verse in this connection is: "Make holy garments for Aaron thy brother, *for splendor and for beauty*" (Exodus 28:2). The very glib statement that is sometimes made that the Greeks believed in the holiness of beauty while the Hebrews believed in the beauty of holiness is a superficial generalization far off the mark.

The Rabbis stress the idea of *hiddur mitzvah* ("adorning the precepts"), i.e., of carrying out the precepts of the Torah in as beautiful a way as possible. (A general Rabbinic awareness of the psychological value of beauty is expressed in the saying in the Babylonian Talmud (*Berakhot* 57b) that a beautiful wife, a beautiful home, and beautiful furniture broaden a man's outlook.) The verse: "This is my God and I will glorify Him" (Exodus 15:2) is read by the Rabbis as "I will adorn Him." This means in the words of the Rabbis (*Shabbat* 133b): "Be beautiful in His presence when carrying out the precepts. Make in His presence a beautiful *sukkah*, a beautiful *lulav*, a beautiful *shofar*, beautiful *zizit*, a beautiful *sefer torah* written for His sake by an expert scribe, using fine ink and a good pen, and wrap it round with fine cloths." While until modern times there was not much secular art among Jews the talents of artists and craftsmen were used in preparing ceremonial objects. Biblical books written by hand, manuscripts adorned with figures and letters, spice-boxes for the *havdalah* ceremony, *menorot* for Ḥanukkah are all well-known examples.

In a remarkable passage Maimonides (*Yad, Issurei Mizbeaḥ,* 7:11) extends the Rabbinic principle. He quotes the Rabbinic list of oils to be used in preparing the meal-offering in Temple times, some of which were finer than others but all of which were fit for use. Maimonides writes:

> *Since they are all fit to be used why are they listed? It is to tell you which is the finest, which average, and which inferior so that one who desires to have merit should overcome his selfish nature and give generously when bringing his offering so that it is from the choicest of that species. Behold, the Torah says: "And Abel, he also brought of the firstlings of his flock and the fat thereof. And the Lord had respect unto Abel and to his offering" (Genesis 4:4). The same applies to whatever is done for the sake of the good God; it should be from the good and the beautiful. If a man builds a synagogue it should be more beautiful than his own house. If he gives food to the hungry it should be from the best and tastiest food on his table. If he clothes the naked he should provide them with the most beautiful garments he can find. If he devotes something to the sanctuary it should be from the finest of his goods, and so it is said: "All fat [i.e., the best] is the Lord's" (Leviticus 3:16).*

A question that has been widely discussed is whether the prohibition of image-making inhibits painting, drawing, and sculpture. The evidence is not too clear or rather it would appear that Jews in different periods interpreted the relevant verses in such a way that some permitted pictorial representation while others prohibited it. Since the verses speak of "sculptured images" there is a much stronger opposition to sculpture than to painting.

A typical Biblical passage is Deuteronomy 4:16–19:

> *Lest ye deal corruptly, and make you a graven image, even the form of any figure, the likeness of male or female, the*

Ornaments for the scrolls of the Law from 17–18th century Italy. At the top are the *rimmonim* (finials) and the crown placed on top of the scroll, and below is the mantle wrapped around the scroll. ▶

likeness of any beast that is on the earth, the likeness of any winged fowl that flies in the heaven, the likeness of anything that creepeth on the ground, the likeness of any fish that is in the water under the earth; and lest thou lift up thine eyes unto heaven, and when thou seest the sun and the moon and the stars, even the host of heaven, thou be drawn away and worship them, and serve them, which the Lord thy God hath allotted unto all the peoples under the whole heaven.

Again the Second Commandment reads (Exodus 20:4):

Thou shalt not make unto thee a graven image, nor any manner of likeness, of anything that is in heaven above, or that is in the earth beneath, or that is in the water under the earth.

From the context in both these passages it would seem that the prohibition is only when the image is made for the purpose of worship, but there is no doubt that not infrequently in Jewish history it has been understood as prohibiting the making of any image.

The Mishnah (*Rosh ha-Shanah* 2 : 8) states that Rabban Gamaliel had a tablet on which were engraved the various phases of the moon for the purpose of instructing witnesses to the advent of the new moon. The Talmud (*Rosh ha-Shanah* 24b) discusses why this should have been permitted and draws, in fact, a distinction between making images for purposes of worship and for other purposes, though the passage states that there are lesser prohibitions, too, even where the purpose is not for worship. Interestingly enough, this passage tells us of a synagogue in Nehardea in Babylonia, in which the Rabbis worshiped, which had a statue, though it was not fashioned by a Jew.

In the light of the Talmudic discussion, the *Shulhan Arukh* (*Yoreh Deah* 141:4–7) rules that it is permitted to paint, draw, or weave in a tapestry the figures of human beings but not to make statues of the complete human form. However, it is permitted to sculpt an incomplete human figure, for example, the head alone or the torso alone. While there are stricter views held by some pietists (some of whom do not even allow a

A page from a Renaissance illustrated manuscript executed in Florence in 1492. This prayerbook incorporated special festival readings including the Book of Ecclesiastes (here illustrated) which is read on the Festival of Tabernacles. ▶

הַיּוֹם הַמֵּדֵיטֵירִינוּ סִיכָל רַע   הַיּוֹם הַנוֹבְרִיס   הַיּוֹם הַשְׁטֵימְבְרֵ
הַיּוֹם הַקוֹסְטֵרִינוּ   הַיּוֹם וְהַפֵּבְרִינוּ   הַיּוֹם הַשְׁטֵרְדִינוּ
הַיּוֹם הַקוֹסְטֵרִינוּ   הַיּוֹם הַּמַרְמֵרִינוּ   הַיּוֹם הַשֶׁמֶשׁ שֶׁל יְשׁוּעָה
הַיּוֹם וְהַמֵּרִינוּ

כְּהַיּוֹם הַזֶּה כְּבֵיתֵנוּ שָׁשִׂים וּשְׂמֵחִים בְּבִנְיַן שָׁלֵם כַּכָּתוּב בַּטָּהוֹב וְהַבְּיוֹתֵנוּ מִלֵּא הָהָר קָרְשִׁי וְ
בְּבֵית תְּפִלָּתֵנוּ שְׁלֵמוּתֵנוּ וְנִבְמֵתֵינוּ לִרְצוֹנֵךְ שֶׁל פִּי בֵּית בִּית הַמִּקְדָּשׁ קָרְמוּ וְלִ
וְכִתוֹב וְיִשְׂרָאֵל אֵל אֱלֹהֵינוּ לַעֲשׂוֹת מַה כָּל הַחֻקִּים הַמִּלָּה לִזְמַנָּהּ מַה גִּיל וְלִיהַבְ לֹ
הַיָּמִים לְחַיּוֹתֵינוּ כְּהַיּוֹם הַזֶּה ''   וּצְדָקָה וּבְרָכָה וַחֲמָירִים וְשָׁלוֹם יִהְיֶה לְפָ

וְסֵדֶר לִלְמֹשָׁה שְׁטַחָה וְסוֹשָׁה וְיוֹם נֶרֶב לַעֲמָרָה שֶׁל קָרֵב שֶׁבַע וְרֵבֵנוּ בְּטַהֲלָה וְהַ
וְהַשְּׁבָּתְבָא בְּחֵילוֹנֵיה בַּטּוֹבָן אֵל הַקֵּבֶר חֶבְּרָה בָּא יְרוּשָׁלֵם וְנִשְׁטַח מַשְׁקָן חֶסְרָי וְיָקֵץ
שְׁלֹשָׁה וְהֶם חַיִּים רְבָר יְרוּשָׁלַיִם וְיִשְׂמְחוּ לְבָן בָּחוּן בָּרֹב נַן וְיוֹבֵל מִלֹּאוֹת וַעֲבָרוֹ לַ
שְׁלֹשִׁים וְיִמְטַשׁ מֵשְׁמָשׁ לְבָל עַבְדֵּינוּ ''וְוַן ל' נִישׁוֹר טַמְבָן שֶׁשָּׁמַן מֵבָהֵרֵי לַאֲחַיּוֹת שֶׁל
קוֹרָה

יְלַחָמָה מְטֵנַטְה שָׁבַע בָּרוּם שַׁנָּתֵי חֲנַיְתָ בַּמֵּיּן לְבֵית הַמִּשְׁבָּחָה
סְבָנֵיבָד יוֹם וְרָדִים שֶׁנָּאַלָ קָהֲלָה זֶה חָי

לְבֵן

הַזְּלָה בֶּן ''וֶה מֶלֶךְ בִּירוּשָׁלָם : הֲבֵל הַבְּלִים וְאָמַר קֹהֶלֶת רַגֵּל וּמָרִים הַבֵל הָבֵל :
יִתְרוֹן לַהֲרִים בְּכָל עֲמָלֵי נִיְהַסֵּל בַּחַת הַשָּׁמֶשׁ : הֲרוּר הֹלֵךְ וְהֹרֵר בָּא וְהָדָּיִ לְמֵי
עֹמָרֵת : זֶרַח הַשֶּׁמֶשׁ וּבָא הַשָּׁמֶשׁ וְאֶל ''קְרָטִי קִי יְחָרֵטֵי נוֹמַהּ וּמֵיחַ הוּא שֶׁךְ ''חֹלֵךְ אֵל
וְסוֹבֵב אֵל ''שָׁתֵן סָבַב סֹבַב הֹלֵךְ הָרוּחַ וְתַל הֲרָיוּ שֶׁב הָרוּחַ ''וַבְבַנְחֲשׁ כָּל הַנְּחֲלֵיס וֹ

photograph of themselves to be taken), the official ruling of the *Shulḥan Arukh* here permits painting, drawing, tapestry-making and the like with human figures. Statues of the complete human body are forbidden by Rabbinic law but busts and torsoes are permitted. It follows that stained-glass windows depicting even the human form are permitted in a synagogue.

Basically, the idea behind the whole legal conception is the avoidance of anything that smacks of idolatry. Some of the ancient Greek writers called the Jews "a nation of philosophers" when they observed the seemingly strange phenomenon of a whole people worshiping an invisible God of whom an image must never be made. Image-making of the divine is an attempt to render permanent a representation of the deity, whereas Judaism teaches that whatever mental image we have of God cannot express the reality and is no more than a fleeting, imaginative glance that must be rejected as soon as it begins to become fixed.

Reference might here be made to two Responsa of Rabbi A. I. Kook (1864–1935) in the collection published under the title *Da'at Kohen*[1]; the first of these[2] is dated 1931. The question put to Rabbi Kook was whether it is permitted in Jewish law to make a bust of a distinguished person the community wishes to honor. Rabbi Kook, in his reply, quotes the ruling of the *Shulḥan Arukh* that it is permitted but goes on to say:

> *In spite of this, however, I must say that while it is possible to find a dispensation in law yet the spirit of the sages is not pleased with it. The spirit of the pure is opposed to all graven images of humans. Happy will be your portion if you are able to dissuade those who wish to set up a graven image even in the form of a bust. Although I felt obliged to expand the different views as they are and to show, too, the reasons for permitting it, I still declare that blessings will fall on whoever refrains from it, arranging the kind of permanent token of honor to a suitable person but one fully appropriate to the spirit of our people and its Torah.*

[1] *Da'at Kohen*, 2nd edition, Jerusalem 1969.

[2] No. 65, pp. 160–2.

The second Responsum (No. 66, p. 162), addressed to the portrait painter Abraham Neumann, is dated 1926. Neumann had asked Rabbi Kook whether there was any objection in Jewish law to painting the portraits of Orthodox Jews. Rabbi Kook remarks that some pious folk did object to being painted or photographed and there are authorities which lend support to their attitude. But the majority of Jews follow the *Shulḥan Arukh* which permits it although, he says, it is still better if only the upper part of the body or the face alone is painted or photographed. There are, of course, many paintings of distinguished Rabbis, some of which, at least, must have been done with their approval.

Artificial Insemination

There are two kinds of artificial insemination, known in the literature on the subject as AIH (where the donor is the husband) and AID (where the donor is a man other than the husband). Important moral questions are involved in the practice of artificial insemination. These have been widely discussed by Rabbis in this century. Obviously, these questions cannot have been considered in the classical sources of Jewish law, even though the Talmud (*Ḥagigah* 15a) does refer to the possibility of a woman becoming pregnant through bathing in water where a man had deposited his semen. (Modern medicine denies, incidentally, that such a pregnancy is possible.) There is also a curious legend that Ben Sira was the son of the prophet Jeremiah, conceived by the latter's daughter in a bath as above.[1] When contemporary Rabbis discuss artificial insemination they can expect to find, therefore, no direct ruling in the earlier sources and can only try to apply the principles found in those sources to the new problem. (From the legend it would appear that impregnation of a daughter with the semen of her father without sexual intercourse is not considered to be incest since Ben Sira was not held to be a bastard. But this is far from necessarily implying that AID would be permitted.)

We examine first the case of AIH. If a woman cannot have a child from her husband except by artificial insemination the majority of the authorities permit it. The only possible objection would be that the extraction of the husband's semen involves the offense of "wasting seed," i.e., masturbation. But in this instance far from the seed being "wasted" it is emitted precisely for the purpose of impregnating the wife and is consequently permitted.

The problems raised by AID are much more serious, and here the vast majority of contemporary authorities forbid the practice categorically. Among the objections raised are that it is an act of adultery even

[1] Louis Ginzberg, *Legends of the Jews,* Vol. VI, pp. 400–402, Philadelphia, 1946.

without intercourse (or, at least, it resembles adultery so closely as to be forbidden even if not technically adultery) and that if widely practiced it might lead to incest in that the same donor might become the natural father of a boy and a girl who later marry. In Talmudic times, for example, even when polygamy was permitted, it was forbidden for a man to marry two women living in different countries for the same reason. Furthermore, it has been argued that, apart from the purely legal considerations, there is something highly unsavory about a married woman becoming pregnant through the semen of a man not her husband. In the case of a single woman there is less objection but the majority of the authorities still frown upon it.

Asceticism

Three differing attitudes have obtained among religious people towards the gratification of physical appetites when their indulgence does not involve any breach of religious law. These may be called the ascetic attitude, the puritanical attitude, and the attitude of thankful acceptance. The first considers abstinence to be a virtue. According to this view, body and soul are in conflict. To indulge one is to frustrate the growth of the other. The ideal is for man to reduce his physical needs to the bare minimum required for his existence. A state of holiness can be achieved by means of fasting and a general mortification of the flesh. The puritanical attitude is not necessarily ascetic. It can be aware of the physical and spiritual dangers of ascetic exercises—ill-health, morbidity, rebellion, masochism, pride, and lack of charity. But it is as uncompromising as asceticism in rejecting any enjoyment of the physical as an end in itself. Macaulay was unfair to the Puritans when he accused them of objecting to bear-baiting not because it gave pain to the bear but because it gave pleasure to the spectators. After all, pleasure from the spectacle of animal suffering is an ugly emotion. But it seems to be true that the puritan mind considers physical pleasure to be somehow unworthy. The physical appetites were implanted by the Creator in order to guarantee the survival of the human species, but they are more in the nature of a necessary evil than a positive good or, in any event, are only good because they can serve as a preparation or condition for higher things. The third attitude sees physical pleasure as a gift of the Creator. Physical pleasure is not the highest pursuit of man but neither is it shameful or sinful or only of value as a means to an end.

Each of these attitudes has had its Jewish adherents, so that one cannot speak of *the* Jewish attitude towards asceticism. There are certainly ascetic tendencies in Jewish thought but they are not the only tendencies and do not belong to the normative forms of Jewish religious expression.

On the whole the Talmudic Rabbis adopt the third attitude, that of grateful acceptance. The Jerusalem Talmud (*Kiddushin* 4:12, end), for instance, states that a man will have to account before the judgment seat of God for every legitimate pleasure he denied himself. This is derived from the verse: "And whatsoever mine eyes desired I kept not from them" (Ecclesiastes 2:10), referring, of course, according to the Rabbis, only to legitimate pleasures. The enjoyment of the Sabbath and festival meals as a religious duty, which the Rabbis enjoin, and the numerous benedictions in which thanks are given to God for food and drink, point to a frank and at times joyous acceptance of physical pleasure. The Jerusalem Talmud (*Nedarim* 9:1) again says in reference to abstinence: "Are not the things which the Torah has forbidden you enough, that you wish to add more to them?"

Yet this is not the whole story, even in Rabbinic times. There are sayings in the Rabbinic literature of a marked ascetic tendency. For instance, it is said of Rabbi Judah the Prince that on his deathbed he raised his ten fingers and declared to God: "It is revealed to Thee that I have not enjoyed the pleasures of this world even with my little finger" (*Ketubbot* 104a). There is the further saying that rather than praying that the words of the Torah should enter his innards a man should pray that food and drink should not enter his innards (*Yalkut, Deuteronomy*, 830). The third-century Palestinian teacher R. Simeon b. Lakish said (*Berakhot* 63b) that the Torah can only be established if a man kills himself for it, i.e., denies himself in order to study it. A saying in a similar vein is (*Avot* 6:4): "This is the way of the Torah. You must eat bread with salt and drink water by measure, and you must sleep on the ground and you must live a life of pain while you toil in the Torah."

Yet nowhere in the Rabbinic literature do we find the advocacy of ascetic exercises which endanger health. Nor do we find there injunctions to torment the body by self-flagellation, the wearing of hairshirts and the like, known to other religions and among some Jews as well in the medieval period. R. Moses Ḥayyim Luzzatto in his *Path of the Upright* summarizes the Rabbinic view accurately when he writes (Chapter 13):

> *You may accept as a true principle that a man should abstain*
> *from things in this world which are not absolutely necessary.*
> *But if, for any reason, a thing is physically indispensable*
> *he who abstains from it is a sinner. To this there is no exception.*
> *And how each particular thing is to be regarded must be left*
> *to each man's discretion. "A man shall be praised according*

to his understanding" (Proverbs 12:18). It is impossible to set
down a rule for all the possible cases, because these are
innumerable, and the human mind, not being able to grasp
all of them at the same time, must deal with each case as
it presents itself.

In the circle of medieval German mystics known as the *Hasidei Ashkenaz* ("Saints of Germany"), on the other hand, we do find asceticism so pronounced that the mortification of the flesh is practiced. There appears to be either a direct influence of Christian monasticism on this movement or, at least, the influence of a strong ascetic mood "in the air" in that part of Europe in that period. As penance for their sins these men would fast for many days, submit to floggings, roll in the snow naked in winter and sit naked in summer while smeared with honey to be stung by the bees.

Among the later Kabbalists there was a good deal of emphasis on ascetic practices. Solomon Schechter in his essay on Safed[1] describes the asceticism of the Kabbalistic circle in this town in the sixteenth century. Some of these men refrained from food and drink during the day and wore sackcloth and ashes. Others fasted each week for two or three days in succession. Others refrained from eating meat and drinking wine except on the Sabbaths and festivals. In Eastern Europe there were to be found many Kabbalists who fasted "from Sabbath to Sabbath."

A reaction set in with the rise of the Hasidic movement in the eighteenth century. The grandson of the Ba'al Shem Tov, the founder of the movement, is reported to have said that the Ba'al Shem Tov introduced a new mystical way, without any mortification of the flesh, in which the three essentials are love of God, love of Israel and love of the Torah.[2] A well-known Hasidic story tells of how a young ascetic came to R. Israel of Ruzhin (d. 1850). It was the young man's boast that he drank only water, rolled in the snow, wore white garments (as a symbol of purity), wore nails in his shoes, and allowed himself to be flogged regularly. The Rabbi took him to the window and pointed to a white horse in the yard. This horse, he said, is clothed in white, wears nails in its shoes, rolls in the snow, drinks only water, and is flogged regularly. Yet it is still only a horse! For all that, some Hasidic masters were ascetics.

---

[1] *Studies in Judaism,* Vol. 2, pp. 202–306.
[2] *Sefer Ba'al Shem Tov,* Vol. II; *Mishpatim,* pp. 68–70.

The Rabbi of Belz (d. 1957), for example, defended his extremely ascetic life by declaring that one who serves God while eating does so during the act of eating but one who serves God by fasting does so all the time.[1]

Asceticism is therefore not unknown in Judaism and many of the great Jewish teachers did follow an ascetic way of life. In the majority of modern interpretations of Judaism, however, asceticism is rejected.

[1] *Ha-Rav ha-Kadosh mi-Belza,* p. 18, Jerusalem, 1967.

Astrology

Judging by the popularity of horoscopes and fortune-telling along with books on the subject, many people still believe in astrology though it is often looked upon as no more than a parlor game. It is notorious that Hitler consulted professional astrologers to guide him in the conduct of the war. They cannot have been very good at it. There is no doubt that in a pre-scientific age, Jews did believe in astrology. The Talmudic Rabbis, for instance, believed in it, though some of them held that the stars had no influence over Jews, who were under direct divine influence. Traces of the belief are still to be found in words used by Jews, notably the expression *mazzal tov*, literally "a good star" (or "planet"). An unfortunate fellow is still called a *shlimazzal*, "one who has no *mazzal*," one on whom fortune does not smile. Even when the belief in astrology was strong, however, it was taught that the Jew should leave the future to God and not, therefore, consult astrologers. The *Shulḥan Arukh*, the standard Code of Jewish Law, states categorically: "One should not consult astrologers, nor should one cast lots (to determine the future)" (*Yoreh Deah* 179:1).

There are two reasons why a belief in astrology lost its respectability in modern times. First, the use of scientific method made astrology increasingly improbable, since empirical investigation does not demonstrate that a man's life is influenced by the stars under which he was born. Secondly, the whole elaborate astrological scheme is based on the notion that the earth is at the center of the universe with the spheres, containing the stars and planets, revolving around it. One of the achievements of modern astronomy was the demonstration that the universe is not geocentric. Before the rise of modern science, astrology did seem to be convincing and a belief in it was entertained by highly sophisticated persons as well as by the credulous.

It is one of the examples, therefore, of the extraordinary independence of mind of the great Maimonides (d. 1204) that virtually he alone in the

Diagram of a sphere, relating the names of the signs of the Zodiac to the months and the seven planets. From a 13th century Hebrew illuminated manuscript.

יה גלגל שיש בו מזלות כתובים ומפרשים

Middle Ages rejected the belief in astrology. In a letter on astrology written by Maimonides in reply to a query from the Rabbis of Southern France,[1] he distinguishes between astronomy, which is a true science, and astrology, which is sheer superstition. He states further that according to our Torah man's fate is determined by God directly and not by the stars, and that, moreover, man has free will and can choose good and reject evil—otherwise the commands of the Torah are meaningless. As for the references to astrology in the Talmud, these cannot be taken literally when they contradict reason. Man was created with his eyes in front and not behind, i.e., he must act according to reason, rejecting astrology even if it is mentioned in Rabbinic sources.

Until modern times very few Jewish thinkers agreed with Maimonides. Nowadays, for the reasons mentioned above, the whole astrological scheme has been rejected by the vast majority of thinking Jews.

[1] This correspondence has been published with an introduction and notes by Alexander Marx in the *Hebrew Union College Annual,* Vol. III, 1926, pp. 311–358.

Autopsies

The question of autopsies has been the cause of much conflict in the State of Israel. Many Orthodox Jews there have vehemently opposed them while pathologists have argued that there is no other way of furthering medical knowledge. The basic legal question concerns the prohibition (mentioned in the Talmud) of *nivvul ha-met* (literally "desecrating the dead," i.e., mutilating a corpse). Can this prohibition be disregarded, and under what conditions?

The classical ruling on the subject was given towards the end of the eighteenth century by R. Ezekiel Landau of Prague.[1] At that time, thanks to the work of John Hunter, London was the center in Europe for anatomy. The question addressed to Rabbi Landau came from London. A man suffering from stones in his bladder was unsuccessfully operated on and died. The doctors wished to perform an autopsy to discover what had gone wrong, in order to operate with success in future cases. The Rabbi who presented the problem of whether or not this would be permitted in Jewish law states that the Jewish scholars in London were divided on the question. Those who permitted it argued that we find in the Bible that Jacob and Joseph were embalmed (Genesis 50:2–3, 26). This involved the making of incisions in the body and yet it was done to honor them. It follows that it is permitted to perform an autopsy, since the fact that society will benefit is in itself an honor to the deceased. A further permissive argument was advanced from the ruling in the *Shulḥan Arukh* (*Yoreh Deah* 363:2) that if a man decreed in his will that he was to be buried in a place different from the place where he was actually buried, it is permissible to disinter the body and accelerate decomposition by using quicklime, so that the skeleton can be reburied. If even this step can be taken to honor

---

[1] Responsa, *Noda Bi-Yhudah, Tinyana. Yoreh Deah,* No. 210.

the deceased, surely an autopsy which will be of benefit to others can be permitted.

The London scholars who thought it forbidden tried to prove their case from a passage in tractate *Bava Batra* (155a) in the Babylonian Talmud. The case discussed there is that of a boy who sold some property from his estate and died soon after. An attempt was made to invalidate the sale on the grounds that the boy was a minor at the time of the sale (a minor has no power to sell in Jewish law). The suggestion was made that the corpse be disinterred in order to discover whether or not the signs of puberty were present. Rabbi Akiva ruled that this was forbidden on the grounds of *nivvul ha-met*. The London scholar who permitted the autopsy retorted that in *Bava Batra* the case concerns property and for financial gain it is indeed prohibited. But an autopsy can save lives and should thus be permitted.

Rabbi Landau argues that if an autopsy is a matter of saving lives it is certainly permissible, since there is no doubt that the prohibition of *nivvul ha-met* cannot override this consideration. But he adds the qualification that there must be a direct connection. If, for example, the autopsy would help someone suffering from the same disease as the diseased, then it would be permitted. But one cannot permit autopsies on the grounds that they may help to save lives at a later date, for if this argument were accepted it would follow that it is permissible for a doctor to desecrate the Sabbath by preparing medicines and the like because one day they may be used to save lives. This is patently absurd, because surely the law does not permit the desecration of the Sabbath in anticipation of such a remote possibility.

Rabbi Landau concludes:

> *Far be it to permit this: even the gentile doctors only use corpses for the purpose of training in the performance of operations if the corpses are those of criminals condemned to death by the courts or those who gave permission while they were alive for this to be done to their bodies. If, God forbid, we permit these things then all corpses should be dissected in order to learn how the internal organs are distributed so that cures can be found for the living. There is, consequently, no need to elaborate on this and there is not the slightest possibility of permitting it.*

This ruling of Rabbi Landau became the official ruling accepted by all later authorities with the exception of one or two bold spirits. These latter have argued that nowadays the whole science of medicine has become so advanced and communications are so much better than in Rabbi Landau's day that every autopsy which doctors consider necessary can be said to benefit the living directly.

There the matter rests at present. It can be seen that there are good grounds for favoring a more permissive attitude toward autopsies, but so far the conservative view has prevailed.

Birth Control

There has been considerable discussion among Orthodox Rabbis on the rights and wrongs of birth control. Practically every important collection of Responsa contains a lengthy consideration of the legal aspects of this question. According to the Rabbis it is a strict religious duty to have children and it is forbidden to "waste seed," i.e., emit semen without purpose. Consequently, the legal discussions are chiefly concerned with whether there are circumstances when these two principles may be disregarded, for it is obvious that birth control negates the first and it is generally assumed that it violates the second.

First there is the duty to have children. This is based by the Rabbis on the verse: "Be fruitful and multiply" (Genesis 1:28). How many children must one have in order to fulfill this obligation? The School of Shammai said two sons, while the School of Hillel, whose view is followed, said a son and a daughter (Mishnah, *Yevamot* 6:6). Although the Rabbis considered it meritorious to have as many children as possible, the practice of birth control after one has a son and a daughter is treated in a more favorable light than attempts to avoid having a family at all.

As for the prohibition against "wasting seed," this does not apply to ordinary acts of intercourse where pregnancy is ruled out, as in the case of an old or barren couple. But where conception is frustrated by artificial birth control methods the question does arise of whether the offense of "wasting seed" is involved. J. Z. Lauterbach, writing from the Reform point of view,[1] argues that the use of contraceptives in the marital act can in no way be construed as masturbation (i.e., "wasting seed"); but no Orthodox Rabbi has taken this view.

The classical passage around which much of the subsequent discussion revolves is found in the Babylonian Talmud (*Yevamot* 12b). In this passage a debate is recorded between the second century teacher R. Meir

[1] *Central Conference of American Rabbis Year Book,* Vol. 37, 1927, pp. 369–384.

and his colleagues, referred to as the Sages. It should be kept in mind that as a general rule the opinion of the Sages is followed against that of R. Meir. The debate centers around the use of an absorbent (*mokh*) as a contraceptive. R. Meir says: "Three women use a *mokh* during intercourse." The "three women" are a minor, a pregnant woman, and a nursing mother, for in these cases pregnancy can be dangerous. The minor's constitution cannot withstand the rigors of a pregnancy. The fetus carried by a pregnant woman is in danger if she conceives again, it being maintained that a second pregnancy is possible. (The fact that medical opinion today repudiates this possibility is not relevant to the argument.) If a nursing mother becomes pregnant her milk stops and this endangers the life of her suckling. Hence in these three instances Rabbi Meir rules that the *mokh* is used in order to prevent conception. But the Sages say: "They [the three women] have intercourse in the normal way and Heaven will have mercy on them."

The above quotations reflect the ambiguous wording of the original Hebrew. The commentators are divided as to its meaning. Does Rabbi Meir mean that the three women *may* use a *mokh* and the Sages that they *must* not use one? Or does Rabbi Meir mean that they *must* use a *mokh*, so that the Sages only disagree with him in holding that the three women are not obliged to use a *mokh* but *may* do so if they wish? Moreover, what precisely is meant by the word *mokh*? Is it a device used to absorb the semen during intercourse or only after unimpeded intercourse has taken place? Adopting the strictest interpretation, some authorities in the early part of the last century refused to permit the use of artificial means of contraception in any circumstances. But the majority of authorities interpret the passage as permitting the use of a contraceptive when doctors are of the opinion that a pregnancy will do serious harm to the wife.

Economic and other reasons for family planning are not recognized as valid, though there is a tendency even among the Orthodox authorities to allow the "pill" to be used on grounds other than serious threat to health (the argument for greater leniency in the case of the "pill" being that here there is no "waste of seed"). Reform and Conservative Rabbis are generally more lenient and permit the use of any contraceptive devices for other reasons as well. However, no Jewish teacher believes that a couple should avoid having children. Jewish teachers still sing the praises of having children, even though Reform and Conservative Rabbis tend to leave the question of how many and how they are to be spaced to the individual couple. This decision should be based on concern for the welfare of one's family and not selfish reasons.

An excellent and comprehensive survey of the whole subject in English can be found in *Birth Control in Jewish Law* by David M. Feldman, New York, 1968.

Birthdays

There is only one reference to a birthday celebration in the Bible: "And it came to pass the third day, which was Pharaoh's birthday, that he made a feast unto all his servants" (Genesis 40:20). Until comparatively recent times birthday celebrations do not seem to have been held by Jews, or, at least, there is no record of them in Jewish literature. The Talmud (*Kiddushin* 72b) lists the birthdays of some famous Rabbis who were born on the day that another famous Rabbi died, thus replacing them, with an implication that there is cause for rejoicing when a good man is born. There are Jews who look askance at birthday celebrations as un-Jewish but, interestingly enough, birthdays are celebrated in some Hasidic circles. From the last century the institution of the *Festschrift*, the book of essays in honor of a scholar's birthday, has been adopted by Jewish scholars. In some places it has become customary for a man celebrating his seventieth or eightieth birthday to be called to the Torah, where special prayers are recited. The form of greeting on the birthday of elderly persons is generally: "May you live to a hundred and twenty" (the span of Moses' life, see Deuteronomy 34:7).

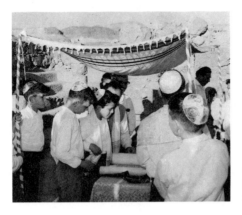

A bar mitzvah at Masada, the ancient fortress in the Judean desert.

Even if the custom of celebrating birthdays has been copied from the non-Jewish world, there is obviously no doctrinal significance in it and hence no laws. Indeed, it is in keeping with Jewish tradition that God be honored for the gift of life. The same applies to the celebration of weddings and other anniversaries. Reference should also be made to the Rabbinic statement on the ages of man (*Avot* 5:21):

> The age of five for the study of the Bible; then ten for the study of the Mishnah; thirteen for the commandments; fifteen for the study of Talmud; eighteen for marriage; twenty for earning a living; thirty for power; forty for understanding; fifty for giving advice; sixty for old age; seventy for grey hairs; eighty for special strength; ninety for bowed back; a hundred—it is as if he had died and passed away.

According to the Rabbis, as can be seen in this passage, the thirteenth birthday is the day on which a boy becomes fully responsible to keep the commandments—hence *Bar* ("son of") *Mitzvah* ("the commandment"). The special Bar Mitzvah celebration dates from the Middle Ages. Girls, according to the Rabbis, are obliged to keep the commandments at the age of twelve—hence the modern celebration of the Bat Mitzvah.

Buddhism

Obviously, Judaism is at complete variance with the Buddhist belief in a multiplicity of gods as well as with the branch of Buddhism that is atheistic. The question to be considered concerns the similarities and differences between Judaism and Buddhism in the ethical sphere and general philosophy of life.

In its common form Judaism is far more activist than Buddhism. It has been pointed out, for example, that both Moses and Buddha were brought up in a king's palace and went out from there to view with horror a world of pain, injustice, and suffering. But while Buddha's enlightenment consists in his realization that desire is the cause of suffering and the aim of man should be to rise above all desire, Moses is moved to fight injustice and help his brethren to emerge from slavery and bondage to Pharaoh. While both Moses and Buddha see man's lot as pitiful, Buddha seeks to encourage neither contentment nor discontent, whereas Moses teaches the kind of divine discontent through which man's condition is improved.

The Buddhist aim is the attainment of Nirvana, a concept that has been given many interpretations but seems to involve the complete loss of the ego and its desires and the idea of the individual becoming totally absorbed in the world spirit. This ultimate aim of Buddhism is at variance with Jewish teachings about the survival of the individual and his possession of an immortal soul. However, there is a doctrine prominent in Ḥasidism and known as *bittul ha-yesh* ("annihilation of the self") which bears a striking resemblance to the Buddhist concept. In Ḥasidic thought man's ego is a barrier between him and God. By forgetting himself in the worship of the Creator man can achieve self-annihilation, a state in which his desire for material things, his pride, and even his yearnings for spiritual fulfillment are all transcended and the soul becomes attached to its source in God. But even here it is God who is at the center of the Ḥasidic longing and not a vague world spirit. Nevertheless, there were Ḥasidic teachers who never used the personal pronoun "I."

For all the differences between Judaism and Buddhism, and while the anti-theistic elements in Buddhism must be uncategorically repudiated from the Jewish point of view, the Jew can admire the marked spiritual emphasis in a good deal of Buddhist life and thought.

Business Ethics

Professor Louis Finkelstein has described Pharisaism as "Prophetism in action." It is perfectly true that the many prophetic teachings regarding justice and righteousness were given concrete expression by the Rabbis of the Talmud. The prophets had urged men to be just. The Talmud discusses in detail what it means to be just in terms of fair business dealings. The Talmudic literature is full of laws governing commercial life: how an employer is to behave toward his employees and the duties of employees to their employer; which prices are legitimate and which constitute overcharging; how false weights and measures are to be avoided; how business contracts are to be drawn up; how conditions of sale are to made binding; what is fair and what unfair competition. These and many other topics receive the most precise treatment in the Talmud in an effort to translate prophetic ideals into the language of the market place.

Of course, economic life in Rabbinic times was vastly different from our own. There were no great corporations in those days, no complicated machinery, comparatively little banking, advertising and commercial loans, hardly any organized labor and no trade unions, no stock exchanges and investments, no insurance policies—none of the problems, in short, which confront the businessman in a highly complex and competitive industrial society. Yet the principles governing business relations are there in the classical sources. Some of these, as expressed in the legal system of the Rabbis, can be mentioned.[1]

---

[1] There is very little literature on this subject in English. Two important surveys are "Jewish Ethics and their Application to Modern Commerce and Industry" by Solomon Goldman, *13th Conference of Anglo-Jewish Preachers,* pp. 17–23, London, 1960; and "Judaism and the World of Business and Labor" by Seymour Cohen, *Proceedings of the Rabbinical Assembly of America,* Vol. 25, pp. 17–44, 1961.

A famous Rabbinic saying is that of the fourth century Babylonian teacher Rava. Rava said that on Judgment Day the first question God asks a man is: "Were you reliable in your business dealings?" Rava was the spiritual leader of the town of Maḥoza on the Tigris, which was adjacent to the capital of the Persian Empire, Ctesiphon, and a renowned commercial center located on the great trade routes. There are many Talmudic references to the wealthy merchants of Maḥoza and it is probable that Rava's saying was a reminder to them to be always scrupulously honest in their business activities.

In Rabbinic law an overcharge (or undercharge) of more than one-sixth of the value of a commodity invalidated the sale (*Bava Meẓia* 30b). When goods were sold it was the delivery of the goods which established the sale and not payment. Consequently, if a man had paid for some commodity which had not yet been delivered, either party could back out of the deal without the courts compelling him to abide by it. But, we are told, the Rabbis frowned severely on such attempts to break one's word, even though there was no technical offense. The courts, therefore, issued a formal and solemn warning to anyone who tried to avail himself of this loophole in the law. The Mishnah (*Bava Meẓia* 4:2) gives us the formula used: "He that exacted punishment from the generation of the flood (Genesis 6:13) and the generation of the Dispersion (Genesis 11:9) will exact punishment from him that does not abide by his spoken word."

To take away a man's livelihood by unfair competition is compared by the Rabbis to adultery (*Sanhedrin* 81a). The second century Palestinian teacher R. Judah forbids a shopkeeper to distribute corn and

Dome-shaped weights of the late Israelite period (c. eighth–seventh century B.C.E.). The four largest are shekel weights, the next two, *nzp (neẓef)*, and the smallest, a *pim* weight.

nuts among children as an inducement. His colleagues permitted it, however, since it could not be considered unfair competition as long as other shopkeepers could do the same or even go one better (*Bava Mezia* 60). A Rabbinic saying has it that to defraud a fellow human being is a greater sin than to defraud the Sanctuary (*Bava Batra* 88b). The law was laid down that a grain merchant must wipe clean his measuring vessels at least once in thirty days so that he always sells the exact measure and not less (*Bava Batra* 88a). To corner the market in vital necessities and thus raise the prices was considered a very serious offense and an example of extreme human wickedness (*Yoma* 83a).

The eighteenth century moralist R. Moses Hayyim Luzzatto in his *Path of the Upright* (pp. 75–76) stresses the need for what he calls "cleanness" with regard to matters of theft and fraud. Luzzatto observes:

> *The Holy One, blessed be He, wants us to be absolutely honest. Thus we read in Scripture, "The Lord preserveth the faithful" (Psalms 31:24). "Open ye the gates that the righteous nation which keepeth the truth may enter in" (Isaiah 26:2). "Mine eye shall be upon the faithful of the land, they that dwell with me" (Psalms 101:6). "O Lord, are not Thine eyes upon truth?" (Jeremiah 5:3). It was Job who, in defending himself against implication of guilt, exclaimed, "Hath my step turned out of the way, or hath mine heart walked after mine eyes, or hath any spot cleaved to mine hand?" (Job 31:7). See how apt is the last remark. He describes a minor theft as something that cleaves to the hand. There are things which come into a man's possession because they happen to cling to his hand, although he does not mean to take them. So, many a man, without actually intending to steal, finds it hard to be absolutely clean handed. This is the case because, instead of the heart controlling the eyes so that they should not desire what belongs to others, the eyes seduce the heart to condone wrong committed for the sake of owning beautiful and desirable things. Hence, Job protested that he had not in this wise erred; his heart followed not his eyes, and therefore nothing cleaved to his hands.*

A man's business affairs should be infused with the spirit of fairness, the Rabbis teach, even where the law has nothing to say on the matter.

The Rabbis base this principle on the verse: "And thou shalt do that which is right and good in the sight of the Lord" (Deuteronomy 6:18). As the great Spanish commentator Naḥmanides (1195–1270) observes in his comments to this verse, the law cannot possibly cover all cases. There are bound to be circumstances where a man can take advantage of his neighbor and get away with it because there is no actual law to forbid the particular malpractice in which he engages. Consequently, Scripture lays down a general principle: "And thou shalt do that which is right and good in the sight of the Lord." Before contemplating any business deal a man should not only consider whether it will be to his advantage or whether it is legal or illegal but whether it is good and right in God's eyes. In Naḥmanides' own words:

> *The meaning of this verse is as follows. First God tells us to keep the statutes and laws which He has commanded us to. And then He tells us that even with regard to those matters concerning which there is no specific command we should see to it that we do only that which is good and right in His eyes for He loves that which is good and right.*

An example of this is the case of *bar meẓra* (literally, "the son of a boundary"), the case of a first option (*Bava Meẓia* 108a–b). If a man intends to sell a field he must give the first option to buy to the man whose field adjoins it, provided the man is prepared to pay the asking price. The man who owns the adjoining field will benefit more than any other purchaser, since he will then have two adjoining fields and save in labor and expenses. According to the strict letter of the law a man can dispose of his property as he sees fit. But if without financial loss to himself he can benefit the owner of the adjoining field and refuses to do so out of malice or to demonstrate his power and rights, then he violates the spirit of our verse.

The Jerusalem Talmud (*Bava Meẓia* 2:5) gives a number of illustrations of how the great teachers behaved with scrupulous honesty even where the strict letter of the law did not cover the case. The disciples of the early teacher Simeon b. Shataḥ bought him a donkey from a Saracen and found a pearl on the donkey which the Saracen had overlooked. Since the Saracen was a heathen the law would have permitted Simeon to keep the pearl, but when the disciples suggested that he should do this he refused and returned the pearl to the Saracen. The Talmud comments that Simeon b. Shataḥ was no barbarian that he should act dishonestly within the law. Simeon b. Shataḥ would rather hear the heathen say "Blessed be the God of the Jews" than have any reward the world has to offer. R. Ḥanina (late second century) similarly told how some aged Rabbis once bought a measure of wheat from a band of robbers and found some coins in it, whereupon they returned the money and the robbers said "Blessed be the God of the Jews." In the same passage the tale is told of a certain Abba Hosea who was in charge of a laundry. The queen once came to the laundry and lost some jewelry there. When Abba Hosea returned the jewels, the queen said: "Keep them. Of what use are they to me! I have many more and much more valuable." But Abba Hosea replied: "Our law orders us to return lost property." And the queen said: "Blessed be the God of the Jews."

The third century Babylonian teacher Rav Judah said in the name of the teacher Rav: "A person is forbidden to keep in his house a measure that is either smaller or larger than the normal capacity." A later Babylonian teacher, R. Papa, argued that this rule would not apply in those places where the Persian authorities controlled the weights and measures, for in these places only those utensils with appropriate seals and marks could be used for weighing and measuring without arousing the suspicion of the authorities. But the Talmud disagrees with R. Papa on the grounds that the customers may call at twilight when people are in a hurry and he may accidentally accept the faulty measure (*Bava Meẓia* 89b). The Jewish communities in both Palestine and Babylon appointed special market commissioners to control weights and measures (*Bava Meẓia* 89b). In Babylon it was the duty of the Exilarch, the leader of Babylonian Jewry, to appoint these market commissioners. Whereas in Palestine their function was to control only weights and measures, prices being left to find their own level, in Babylon the commissioners were expected to control prices as well. When Rav returned from Palestine to his native Babylon in the year 219, we are told (Jerusalem Talmud, *Bava Batra*, 5:2), he was appointed by the Exilarch to the position of market commissioner. Rav refused to control market prices, preferring the Palestinian system, whereupon he was imprisoned by the Exilarch.

In modern times numerous tales have been told of the exemplary business integrity of R. Israel Meir ha-Kohen (1838–1933), known as the Ḥafeẓ Ḥayyim (after the title of his first book). Even if some of these tales are legendary, the fact remains that the Ḥafeẓ Ḥayyim, though an outstanding talmudist, occupied no official rabbinic position, preferring to earn his living in commerce but with extraordinary devotion to the highest ideals of honesty. Dov Katz[1] has collected some of these anecdotes. When he was a young man the Ḥafeẓ Ḥayyim together with his wife opened a small general store. He refused to keep in the store any goods that were not fresh or perfect. To make sure that he was giving good value he would always add a little to whatever was bought. Fearful that too many customers were buying at his store and thus depriving other storekeepers of their revenue, he used to close the store at midday. A non-Jewish customer once left behind a herring he had bought and the Ḥafeẓ Ḥayyim was unable to discover his identity. To make sure that he was not guilty of theft he distributed a fresh herring to each one of his non-Jewish customers on the next market day when they came to buy. When he became a renowned author, publishing and selling his own books, the Ḥafeẓ Ḥayyim would spend months at the printers in far-off Warsaw in order to make sure that each copy sold had no faults in the binding, paper or print. He also took extreme measures to see that the employees at the printing house received a fair wage for their labor and were always paid on time. He would do his utmost to avoid sending by hand books that had been ordered by post, and whenever such a delivery by hand was made he would buy stamps of the equivalent value and destroy them in order not to cheat the post office. When wealthy admirers wanted to give him gifts of money to enable him to live with dignity, the Ḥafeẓ Ḥayyim would always refuse, his argument being that if they only knew what he was really like they would not be in such a hurry to give him gifts and by taking their money he would be guilty of misrepresentation.

Of course, the Ḥafeẓ Ḥayyim was a saint in a small town and it would be absurd to expect the average businessman in the big city to be a saint. Every businessman knows how difficult it is to be scrupulously honest, especially when engaging in the type of commercial activity where refusal to be ruthless often results in failure. There are many sharp practices that are an outgrowth of the kind of society in which we live and it sometimes seems almost impossible for the honest individual to swim against the tide. There are whole areas of commercial life where the problems still await their solution. For all that, the Jewish ideals of justice, righteousness, and integrity ought to be the ideal of the Jewish businessman. In fact, he should conduct his affairs in such a way that people will be moved to say: "Blessed be the God of the Jews."

[1] *Tenu'at ha-Musar,* Vol. IV, pp. 117–139, Tel Aviv, 1963.

Capital Punishment

The most important passage in the Rabbinic literature regarding capital punishment is found in the Mishnah (*Makkot* 1:10):

> *A Sanhedrin which executes [a criminal] once in seven years is known as destructive. Rabbi Eleazar son of Azariah says: Once in seventy years. Rabbi Tarfon and Rabbi Akiba say: If we had been members of the Sanhedrin no man would ever have been executed. Rabban Simeon son of Gamaliel says: They [Rabbi Tarfon and Rabbi Akiva] would have been responsible for the proliferation of murderers in Israel.*

The first thing to be noted is that the discussion in this passage is purely academic. There is a good deal of uncertainty about the actual nature of the Sanhedrin when it did function, but in any event we are told that the right to inflict capital punishment was taken away from the Sanhedrin by the Romans 40 years before the destruction of the Temple (*Sanhedrin* 41a). All the teachers mentioned in the Mishnah flourished at a time when the Sanhedrin had been defunct for about 150 years. For all that, the opening statement that it was rare for a criminal to be executed by the Sanhedrin may well be an authentic tradition to this effect.

Rabban Simeon son of Gamaliel's argument is the stock argument of the anti-abolitionists even today. Capital punishment is the most powerful deterrent and its abolition will only lead to an increase in crimes of violence and murder. Rabbi Akiva and Rabbi Tarfon argued otherwise. In the Babylonian Talmud (*Makkot* 7a) it is suggested that Rabbi Tarfon and Rabbi Akiva would have accomplished their aim by putting questions impossible to answer to the witnesses of the crime. It is interesting to find these Rabbis advocating the abolition of capital punishment even though the Bible sanctions the punishment in a number of instances. They evidently believed that the Biblical law was intended as a solemn warning as to the extreme seriousness of the crime but that the courts were justified in circumventing the law, so that it becomes a dead letter. A good illustration of this method of procedure is the Rabbinic treatment of the Biblical law regarding the stubborn and rebellious son (Deuteronomy 21: 18–21) who was to be stoned to death and the city that turned to idolatry which was to be razed and whose inhabitants were to be destroyed (Deuteronomy 13: 13–19). The Talmud (*Sanhedrin* 71a) declares that these punishments were never actually carried out nor are ever likely to be carried out and are recorded in the Torah for one purpose only, that we might study them and benefit from doing so. It is typical of Rabbinic law and thought that the written text of the Bible is not followed slavishly but is interpreted and reinterpreted by Jewish scholars and teachers in order to preserve its dynamism. The Rabbinic teachers did not argue that since the Bible advocates capital punishment no more can be said on the question.

According to another statement in the Talmud (*Sanhedrin* 52b), the Sanhedrin can only function while the Temple is standing, so that after the destruction of the Temple it was illegal for any Jewish court to inflict capital punishment. It is true that where emergency measures of great severity are required the courts are empowered to act "illegally" and inflict capital punishment (*Sanhedrin* 46a). Some medieval communities availed themselves of these emergency powers. In medieval Spain, for example, there are cases recorded of informers who endangered the very existence of the Jewish community being executed. But for many centuries now no Jewish court has ever inflicted the death penalty and, as we have seen, it is indeed illegal for a Jewish court so to do.

Writing in 1932 from the strictly Orthodox point of view, Rabbi Isaac Herzog[1] replies to the objection that if Jewish law were restored in a future Jewish state, the Jewish people would become isolated from the civilized world, since the Hebrew penal code prescribes the death penalty for purely religious offenses. Rabbi Herzog points out that, in Rabbinic law, there are so many technical restrictions as to make an execution for purely religious offenses a virtual impossibility. Even with regard to homicide there is a definite tendency, as we have seen, to forgo capital punishment. Rabbi Herzog also points out that no Jewish court is empowered to inflict the death penalty unless the Temple

---

[1] *The Main Institutions of Jewish Law,* 2nd edition, Vol. I, note 3, pp. xxii–xxiv, London, 1965.

is standing and the sacrificial cult restored, which, he says, cannot happen until the Messianic age. He writes:

> *Even if all the tremendous practical obstacles which prevent the rebuilding of the Temple were removed, the sacrificial cult could only be restored under prophetic directions, and this presupposes a supernatural divine manifestation. Until that will have taken place, no Jewish court could inflict the death-penalty even for the crime of homicide. The difficulty in question is therefore a matter which could only arise in the* Messianic *age and need not enter into any practical calculations affecting the reconstitution of the Jewish State in Palestine. But, of course, in view of the actual position the idea of a Jewish State in Palestine (as distinct from a National Home), quite irrespective of the restoration of the Temple, is, in itself, rather a* Messianic *hope than a question of practical politics.*

History has, of course, refuted Rabbi Herzog's contention in this last sentence, and he himself became the first Chief Rabbi in the State of Israel. But the rest of what he has to say is pertinent. In fact, except for the offenses of treason and genocide, capital punishment has been finally abolished in the State of Israel.

The question of whether Judaism would have Jews living outside Israel support abolitionist or anti-abolitionist policies in the countries in which they reside is rather more complicated. From the evidence produced here it would seem to be suggested that the abolitionists are closer to the Jewish spirit and should be supported. However, there is no dogmatic statement to this effect, and sincere anti-abolitionists, convinced despite the weighty statistical evidence to the contrary that the death penalty is a deterrent, do have Rabban Simeon son of Gamaliel on their side and can support this policy with a clear conscience.

Careers

The Rabbis attach great importance to the earning of a livelihood through a regular trade or occupation. In a second century source (*Kiddushin* 29a) it is said that one of the obligations a father has toward his children is to teach them a trade. Rabbi Judah says that a father who does not teach his son a trade teaches him robbery, i.e., if the son cannot earn a living when he grows up he will resort to criminal activities.

The classical statement in the Rabbinic literature (dating from the second century) on the attitudes of the Palestinian Rabbis toward different occupations is found in the Mishnah (*Kiddushin* 4:14):

> *Rabbi Meir says: A man should always teach his son a craft that is clean and easy and he should pray to Him to whom riches and possessions belong. For there is no craft without both poverty and riches. For poverty is not the result of a craft nor are riches the result of a craft but it all depends on a man's merit. Rabbi Simeon son of Eleazar says: Have you ever seen an animal or bird following a craft? Yet they have their sustenance without care and they have been created only to serve me. So, I, who have been created to serve my Maker, should certainly find my sustenance without care. But because I have done evil I have interfered with my sustenance. Abba Guryon of Sidon says in the name of Abba Guria: A man should not teach his son to be an ass-driver, or a camel-driver, or a barber, or a sailor, or a shepherd, or a storekeeper, for their craft is the craft of robbers. Rabbi Judah says: The majority of ass-drivers are wicked; the majority of camel-drivers are good men; the majority of sailors are saints; the best of doctors will go to Hell; and the worthiest of butchers is a partner of Amalek. Rabbi Nehorai says: I would leave aside all the crafts in the world to teach my son the Torah alone.*

It must be first appreciated that these sayings date from a period of economic decline in Palestine when the land had been thoroughly devastated as a result of the wars with Rome. At such a time the trades and occupations open to Jews were comparatively few. In the literature produced in this period there are no references, for instance, to Jews engaging in commerce on a large scale.

Rabbi Meir's saying about a clean and easy craft is intelligible. The Talmud comments that while the world needs both the tanner and the dealer in perfume it is better to be the latter than the former. There follows in the Mishnah short homilies by Rabbi Meir and Rabbi Simeon ben Eleazar to the effect that while man's own efforts are required it is God's blessing which determines whether or nor he will succeed, and the blessing depends on the way he conducts himself. Abba Guryon then gives a list of the trades of which he disapproves on the grounds that the men who follow them frequently take unfair advantage of their fellows. The meaning is evidently that they overcharge for their service. Ass-drivers, camel-drivers and sailors, for example, are all in trades connected with transport and their fares are too high. Why a barber should have been included is far from clear. In some texts the word *sappar* ("barber") does not, in fact, appear, and instead the trade of "wagoner" is mentioned. (It is possible that the word *sappar* was accidentally inserted in the Mishnah text by a careless scribe, influenced by the similar word *sappan* ("sailor") in the Mishnah.) A storekeeper was held to be dishonest because of the many opportunities he had of using false weights and measures, diluting his wine and the like. But why a shepherd should have been disapproved of is also not clear. After all, in the Bible Moses and David were shepherds and the Psalmist declares: "The Lord is my shepherd." The famous French commentator, Rashi, remarks, following a passage in the Talmud, that the reference is to a man who acts as a shepherd for his own flock, and the reason he is suspect is because he allows the flock to graze on lands belonging to others. But modern scholars have suggested that the real reason for the disapproval of the shepherd is that the Jewish teachers wished to improve the economic condition of the community by encouraging people to plant trees again. The sheep and goats led to pasture would eat the young shoots and prevent their growth.

Rabbi Judah refuses to accept the blanket disapproval expressed by Abba Guryon. Ass-drivers are suspect but not camel-drivers, perhaps because the latter were contracted for far longer journeys and had less opportunity to cheat their customers. But Rashi comments that camel-drivers were forced to journey into the desert and their exposure to danger made them God-fearing. According to Rashi, this is why the majority of sailors are "saints," the perils they encounter being even more extreme than those of the camel-drivers. The pious sailor with Bible in hand is known, of course, in Western culture. The disapproval of doctors is noteworthy, and is probably based on the many unskilled practitioners who risked the lives of their patients for personal gain. Rashi understands the disapproval of butchers on the grounds that they frequently pass off as kosher meat that is really not. But the expression "a partner of Amalek" suggests rather that they were frowned upon because the killing of animals (butchers in Talmudic times slaughtered the animals as well as selling them) made them callous and indifferent to suffering.

Rabbi Nehorai's saying seems strange. It is contrary to the general trend of Rabbinic thought to earn a living by studying the Torah without having a craft. There were no professional Rabbis in those days. Many of the Talmudic Rabbis earned their living as artisans or small traders. It has been suggested that Rabbi Nehorai only refers to a particularly gifted boy. In that case, says Rabbi Nehorai, the father is well-advised to support his son without bothering about his future and so encourage the boy to amass great learning and wisdom.

Although these teachings are found in the Mishnah, which enjoys the greatest authority, there is no mention of them in any of the great codes of Jewish law and they were completely ignored during the Middle Ages. Some of the greatest medieval Jewish teachers, like Maimonides and Naḥmanides, earned their living as physicians, and others were storekeepers. There appears to have been the fullest appreciation that the Mishnah was laying down basic principles but not legislating for all time. The particular trades disapproved of were held to be un-worthy only against the particular social and economic background of the second century Jewish community in Palestine. In other periods, these trades can become respectable and others far less so.

The principles for choosing a career nowadays nonetheless emerge clearly from the Mishnah. First, a man is fully justified in seeking a career for himself. God's help is essential but man is obliged to make the effort. Secondly, in choosing his career he should favor an occupation of benefit both to himself and society and should avoid choosing one that offers temptations toward dishonesty or has a corrosive effect on the character. Finally, the sense of vocation should be encouraged. Not all people are drawn to the same type of work. There is sound wisdom in the Hasidic saying that every man has his own "soul-root" and should pursue in life that course which is in accord with it.

Censorship

It would be untrue to say that Judaism has known nothing of censorship. Especially in the Middle Ages Jewish teachers banned books. These teachers would have seen their acts as admirable and necessary for the defense of the faith. Most of us today accept the principles of freedom and tolerance but this is chiefly the result of the efforts of thinkers and writers like Milton, Spinoza, John Locke, and John Stuart Mill. Nevertheless, Judaism does have a better record in this matter than other Western faiths, partly, no doubt, because Jews did not have the power to impose censorship and because Jews learned from their own bitter experiences of having their writings censored and banned by others.

Page of *Seder R. Amram* showing censored portion of *Aleinu* prayer, Spain, 14th–15th century. In the Middle Ages the prayer was censored by Christians as containing an implied insult to Christianity. They claimed that the verse "for they prostrate themselves before vanity and emptiness and pray to a God that saveth not" was a reference to Jesus. The censors remained adamant even when it was pointed out that the phrase is found in Isaiah (30:7; 45:20), and that the prayer is probably pre-Christian.

The earliest and best-known statement recording a ban on books is found in the Mishnah (*Sanhedrin* 10:1). Rabbi Akiva says that one who reads "external books" will have no share in the world to come. It is almost certain that the "external books" referred to are the books of the Apocrypha. Moreover, the term for "reading" (*ha-kore*) is the one generally used in the Rabbinic literature for reading in public worship. Consequently, the aim of Rabbi Akiva is to discourage in the strongest terms the public reading of the Apocryphal books because to do this would place them on a par with the books that had been formally admitted into the Bible. The whole passage has to be seen against the background of a careful sifting by the Rabbinic teachers of the literature that had been produced by Jews up to their day. Some of this was recognized as inspired literature, as sacred scripture, while some of it did not seem to the Rabbis to have this sacred character. The demarcation line between sacred and non-sacred literature had to be drawn very firmly. Hence some books were called "external" in the sense that they did not belong to the collection of Biblical literature. But there was no ban on the private reading of these books and, indeed, the Talmud occasionally quotes from one of them, the book of Ben Sira, in approval of some of its wisdom.

In the Middle Ages, however, the term "external books" was understood as referring to any books that could be harmful to faith and morals. Maimonides in his Code of Law (*Yad, Akkum* 2:2) understands the term as referring specifically to works on idolatrous worship. However, in his *Guide for the Perplexed* (III, 29) Maimonides is not content with giving a full list of these books, which he had himself read, but argues that their study is essential if we are to understand the nature of the Torah laws aimed against idolatry. Evidently Maimonides makes a distinction between reading these books out of a penchant for idolatrous worship and reading them for the purpose of knowing the enemy. An extreme interpretation of "external books" is given by R. Obadiah of Bertinoro (15th century). This Italian scholar writes in his commentary to the Mishnah which speaks of "external books":

> External books. *By this is meant the works of heretics, for example, the books of the Greek Aristotle and his associates. Included in the prohibition is one who reads the histories of gentile kings, love poems, and erotic writings, works in which there is neither wisdom nor advantage but which are only a waste of time.*

The great legal authority R. Joseph Caro (1488–1575), author of the *Shulhan Arukh*, tried to ban the work *Me'or Einayim* by his contemporary Azariah de Rossi because of its claim that the Talmudic Rabbis were occasionally ill informed on historical matters. R. Joseph Caro in his *Shulhan Arukh (Orah Hayyim* 307:16) also rules:

> *It is forbidden to read on the Sabbath the mocking poems and parables of secular works and erotic works, the book of Immanuel (of Rome) for instance. And the same applies to works of military exploits. Even on a weekday it is forbidden on the grounds of "sitting in the seat of the scoffers" (Psalms 2:1). One who reads these works also offends against the verse: "Turn ye not unto idols" (Leviticus 19:3), which means (according to the Rabbis): "Do not empty your mind of God." In the case of erotic works there is the further prohibition of inciting the evil inclination. The authors of these works and those who make copies of them, and, it goes without saying, those who print them, are guilty of causing the public to sin.*

R. Moses Isserles, in his notes to the *Shulhan Arukh,* shows a more lenient attitude. If, he says, secular books are written in Hebrew it is permitted to read them even on the Sabbath. Elsewhere (*Yoreh Deah* 246:4), however, he strictly forbids the reading of heretical works.

There are many instances of the banning of books on the grounds of heresy. After Maimonides' death some of his opponents placed a ban on his works. Others banned the reading of philosophical literature for persons under 40 years of age. Hasidic works were banned by their opponents. The first Hasidic work to be printed—*Toledot Ya'akov Yosef* by R. Jacob Joseph of Polonnoye—was publicly burned. The Hasidim retaliated by buying up as many copies as they could of anti-Hasidic polemical writings and destroying them. With the rise of the Haskalah ("enlightenment") movement there was a ban in both Hasidic circles and among their opponents on the reading of the books produced by the Maskilim. A number of Rabbis forbade the reading of Moses Mendelssohn's work as well as the *Biur*, the commentary to the Bible produced by the members of his circle. Reform writings were also placed under a ban by Orthodox Rabbis. In the United States a number of Orthodox Rabbis burned publicly the prayer book compiled by Mordecai Kaplan.

But it remains true that censorship is favored by very few Jews today. We live in a world where ideas are not weakened by an attempt to deny their existence. Yet even the most liberal of thinkers would argue that there must be some kind of censorship. In most civilized countries it is not permitted by law to advocate criminal activities. To take an extreme example, hardly anyone would defend the publication of a book which gives advice on how to commit the perfect murder and get away with it. For the rest it is a matter of balance among the values we cherish—one of which is man's freedom to record and publish his thoughts for others to read.

Change of Sex

The Talmud contains many references to the *hermaphrodite (androgynos)*, one having the organs of both sexes, and the *agenosomus (tumtum)*, one having the organs of neither sex. There are numerous discussions, mostly of an academic nature, on the legal status of such persons, for example, whether they are to be considered in law as men or women or as a third sex. But these have nothing to do with change of sex. The only reference in the whole of the Rabbinic literature to something approaching a change of sex is the story of the man whose wife died, leaving him with an infant for whom he was unable to afford a nurse. A miracle occurred and his breasts became a woman's, so that he himself was able to suckle the child. One Rabbi expressed his admiration for a man for whom such a miracle had been wrought but another exclaimed: "How inferior such a person is that the order of creation was changed on his behalf" (*Shabbat* 53b). But the story does not really speak of a change of sex. The man remained essentially a man. By a miracle, too, it was believed, the sex of an embryo could be changed. This is said (*Berakhot* 60a) to have happened to the child carried by the Matriarch Leah. Leah, out of compassion for her sister, who had no sons, prayed to God that the child she was carrying should be a girl, and even though it was a male God changed its sex and Dinah was born. The Mishnah (*Berakhot* 9:3) quotes a prayer of a husband that his pregnant wife should give birth to a boy as an example of a "futile prayer." If the embryo is male no prayer is needed. If the embryo is a female then prayer cannot change it unless through a miracle for which it is forbidden to pray.

From all this it follows that the ancients did not entertain the possibility of a real change of sex in adult persons. It would seem that in some rare cases today medical treatment is able to effect a real change of sex or it may take place by natural means. There has been no discussion in the Responsa literature of the legal status of a person who has undergone such a sex change. The likelihood is that Jewish law would recognize the change and the legal status of the person who has undergone such a change would be that of the sex into which he or she has changed. But the whole topic remains problematic.

Charity

The Bible, the Talmud, the Codes, and the moralistic literature all emphasize the need to care for the poor. Teachings on the privilege and duty of charity are too numerous to be recorded in detail. A key text is Deuteronomy 15: 7–11. In this context the reference is to the "year of release," the seventh year, when debts were to be cancelled (Deuteronomy 15: 1–2). A wealthy man, otherwise well disposed toward the poor, might be tempted to refuse to lend a poor man money when the year of release is at hand because his debt might be forfeited. Scripture admonishes sternly against this. But the text was interpreted in Jewish tradition as also indicating a general attitude toward aiding the poor. The relevant verses read:

> *If there be among you a needy man, one of thy brethren, within any of thy gates, in thy land which the Lord thy God giveth thee, thou shalt not harden thy heart, nor shut thy hand from thy needy brother; but thou shalt surely open thy hand unto him, and shalt surely lend him sufficient for his need in that which he wanteth. Be wary that there be not a base thought in thy heart saying: The seventh year, the year of release, is at hand; and thine eye be evil against thy needy brother, and thou give him nought; and he cry unto the Lord against thee, and it be sin in thee. Thou shalt surely give him, and thy heart shall not be grieved when thou givest unto him; because that for this thing the Lord thy God will bless thee in all thy work, and in all that thou puttest thy hand unto. For the poor shall never cease out of the land; therefore I command thee, saying: Thou shalt surely open thy hand unto thy poor and needy brother, in thy land.*

Every Jewish community has had an organized system of relief for the poor, the members being taxed for this purpose. In addition,

A Jewish soup kitchen at Spitalfields, in London's East End, 1879.

private donors gave of their wealth in order to assist the poor. Perhaps the most remarkable feature of all this is that the many Talmudic rules and ideals were codified by Maimonides and his successors and became part of official Jewish law. Consequently, we find a whole section of the *Shulḥan Arukh (Yoreh Deah* 247–259) devoted to almsgiving in all its ramifications. A useful way of studying Jewish attitudes to charity is to examine in detail this section of the *Shulḥan Arukh,* all of whose teachings are based on the statements in the classical sources. We cannot quote the whole section for considerations of space, but here in translation are some of the more important rules:

247:1. It is a positive religious obligation for a man to give as much charity as he can afford. We have been commanded positively to do this many times in the Torah. There is also a negative precept which warns against hiding oneself from this obligation, as it is said: "Thou shalt not harden thy heart, nor shut thy hand" (Deuteronomy 15:7). Whoever hides himself from this obligation is called a scoundrel and it is as if he had worshiped idols.

247:33. God has compassion on whomever has compassion on the poor. A man should think to himself that he asks of God all the time to sustain him and just as he entreats God to hear his cry so he should hear the cry of the poor. He should also think to himself that poverty is a fate that overtakes all sooner or later so that one day he or his son or his grandson will be in need and whoever has compassion on others compassion is shown to him.

248:1. Every person is obliged to give charity. Even a poor man who is himself supported by charity is obliged to give from that which he receives.

248:7. If a man without adequate means gives more charity than he can afford or if he himself deprives himself in order to give to the charity collection because he fears embarrassment, it is forbidden to ask him for donations and the charity collector who puts such a man to shame by soliciting a donation will be punished by God.

249:1. What is the amount one should give? If a man can afford to do so he should satisfy the needs of all the poor who require help. If he cannot afford so much, then, if he wishes to carry out his duty in the best way possible, he should give up to a fifth of his wealth. A tenth of his wealth is the average amount and one who gives less that this is ungenerous. The fifth referred to means a fifth of his capital on the first year and from then onward a fifth of the profits every year. But a man should not give away more than a fifth of his wealth, so as to avoid becoming himself a recipient of charity. This applies only during a man's lifetime, but on his deathbed a man is allowed to give as much to charity as he wishes. A man should not use his tithe for charity for religious purposes, to give candles to the synagogues, for instance, or for some other religious purpose, but he should use it only for the relief of poverty.

249:3. A man should give charity cheerfully and out of the goodness of his heart. He should participate in the grief of the poor man and speak words of comfort to him. But if he gives in an angry and unwilling spirit he loses any merit there is in giving.

249:5. If a man can encourage others to give his reward is even greater than that of the man who gives.

250:1. How much should be given to a poor man? "Sufficient for his need in that which he wanteth" (Deuteronomy 15:8). This means that if he is hungry he should be fed; if he has no clothes he should be given clothes; if he has no furniture, furniture should be bought for him. Even if he was accustomed to ride a horse with a slave running before him when he was rich and he has now become poor, a horse and slave should be bought for him. So, too, every poor person should be given that which is appropriate for him. One whose needs are for a morsel of bread should be given a morsel of bread; a whole loaf, he should be given a whole loaf; a bed, he should be given a bed. One who needs to be given bread hot from the oven should be given bread hot from the oven. One who prefers bread that is cool should be given bread that is cool. One who needs to be spoonfed should be spoonfed. If the poor man has no wife and wishes to marry, he should be given the means wherewith to marry. A house should be rented for him, a bed and other furniture should be purchased for him, and then a wife found for him. But it would seem right to say that all this only applies to the distribution of charity or to the community operating as a unit. An individual is not obliged to give the poor man "sufficient for his need" but the poor man should make his sufferings known to the community. If this is not possible, the individual should give him what he needs if he can afford to do so.

251:3. It is considered as an act of charity if a man gives to his grown-up sons and daughters, whom he has no legal obligation to support, in order that the sons might study the Torah and the daughters be trained to follow the right path. The same applies to a son who gives gifts to his parents when they need them. Indeed, a man should give to his children and his parents before he gives to anyone else. A man should give to his relative, even if he is neither a son nor a parent, before giving to anyone else. A brother of one's father comes before a brother of one's mother. The poor in a man's own household comes before the poor of the town in which he resides. The poor of the town in which he resides come before the poor of another town and the poor in the land of Israel come before the poor in lands outside Israel. A man's own livelihood comes before that of any other person, so that he is not obliged to give charity until he has secured a living for himself. He should then support his parents if they are poor and they have precedence over the support of his [grown-up] children. He should then support his children and they have precedence over his brothers. They have precedence over his other relations and his relations have precedence over his neighbors, his neighbors over the other poor of the town, the poor of the town over the poor of other towns. The same applies to ransoming them if they have been captured [by bandits].

251:5. Once a man has given money to the charity collection neither he nor his heirs any longer have a say in the matter and the community can do with the money what they consider to be right in the eyes of God and man.

251:10. If a man asks to be fed no investigation should be undertaken to see whether or not he is a fraud but he should be fed without further ado. But if a man asks to be clothed it is necessary first to investigate whether or not he is a fraud. If, however, his status is known he should be given clothes without further ado.

255:1. A man should always try to avoid being the recipient of charity. He should rather live a life of pain than be supported by others. Thus the Sages advised: "Turn thy Sabbath into a weekday [eating only weekday meals] and do not be in need of others." Even if an honorable sage became poor, rather than be supported by others, he should work at a trade, even if it involves coarse work.

255:2. Whoever does not need to take charity but tricks the people into giving him will not die before he becomes truly in need of others. Whoever needs to receive charity and cannot survive unless he takes it, an old or sick person, for example, or a sufferer, and is too proud to take it, such a person is a shedder of blood and he is guilty of suicide. All he has for his pains are sins and transgressions. Whoever needs to take but torments himself, is patient, and lives a life of pain in order to avoid being a burden on the community will not die before he supports others. Concerning him it is said: "Blessed is the man that trusteth in the Lord" (Jeremiah 17:7).

Thus far, the rules as recorded in the *Shulḥan Arukh*. Reference should also be made to Maimonides' famous eight degrees of charity, one higher than the other (*Yad Mattenot Aniyim* 10:7–14). The lowest degree of all is for the giver to be glum when he gives to the poor. The next is when he gives cheerfully but not as much as he should give. The next highest is when he gives to the poor cheerfully and gives as much as he should but only when the poor man asks him. Next in degree is when he gives without having to be asked. Higher still is when the donor does not know which of the poor are the recipients of his charity, i.e., when he places the money in a certain place and the poor come and take it. Higher still is when the poor man does not know to whom he is indebted, i.e., the donor sends the money anonymously. Higher still is when neither the donor nor the poor know one another's identity, i.e., when the money is given for distribution to the community chest. Highest of all is when a man is prevented from becoming poor by being given a loan or a job so that he can adequately support himself.

A striking aspect of the laws of charity is their realism. A man must not use charity as an excuse for neglecting his own family nor must he impoverish himself by giving too much away because this only aggravates the problem of poverty. The charity collectors and distributors are obliged to make investigations but not in a heartless way and never when the demand is for food. It is better to take the risk of giving to a fraudulent claimant than to allow a hungry man to remain unfed. The townspeople must first look after their own before considering "the poor of other communities." But side by side with this realistic approach is a lofty idealism in which men are asked to make heavy sacrifices for the good of the unfortunate.

It follows from all this that Judaism would certainly approve of social measures aimed at the eventual abolition of poverty. Maimonides' highest degree still holds good. Man should love the poor but hate poverty and work for its total abolition. Whether a form of society can ever be developed in which there are no poor is a question for visionaries and dreamers. But it is the visionaries and dreamers more than anyone else who have been responsible for the improvement of society. Having the dream in mind, Judaism would have us work within the framework of our present social institutions to do all we can to alleviate suffering and help others to lead lives of happiness, prosperity, and dignity.

Christianity

The doctrinal differences between Judaism and Christianity cannot be bridged, making it impossible for anyone to be a believing Jew and a devout Christian at one and the same time. The Christian doctrines of the Trinity, the Incarnation, the Virgin Birth and the Atonement have always been looked upon by Jews as running completely counter to the pure monotheism taught by Judaism. On this all Jews are agreed, even those who admire the personality of Jesus and the Christian ethic and who accept the idea that Christianity has an important role to play in God's world. Christianity holds that this faith has taken the place of Judaism, that the New Testament is the fulfillment of the Old. Judaism asserts that the Torah never has been and never will be superseded and that there is only one "Testament." Christianity teaches that Jesus was the Messiah and that we are now living in a redeemed world. Judaism says, in the words of the Rabbi who looked out of the window when told that the Messiah had come: "Nothing has changed!"

Other alleged differences between the two faiths are far more problematic. It is frequently said, for instance, that Judaism is a religion of justice while Christianity is a religion of love. Aḥad Ha-Am used this theory to formulate his view of the complete incompatibility of the Jewish and Christian ethic. But while there may be slight differences of emphasis in this matter between the two faiths, it is obvious that Judaism knows of love and Christianity of justice. Again it is said that Judaism is centered around the group while in Christianity the individual is of supreme importance. It is true that Judaism stresses the idea of peoplehood and Christianity the role of the individual, but here too it is incorrect to generalize. The same applies to the contention that Judaism is a religion of law while Christianity believes in the free choice of the individual in each particular situation. Naturally it is true that Christianity knows nothing of the concept of Torah, but there are laws which Christians are expected to obey and there are many situations where the Jew has to decide freely how the law would have him act. In the matter of original sin it is no doubt true that Christianity is bound to emphasize the doctrine because of its teachings about Jesus and the Savior. But there are Jewish teachings, too, or, at least, teachings put forward by some Jews, which speak of man's inherent sinfulness and even of sinfulness inherited from Adam. The conventional distinction, that Judaism believes that a man is a sinner because he sins while Christianity believes that a man sins because he is a sinner, is also a generalization which should not be pressed too far. Finally, it is true that in Christianity, at least in many of its versions, celibacy is a high ideal while in Judaism to marry and have children is a religious obligation. Yet there have been examples (not many, to be sure) of Jews, like the second-century teacher Ben Azzai, who could not bring themselves to marry because "their soul was in love with the Torah."

In all these matters Judaism and Christianity have developed in different directions and it would be very surprising if differences in

Disputation between Jewish and Christian scholars, from a woodcut by Johann von Armssheim, 1483.

emphasis had not emerged. But the differences are not really doctrinal and individual temperament as well as social background have been at work in influencing both Jewish and Christian teachings.

As for the things Judaism and Christianity have in common, they are many. Both religions have the Hebrew Bible as sacred scripture. The Psalms are used in the liturgies of both faiths. There are many resemblances in the form of worship; the reading of scripture; the particular chants; the use of words like "Amen" and "Hallelujah"; the priestly blessing; the structure of the house of worship. Both religions hail God as "Father" and both believe in the Fatherhood of God and the Brotherhood of Man. Both faiths believe that man should strive to be holy, to practice justice and righteousness, to walk humbly with God. Again, both religions believe that man is created in the image of God and that he has an immortal soul.

It is against all this that we must approach the much-discussed question of whether there is such a thing as a common Judeo-Christian tradition and whether dialogue between the two faiths is possible and if possible whether desirable. The answer to these questions depends on whether the real differences between the two faiths are such as to render them completely different, so that to speak of a dialogue or a common tradition is to blur distinctions which the adherents of both faiths consider of the utmost significance and for which they have been prepared to offer up life itself. Jews today are divided in their attitudes. Thinkers like Buber and Rosenzweig have explored the possibility of both dialogue and common endeavor. In various countries there are organizations of Christians and Jews which cooperate fruitfully in many fields while both their Jewish and Christian members refuse to engage in any attempts at proselytism and respect real differences. Nevertheless, there are Jews who find such a dialogue distasteful and even harmful to faith. In this matter, as in so many others, it is not so much a question of what Judaism has to say as a question of how Jews feel they should behave, and quite naturally there are sincere differences of opinion.

Civil Disobedience

The prophet Jeremiah, advising the Babylonian exiles on their attitude to the land of their exile, remarks (29:7):

> And seek the peace of the city whither I have caused you to be carried away captive, and pray unto the Lord for it; for in the peace thereof shall ye have peace.

In *Ethics of the Fathers* (*Avot* 3:2) we read:

> R. Hanina, the deputy of the priests, said: "Pray for the peace of the government; for, except for the fear of that, we should have swallowed each other alive."

R. Hanina lived in Temple times and survived the destruction of the Temple. This makes his saying extremely significant, for while Jeremiah is thinking of a government in a foreign land where Jews have found hospitality, R. Hanina can only have been referring to the Roman government in the holy land. His saying has to be understood against the background of Roman conquest. In his day it was evidently appreciated that rebellion against Rome was doomed to failure, and so R. Hanina preferred even a foreign and hostile government to complete anarchy. At different periods during the Roman occupation of Palestine there was far less acquiescence to Roman domination. More than once the Jews rose in revolt against Rome, as the history of the period clearly informs us. The Bar Kokhba rebellion is the best known of all. Rabbi Akiva hailed Bar Kokhba as the Messiah and Rabbi Akiva himself refused to obey the Roman decree against teaching the Torah, suffering, according to the traditions, a martyr's death for his efforts. While some of the Rabbinic teachers praised Rome for all that had been achieved in terms of better roads, bathing facilities, splendid buildings and the like, others declared that these achievements were for Roman advantage and Jews should not accept the situation.

A famous ruling of the great third century Babylonian teacher Samuel is relevant to the question. Samuel rules (*Nedarim* 28a; *Gittin* 10b; *Bava Kama* 113a) that *dina de-malkhuta dina* ("the law of the kingdom is law"), i.e., the Jew is obliged to obey the law of the land in which he resides just as he is obliged to keep Jewish law. This ruling established an important principle of conduct for Jews in all the lands of the Exile. While the ruling was interpreted in different ways, it can be said that, generally speaking, Jewish citizens were faithful to the laws of their host country and looked upon such loyalty as an important religious duty. Historically considered, it is noteworthy that Samuel gave his ruling in Babylon, where, in his day at least, Jews were treated well and accepted as citizens of the Persian Empire. Although the Babylonian Talmud seems to imply that Samuel's ruling was not his own but was known among the earlier teachers in Palestine, and although some Christian scholars have understood Jesus' "render unto Caesar" to be an application of his ruling, Louis Ginzberg[1] has convincingly argued that, in fact, none of the Palestinian teachers ever accepted Roman domination to the extent of adopting the laws imposed by the Romans as religiously binding upon Jews.

Very revealing in this connection is the statement in the Mishnah (*Nedarim* 3:4), dating from Temple times, that if "murderers, robbers, or tax-collectors" wish to seize one's goods it is permitted to take a false oath to the effect that the goods belong to the king's household in order to frighten them off. (The false oath referred to does not mean an oath in the name of God, which would violate the Third Commandment.) The Babylonian Talmud objects, in fact, to Samuel's ruling that: "the law of the kingdom is law." But it is probable, as Ginzberg says, that the Mishnah, refusing to recognize the right of Rome to impose discriminating taxes against the Jews in their own land, looks upon the tax-collectors as robbers and so permits even drastic methods of misleading them. This license would not, of course, extend to authorized tax-collectors in Babylon and other lands where the laws of the land had to be obeyed.

It is clear from a number of passages that where the practices of the governing body are iniquitous they should be resisted. When Moses observes an Egyptian task-master mercilessly flogging a Hebrew slave,

---

[1] Louis Ginzberg, *Mekomah shel ha-Halakhah be-Ḥokhmat Yisrael,* pp. 10–11, Jerusalem, 1931.

he has no compunction about slaying the Egyptian (Exodus 2:11–12). There are those who criticize this attitude and look upon Moses' act as murder. But surely the analogy is with a concentration camp guard beating a poor inmate with murderous intent. It is an odd sort of morality that would dare to charge with murder a brave man who sprang to the defense of the victim even if it meant killing the guard. Solomon Goldman[1] rightly comments:

> To which we, who have seen the flower of the Kulturvoelker, might add, for the benefit of those who have contended that Moses had acted without authority, from excess of passion, and that the act was consequently unjustifiable, we might add that in condemning a people to slavery and death the Egyptian had made a mockery of law and its administration. For Moses to have tried to bring the Egyptian before an Egyptian court of justice would have made as much sense as if Dr. Leo Baeck had attempted, between the years 1933 to 1945, to plead a Jew's case in a German court against a Nazi official. All that the one or the other would have achieved would have been to put their lives in jeopardy. The victims they could not have saved, and for the aggressors they would most certainly have won promotion.

There is hardly any need to refer to the instances of the Hebrew prophets rebuking the kings when these abused their powers to commit acts of injustice. Nathan rebukes David (II Samuel 12:1–15); Elijah castigates Ahab (I Kings 21:17–24); Amos defies Amaziah the priest of Beth-el and his master Jeroboam king of Israel (Amos 7: 10–17).

There is certainly, then, enough support in the Jewish sources for resistance to the demands of a tyrannical and iniquitous government. The difficulty in most of the situations in which civil disobedience is advocated is to determine when a government is tyrannical and iniquitous. Jews living in democracies have to be especially careful in assessing the rights and wrongs of civil disobedience. If anarchy is to be avoided it is essential for the individual to obey the law even if he finds it disagreeable. There are in a democracy legal ways of seeking to change the law. Certainly a Jew should not associate with those who openly proclaim the aim of destroying society. The evils that would result if

---

[1] Solomon Goldman, *From Slavery to Freedom,* p. 123, New York, 1958.

such an attempt were successful far outweigh the existing evils. For all that, if a man's conscience persuades him that the law is so evil that it cannot be tolerated then civil disobedience is called for. In our very complex society this should be seen as the very last resort. Indeed, there are few situations in which men of good-will can give this course of action their unqualified approval.

Class Distinctions

On *a priori* grounds it seems reasonable to assume that Judaism, with its strong emphasis on justice, does not in principle tolerate social distinctions between classes. But human nature being what it is, there have been class distinctions in Jewish life. These have been tolerated and even at times encouraged by the Jewish teachers, though they have rarely been seen as a permanent ideal. Especially with regard to marriage there has been a good deal of emphasis on *yihus* ("good stock"), and this inevitably resulted in a certain degree of snobbery.

A passage in the Mishnah (*Kiddushin* 2:3) says that if a man, when marrying a woman, gives her to understand that he is a Kohen (a priest) and it later turns out that he is only a Levite, then the marriage is invalid. It can be assumed that she wishes to marry a priest and hence he has misled her. The same Mishnah states that if he gave her to understand that he was a Levite but was in reality a priest, the marriage would similarly be invalid because, as the Talmud observes, she may not want "a sandal too big for her foot." There is no doubt that the aristocracy of the priests was held in high esteem even after the fall of the Temple. However, it is also true that gradually the aristocracy of learning superseded that of the priesthood. This substitution is reflected in another Mishnah (*Horayot* 3:8) in which it is said that a scholar who is a bastard takes precedence over a High Priest who is an ignoramus.

In a Talmudic passage (*Pesahim* 49b), probably dating from the second century, it is stated:

> *Let a man sell all he has and marry the daughter of a scholar.*
> *If he cannot marry the daughter of a scholar, let him marry*
> *the daughter of one of the great men of the generation (i.e.,*
> *a Jewish leader). If he cannot marry the daughter of one of*
> *the great men of the generation, let him marry the daughter*
> *of one of the heads of the synagogues (a local communal*

*leader). If he cannot marry the daughter of one of the heads
of the synagogues, let him marry the daughter of a charity
treasurer. If he cannot marry the daughter of a charity
treasurer, let him marry the daughter of a schoolteacher.
But let him never marry the daughter of an ignoramus.*

Reference should be made to the theory of Louis Ginzberg (though
many scholars today consider it to be too sweeping and unsupported
by evidence) that the two great schools of Shammai and Hillel, which
flourished at the beginning of the common era, really represented two
different social classes. According to this view, the School of Shammai
represented the upper classes, the wealthy men, the men of substance,
while the School of Hillel represented the artisans, the working men,
and the small traders. The many debates between the two schools are
thus seen as attempts to legislate for two different social classes. To
give one example of how his theory operates, the School of Shammai
only permits a man to divorce his wife if she has been unfaithful, but
the School of Hillel allows divorce even on other grounds (Mishnah
Gittin 9:10). The School of Hillel rules that for the act of marriage to
be effected through the formal delivery of an object of value, that object
need be worth no more than a *perutah*, the smallest coin of the realm.
But the School of Shammai declares the marriage to be invalid unless the
object is worth at least a *dinar*, a coin of much higher value (Mishnah
Kiddushin 1:1). If the theory is accepted that the two schools were legislating for two different social classes, it all fits neatly into place. Among
higher social classes the woman generally enjoys a far higher social
standing. Thus, according to the School of Shammai, a wife can only
be divorced for unfaithfulness and it is degrading to give her a small coin,
even for the formal act of marriage.

It is interesting to observe how Talmudic attitudes received expression
during the Middle Ages. The *Shulḥan Arukh (Even ha-Ezer* 2) quotes
from the Talmudic passage cited above verbatim but adds that the
ignoramus, whose daughter is never to be married, refers only to an
ignoramus who is not an observant Jew (paragraph 6). Furthermore, an
ignoramus should not marry the daughter of a Kohen, but it is highly
meritorious for a scholar to marry the daughter of a Kohen because
then learning and priestly stock will be intermingled (paragraph 8).
Although there are passages in the Talmud which frown on marriage for
the sake of money, it is stated (paragraph 1) that this only applies to an

unworthy match; otherwise, a marriage for the sake of money is permitted. In fact, it seems certain that marriages were frequently arranged during the Middle Ages to perpetuate the class distinctions between the learned and wealthy on the one hand and the unlearned and poor on the other. The phenomenal success of the Hasidic movement in the eighteenth century may at least partly be explained as a revolt of the lower social classes against the dominance of the rich and the learned. But ironically, the later Hasidim developed their own ideas about *yihus* and the Hasidic masters would only allow their children to marry into one another's families, so that again social distinctions were emphasized.

Here and there protests were heard against the whole idea of *yihus*. A well-known story tells of a great Rabbi whose father was a simple tailor. At a Rabbinic gathering each of the Rabbis prefaced his remarks by a reference to a saying of his "saintly father." The tailor's son began by saying: "My saintly father said that it is better to make a suit specially for a child than cut down one of his father's old suits to fit him."

Generally speaking, class distinctions are fast becoming a thing of the past in Jewish life.

Common Sense

There is an old Jewish saying that common sense is "the fifth *Shulḥan Arukh*." The reference is to the fact that the *Shulḥan Arukh*, the standard code of Jewish law, is divided into four sections, each dealing with a vast portion of the law. But there is a great difference between the law as recorded in black and white and its application in daily life. The Rabbis, whose decisions are based on the *Shulḥan Arukh* and who look up the relevant section of the Code when confronted with a problem, are expected to avail themselves of common sense as well in order to make their decisions reasonable. This idea of the basic "rightness" and reasonableness of the law is expressed in the Book of Deuteronomy (4:5–8):

> *Behold, I have taught you statutes and ordinances, even as the Lord my God commanded me, that ye should do so in the midst of the land whither ye go in to possess it. Observe therefore and do them; for this is your wisdom and your understanding in the sight of the peoples, that when they hear all these statutes, shall say: "Surely this great nation is a wise and understanding people." For what great nation is there, that hath God so nigh unto them, as the Lord our God is whensoever we call upon Him? And what great nation is there, that hath statutes and ordinances so righteous as all this law, which I set before you this day?*

The Rabbis have a term for common sense. This is *sevara* (from the Aramaic root *sevar*, "to think"), and is used by the Rabbis in their debates. A few examples from the Talmudic literature can be quoted. When a Rabbi quoted a scriptural verse to support the legal principle that the onus of proof falls on the plaintiff rather than the defendant, (i.e., that possession cannot be denied without conclusive proof), the famous Babylonian teacher R. Ashi objected that no scriptural proof is required since it is a matter of common sense. As R. Ashi puts it: "One who is in pain visits the house of the doctor" (i.e., the doctor does not go knocking on doors to see if anyone is sick but he has to be called by those who are sick or they visit him). From this passage (*Bava Kama* 46b) and similar ones we note that in the Rabbinic view a matter derived from common sense has the full force of a law stated explicitly in Scripture. In another passage (*Pesaḥim* 25b) it is argued that while an act otherwise forbidden may be performed in order to save a life, this does not apply to the crime of murder. If A were told that unless he kills B his own life would be forfeit, he would not be allowed to save his own life by murdering B. This is said to be a *sevara*. "How do you know that your blood is redder; perhaps his blood is redder." It is unreasonable to suggest that murder may be committed in order to save a life, since a life is lost in the very commission of the crime. The only justification would be that the life of the murderer is of greater value than the life of his victim, which is something that no one can possibly ascertain.

In *Sanhedrin* (29a) a scriptural verse is quoted to demonstrate that a judge who is an enemy of a man cannot try that man's case. What if the judge is a close friend of the man? The Talmud replies that the answer can be derived from the first case by a *sevara*. Why is the judge who is an enemy disqualified? Because his attitude makes him biased against the man. By the same token the judge who is a close friend is disqualified because his attitude makes him biased in the man's favor. Similarly, a *sevara* is used (*Kiddushin* 13b) to demonstrate that a widow may remarry. The reason a married woman may not marry another man is because she already has a husband. It follows by the use of a *sevara* that the widow who no longer has a husband may remarry.

Jewish philosophy can be seen largely as an attempt to explain Judaism in a reasonable manner. The fact that not everything that seemed reasonable to thinkers in past ages necessarily seems reasonable to us is beside the point. Behind the deliberations of these thinkers is confidence in the power of reason, and much effort has been put into finding proper perspectives where traditional teachings apparently conflict with what seems common sense.

Compassion

The old Rabbinic Midrash, the *Sifrei*, speaking of the ideal of the imitation of God, comments on the verse: "To love the Lord your God, to walk in all His ways" (Deuteronomy 11:22). According to the *Sifrei*, to walk in God's ways means: "Just as He is called 'Merciful' be thou merciful; just as He is called 'Compassionate' be thou compassionate." Compassion (*rahamanut*) has always been a Jewish trait. Its opposite, cruelty, has always been abhorred by Jews. A man who has no compassion thereby demonstrates that he is not a descendant of Abraham or of those who stood at the foot of Sinai (*Bezah* 32b). One of the ways in which a Jew is distinguished is through his compassion (*Yevamot* 79a). Women are especially endowed with the quality of compassion (*Megillah* 14b). They are more easily moved to tears than men. They should be spoken to gently. God, say the Rabbis, told Moses to speak the word of God in harsher accents to the men but with gentle accents to the women (*Mekhilta* to Exodus 19:3).

The word *rahamanut* has an interesting etymology. (It might be mentioned that the name Rahamim is frequently given to a child by Eastern Jews.) The word appears to be derived from *rehem* ("womb"). Thus the meaning of *rahamanut* is either "brotherly feeling" (of those born in the same womb) or "motherly feeling." It is worth noting that although God's love for man is generally expressed in the Bible in terms of a father's love for his children, the prophet, speaking of God comforting mourners, uses the figure of a mother comforting her children. "As one whom his mother comforteth, so will I comfort you" (Isaiah 66:13).

In the Jewish tradition there are only two limits to compassion. The first is with regard to justice. A judge must apply the principles of the law without regard to persons. It would be as wrong for him to give a favorable judgment to a poor litigant when the law opposes it as it would be for him to give a favorable judgment to a rich litigant when the law opposes it. Certainly, as a man it is his duty *after* the case has been decided to help the poor, but in his function as judge only the dictates of strict justice must be applied. Unless this principle is acknowledged there can be no law, for the judge will be swayed by his emotions. Most civilized peoples appreciate that hard cases make bad law. In the name of compassion itself the judge must decide in accordance with justice alone, for, were the law to fail, the unjust would find no hindrance to the realization of their schemes. To be sure, justice must be tempered with mercy, but where compassion can only be shown to a litigant at the expense of his fellow, justice and not compassion must prevail. This is implied in the remarkable biblical verse: "Neither shalt thou favor a poor man in his cause" (Exodus 23:3). That is why R. Akiva says: "They may not show pity in a legal suit" (Mishnah *Ketubbot* 9:2). The Talmud (*Sanhedrin* 6b) remarks that in rendering legal judgment King David used to acquit the innocent and condemn the guilty; but when he saw that the condemned man was poor, he helped him out of his own purse, thus executing justice and charity at the same time.

The second limit to compassion is to those who themselves lack compassion and practice cruelty. "He who is compassionate to the cruel," said one of the Rabbis, "will, in the end, be cruel to the compassionate" (*Yalkut*, Samuel 121). Judaism does not teach that all hatred is evil. The hatred of evil is a good: "O ye that love the Lord, hate evil" (Psalms 97:10).

Apart from these two instances Judaism considers compassion to be among the highest of the virtues. The good heart is a heart moved to have compassion on all God's creatures.

Corporal Punishment

Flogging as a punishment is mentioned in the Book of Deuteronomy (25: 1–3). The whole of Chapter 3 of *Makkot* in the Talmud is devoted to the rules governing this type of punishment, called *malkut* ("blows"). According to the Rabbis the punishment is meted out to whomever violates a stricture in the Torah ("thou shalt not") in which an action is involved. The number of lashes given were thirty-nine. The instrument used was an ox-hide strap. Provided that the doctor of the court agreed that the victim could bear the punishment, twenty-six lashes were given on the naked back and thirteen on the naked chest while the victim

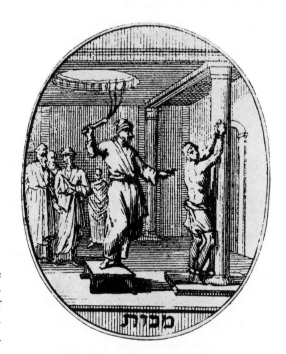

Engraving for the tractate *Makkot*, showing a flogging, from a title page of the Hebrew-Latin Mishnah, Amsterdam, 1700–04.

was bound to a post. The punishment was administered to women as well as to men.

All this certainly seems very brutal. The question to be considered, however, is whether these rules were followed in actual practice or whether they were purely theoretical. There is a good deal of evidence that in the main it was all theoretical. For instance, according to Rabbinic law, the penalty is only incurred when the offender commits the forbidden act in the presence of two witnesses, who have to warn him beforehand that if he persists in the act in their presence they will testify against him. In these circumstances, it is not likely that many offenders would have been punished in this way. But this is not the whole story. In addition to the formal penalty of *malkut* the courts could administer a flogging known as *makkat mardut*, ("the blows for rebellion") for certain offenses if it saw fit, and this type of flogging seems to have been administered not infrequently.

As late as the second half of the eighteenth century floggings were administered by the courts in Eastern Europe and adjacent to many synagogues were pillories (called by the Polish name *kuna*) in which offenders were placed. The preacher Abba of Glussk, for instance, once expressed some critical views regarding the Midrash and Rashi in the presence of the great Gaon of Vilna. The Gaon was horrified and broke off the conversation. Before long two messengers of the court dragged the poor preacher from his lodgings to appear before a court of seven elders, the leader of which declared him guilty. In a letter to Moses Mendelssohn, Abba of Glussk describes what followed[1]:

> *The old man thereupon made a sign with his hand, and the two henchmen of the evil one seized and led me out into the courtyard. Then I heard from the lips of the same old man the decision of the court, that on account of defaming the sages of olden times I was condemned to forty strokes, which the two myrmidons administered to me on the spot. But their rage was by no means assuaged by this, for I was led to the threshold of the synagogue and my neck was enclosed within the iron rings attached to the wall, so as then to expose me to the people, with a piece of paper on my head bearing the words: "This man has been punished for scoffing at*

[1] Israel Cohen, *History of the Jews in Vilna,* pp. 224–5, Philadelphia, 1943.

the word of our holy teachers." Everybody who came for the afternoon service stopped and called to me: "Traitor to Israel!" But even more; they spat nearly into my face, so that the spittle really flowed in streams. Thou knowest well that Vilna is not Berlin, and that the people here go to prayer in crowds. After the evening service was over, I was conducted outside the city and obliged to depart.

Whatever the situation may have been in the past, corporal punishment has now disappeared from Jewish life. In the State of Israel there is no corporal punishment in the prisons and no Rabbinic court anywhere in the world today would dream of administering this form of punishment.

What of corporal punishment in schools and in the home? Throughout the ancient world, so far as we can tell, child-beating was held to be an essential ingredient in the educational process, and the Jews were no exception. The Book of Proverbs (13:24) declares: "He that spareth his rod hateth his son; but he that loveth him chastiseth him betimes." The idea of the father beating his child because of his love for him is behind the verse: "And thou shalt consider in thy heart, that as a man chastiseth his son, so the Lord thy God chastiseth thee" (Deuteronomy 8:5). The Book of Proverbs again declares: "The rod and reproof give wisdom; but a child left to himself causeth shame to his mother" (Proverbs 29:15); and: "Correct thy son, and he will give thee rest; yea, he will give delight unto thy soul" (Proverbs 29:17). On the basis of the latter verse the ruling was given (*Makkot* 5a) in Talmudic times (though from the context it is clear that the ruling was only a theoretical one) that if a father or a teacher beats a child, and the child dies as a result, there is no crime of manslaughter, even if the child is being flogged as an incentive and not because he is badly behaved. However, against all this has to be set the advice of the famous Babylonian teacher Rav that children in a school were only to beaten with a small strap like the lace of a shoe (*Bava Batra* 21a). Following this, Maimonides (*Yad, Talmud Torah* 2:2) writes: "Children are to be brought into the school at the age of six or seven, depending on the child's physical fitness and health. Children must not be sent to school at an earlier age. The teacher should beat them in order to exercise control but he must not beat them cruelly as if he were their enemy. Consequently, he must not use a cane or a stick to beat them but only a small strap."

Unfortunately, these sensible ideas were frequently overlooked and harsh discipline was certainly not unknown in the Jewish schools of the past.

In modern times the corporal punishment of children has come to be looked upon with increasing disfavor by educationalists, though some teachers still believe that in the case of thoroughly unruly children who can disrupt the school there is no alternative. It should also be said that psychologists have called attention to the permanent harm corporal punishment can do to children in awakening sado-masochistic feelings in later life.

Cremation

The practice of cremation as a means of disposing of a corpse was known in the ancient world, but it was not until the last century that the practice became widespread. There is no doubt that the traditional Jewish method was burial in the ground or in mausoleums. Nowadays Reform Judaism generally sees little to object to in cremation, though it normally encourages burial. Orthodox and to a very large extent Conservative Judaism frowns severely on cremation. In Orthodox Responsa published during this century and the last there is nothing but disdain for Jews who state in their wills that their bodies should be cremated.

Orthodox objections to cremation are on a number of grounds, some of them more convincing than others:

1) Cremation was a pagan practice in ancient times and is consequently associated with the idolatrous myths and beliefs against which Judaism has successfully fought. Even an innocent practice can become tainted through association.

2) In the Book of Deuteronomy (21:23) it is said that even the body of an executed criminal must be buried. The Talmud (*Sanhedrin* 46b) discusses the Scriptural evidence for burial and observes that no conclusion can be drawn from the fact that the Patriarchs were buried, since this might have been simply to conform to the custom of the times. However, the conclusion reached is that burial is a *mitzvah*, a religious duty, and where cremation takes place the *mitzvah* has not been fulfilled.

3) It is forbidden in Jewish law to mutilate a corpse (*Ḥullin* 11b). When the corpse is buried decomposition takes place as a natural process, unlike the case of cremation. In the latter case, the remains of a human being are intentionally destroyed. In this connection the analogy with a scroll of the Torah is relevant. Even when a Sefer Torah is no longer fit for use, it is buried in the earth out of reverence rather than directly destroyed. Although the analogy is not too exact (a scroll

is sacred whereas a corpse is a source of contamination; see Numbers 19:14), the point is that delicacy of feeling should preclude anything but a reverential disposal of what was once a human being.

4) It is recorded in Talmudic legend (*Gittin* 56b) that Titus ordered his body to be cremated and his ashes scattered to avoid the judgment of God. Consequently, an argument has been advanced that anyone who wishes his body to be cremated thereby demonstrates a lack of belief in the resurrection of the dead and in God's judgment. This is the weakest of all the arguments against cremation. Many believing Jews do not understand the doctrine of the resurrection of the dead in the crude, literal sense, and even those who do cannot believe that it is not within the power of God to reconstitute a body that has been cremated, just as it lies within His power to reconstitute a body that has decayed after burial. The notion that there is a small bone in the body which does not decay and from which the resurrected body is reconstituted (making cremation forbidden because it destroys this bone) belongs to folklore. The Jews who perished in the gas chambers and whose bodies were burnt in the crematoria are surely not denied their place in the Hereafter because they were not buried.

5) Cremation is opposed to tradition, and it is wrong to depart from the custom of burial which Jews practiced for thousands of years.

The arguments of those who oppose burial and advocate cremation because graveyards take up too much space do not have much to commend them. The amount of land involved is infinitesimal and graveyards are usually situated in the countryside. In any event, crematoria usually have spacious gardens attached to them which also occupy space. Another argument is that the quick disposal by cremation which the bereaved family does not witness spares their feelings. Apart from the dubiousness of this proposition, Judaism does not wish us to close our eyes to the darker side of human existence and the mortality that is man's lot. Judaism does not encourage a morbid preoccupation with death, but it does encourage a healthy realism in which the inescapable fact of death is faced courageously.

A question discussed in a number of Orthodox Responsa is whether the ashes of a cremated person may be buried in a Jewish cemetery. Some authorities forbid this, while others permit it. The practice of the Orthodox community in Great Britain, for example, is to permit the burial of the ashes in the cemetery provided that they are placed in a regular coffin.

Democracy

So far as we can tell the ideal form of government envisaged in the Biblical sources is a theocracy. When, for example, Moses accepts the advice of his father-in-law Jethro to appoint leaders to judge the people (Exodus 18), he first has to obtain God's consent and then Moses, with the authority given to him by God, selects the judges himself. Moses' successors, Joshua and the Judges, are similarly leaders in whom "the spirit of the Lord" resides, i.e., men whom God has inspired to act as leaders. From the time of Saul and David, however, the form of government is a monarchy, though, as has long been recognized, there is a certain ambiguity in the sources as to whether the monarchy is thought of as a divinely ordained institution or a mere concession to the people, who desired to have a king "like the other nations."

The relevant passage in the Book of Deuteronomy (17:14–20) is understood by the second century teacher R. Judah to mean that it is a religious duty for the people to have a king, but his contemporary R. Nehemiah disagrees (*Sifrei* to Deuteronomy 17:14). In any event the passage states that the king was to write a copy of the law and study it "that his heart be not lifted up above his brethren." The king and his subjects are brothers.

On the other hand, in the first book of Samuel (Ch. 8) Samuel tells the people that God was displeased when they wanted a king and that this implied a rejection of God's rule. In this chapter (verses 13–18) there occurs a fiercely anti-monarchic denunciation in which the prophet spells out the autocratic powers of the king:

> *And he will take your daughters to be perfumers, and to be cooks, and to be bakers. And he will take your fields, and your vineyards, and your oliveyards, even the best of them, and give them to his servants. And he will take the tenth of your seed, and of your vineyards, and give to his*

105

officers, and to his servants. And he will take your men-
servants, and your maid-servants, and your goodliest young
men, and your asses, and put them to his work. He will take
the tenth of your flocks; and ye shall be his servants. And
ye shall cry out in that day because of your king whom ye
shall have chosen you; and the Lord will not answer.

Very interesting in this connection are the remarks of Isaac Abravanel
(1437–1508) in his commentary to the passage in Deuteronomy. A
republic, remarks this commentator, is to be preferred to a monarchy,
since when power is shared abuses can be corrected but when all power
is in the hands of one man there is dictatorship. Elected officers have to
give periodic accounts to those who elect them but a king is only responsible to himself. Those countries, continues Abravanel, where the
administration is in the hands of kings are full of corruption. But those
countries where the administration is in the hands of temporary rulers
are governed wisely. Abravanel gives as an illustration the states of
Venice and Florence in his own day. Admittedly, says Abravanel,
there are some monarchies in which the powers of the king are curtailed
and here the harm is far less. Best of all, however, is a situation where
there is no king at all.

After the destruction of the Second Temple the leadership of the
Palestinian community was vested in the Patriarchate. In Babylon,
the second great center of Jewish life, the Exilarch was a kind of king over
the Jews with authority granted to him by the Persian rulers. At a later
period, although in theory the democratic principle was at work in
Jewish communities—education, for example, was open to all classes
and leading scholars came even from the poorer classes—in practice
it was very frequently the rich who were the real leaders of the community. Salo Baron[1] has observed:

> *There has been a great deal of rhetoric concerning the "demo-*
> *cratic" features of the old type of Jewish community. Even a*
> *cursory glance at Jewish communal history must persuade the*
> *unprejudiced observer that the term "democratic" as here*
> *applied has a meaning entirely different from that used for*
> *the political organisms of our day. The simple facts are that*
> *the bulk of world Jewry, even after the second fall of Jerusalem,*

[1] *Salo Baron, The Jewish Community,* Vol. 1, pp. 27–28, Philadelphia, 1945.

was for several centuries subject to the control of the Palestinian patriarchate.

Simultaneously, that part of Jewry which was under the Parthian and Persian empires was under the control of the Babylonian Exilarch until the beginning of the second millennium C.E. After the suppression of the patriarchal office, all Jews lived under the exilarch. It is obvious that both the patriarchate and the exilarchate had all the basic features of hereditary monarchy. Although the prerogatives of the Jewish leaders, unlike those of other oriental potentates, were curtailed by competing powers of scholars and of individuals who wielded influence at various courts (the so-called shtadlanim), *one can hardly speak of a democratic regime at any time in this long epoch. In medieval and early modern Europe, on the other hand, the frequent concentration of wealth gave a preponderant share in communal administration to a few families, which often determined communal affairs against the clear wishes of the majority. In early modern Holland, Germany and Poland, particularly, the steady growth of communal oligarchy had practically eliminated all vestiges of constitutional democracy which were retained in formal statutes.*

While there are many references in the Talmudic literature to local government—for example, taxation, the police force, market controls, and the like—there are no rules about how the mayor and town council are to be elected and, indeed, we have no evidence as to how elections to communal offices were conducted. The best-known reference is to the sale of communal property, such as the town synagogue, "by the seven good men of the city in presence of the city's inhabitants" (*Megillah* 26a), but while the democratic principle appears to be implied in the latter stipulation there is no evidence as to how the "seven good men" were elected.

In the realm of scholarship, however, the democratic principle did obtain. Not only was a court case decided by a majority vote of the judges (*Ḥullin* 11a) but in legal disputes among scholars the majority opinion was followed, with even a voice from Heaven in favor of the minority being considered ineffective (*Bava Meẓia* 59b). R. Meir was so brilliant that his colleagues were incapable of grasping his full meaning and for that very reason their view is followed and not his (*Eruvin* 13b).

When great issues were at stake—the primacy of study or practice, for example—the matter was put to a vote and decided by a majority (*Kiddushin* 40b).

In our kind of world, where the alternatives to a democratic form of government are a dictatorship or totalitarian state, democracy would seem to be preferable. It is not that the majority is always right or even that the majority is more likely to be right but that men have a right to govern themselves. Where majority and minority interests are in conflict the decision rests with the majority simply because it is better that the wishes of a majority as to what is best for them should be heeded. In a sound democracy, moreover, minority rights are adequately safeguarded. As John Stuart Mill has said: "If all mankind minus one, were of one opinion, and only one person were of the contrary opinion, mankind would be no more justified in silencing that one person, than he, if he had the power, would be justified in silencing mankind." There are important Jewish principles at stake in this matter: the rights of the individual created in the image of God; the free choice of the individual, which enables him to choose his way of life; the divine injunction for men to love one another; the equality of all citizens under the law. The Pentateuchal legislation is full of appeals to the rights of all men: "One law and one ordinance shall be both for you, and for the stranger that sojourneth with you" (Numbers 15:16). Totalitarian systems in which the state becomes virtually an object of worship is the modern form of idolatry against which the Hebrew prophets fulminated. It is not at all surprising, therefore, that the State of Israel, founded by Jews, is a democratic state.

Dignity

A religion which teaches, as Judaism does, that man is created in God's image, is bound to affirm human dignity. In the Creation narrative at the beginning of the Book of Genesis man is created after all other creatures, as if to suggest that man is the culmination of all created things, the being above all others in whom God takes delight.

Even the dignity of a criminal must be preserved. His corpse must not be left hanging overnight on the gallows (Deuteronomy 21:23). The Talmud records (*Sanhedrin* 46b) the remarkably bold, anthropomorphic parable on the verse: "For he that is hanged is a degradation of God" (Deuteronomy 21:23). It is compared to the case of twin brothers who closely resembled one other. One became king, the other was arrested for robbery and hanged. Whoever saw him on the gallows thought that the king was hanged! Similarly, when a criminal was flogged care had to be taken not to add to the prescribed number of strokes: "Otherwise, if they go further and exceed this number, your brother will have been publicly degraded" (Deuteronomy 25:3).

The technical Rabbinic term for human dignity is *kevod ha-beriot*, literally "respect for human beings." "Great is *kevod ha-beriot*" is a Rabbinic saying (*Berakhot* 19b). Based on this are the Rabbinic rules concerning a corpse with no relatives to bury it — *met mitzvah* ("a corpse the burial of which is a religious obligation"). Even a man on his way to bring his paschal lamb is obliged to forego his duty and attend to the *met mitzvah* (*Berakhot* 19b–20a) because it is degrading to leave a corpse unburied even for a short time. Similarly if an elder who would not normally attend to an animal finds his neighbor's ox or ass straying, he is exempt from the obligation to look after it until the owner is found (*Berakhot* 19b). His dignity has to be safeguarded.

Some persons are especially singled out for dignified treatment—parents, for example. In tractate *Kiddushin* (31b) we read:

> *Our Rabbis taught: How are we to understand respect for parents and honor of parents? Respect means that a son should not stand or sit in his father's place, that he should not contradict his father's opinions and that when his father argues with another person he should not take it upon himself to decide which of them is right. Honor means that a son should provide his father with food and drink, with clothes and garments, and should assist him as he enters a room.*

Aged persons and scholars should be treated with special respect. The Rabbis apply the verse: "Thou shalt rise up before the hoary head, and honor the face of the old man" (Leviticus 19:32) to scholars as well as to the aged, and rule that one should rise to one's feet as a token of respect whenever an old man or a scholar passes by (*Kiddushin* 32b). Some of the Rabbis would show respect even to aged pagans because, they argued, they have been through so much in their long lives (*Kiddushin* 33a). With delicacy of feeling, the third century Palestinian teacher R. Joshua b. Levi ordered his sons to show respect to a senile scholar who had forgotten his learning through no fault of his own. He noted that the broken tablets of the law were placed in the ark together with the unbroken ones (*Berakhot* 8b).

One of the great Jewish exponents of man's worth and dignity was the head of the yeshivah of Slobodka Rabbi Nathan Zevi Finkel (1849–1927). His ideas about the dignity of man found expression in his personal life. It is reported that the doctors who examined him when he was sick found it very difficult to persuade him to show his tongue because it is disrespectful to stick out one's tongue at a human being. Rabbi Finkel respected the image of God in every man. He would frequently go to the railroad station to help people with their luggage and speed them on their way. A gypsy caravan once passed by and he walked a little of the way with them to show his respect. Rabbi Finkel claimed to have found his attitude toward human dignity clearly stated in the saying of Rabbi Akiva in *Ethics of the Fathers* (*Avot* 3:14):

> *Beloved is man for he was created in the image of God; still greater was the love in that it was made known to him that he was created in the image of God, as it is written: "For in the image of God made He man" (Genesis 9:8).*

Divorce

The law as recorded in the Book of Deuteronomy (24:1–4) speaks of a man divorcing his wife and not of a wife divorcing her husband. The reason for this is that in ancient Jewish law a man could have more than one wife. In a polygamous society it is the wife who is bound to her husband, and while he can take another wife she cannot take another husband. Consequently, the bond between a man and his wife can only be severed when the husband gives his wife a "bill of divorcement," later called a *get* (the word means "document"). It appears from the law as stated in Deuteronomy that the husband can divorce his wife against her will. In modern times Reform Judaism has protested against this inequity and many Reform Rabbis have dispensed with the *get* altogether, relying in matters of divorce on the civil courts. It is only right, however, to note that in traditional law there can be traced a number of successive enactments all of which were intended to favor the wife and prevent discrimination against her. Foremost among these is the institution of the *ketubbah*, the marriage contract, in which a settlement is made by the groom so that in the event of his divorcing his wife (or her becoming a widow) she will be provided for. The need to pay the amount specified in the *ketubbah* acted as a check against easy divorce against the wishes of the wife. Furthermore, the Rabbis rule that in certain circumstances the wife could institute divorce proceedings; although it is the husband who actually gives the *get*, he can be coerced by the courts to consent to give it. This kind of consent by coercion was recognized as valid in order to enable the wife to regain her freedom to remarry (*Kiddushin* 50a). Among the instances mentioned in the Mishnah (*Ketubbot* 7:10) where a husband can be compelled to divorce his wife are when he becomes afflicted with an abhorrent disease or when he engages in an unpleasant occupation such as a tanner.

Among the enactments attributed to Rabbi Gershom of Mainz (d. 1028) are the prohibition of polygamy and divorce against the

Four scenes illustrating the process of divorce in a *bet din*, from Johann Boden-schatz' *Kirchliche Verfassung der heutigen Juden*, 1748–49. Above: (left) a woman weeps as the scribe prepares to write the *get*. The husband speaks to two members of the court; (right) scene of the *bet din* with the rabbis examining the bill of divorcement. Witnesses stand in the background. Below: (left) the husband throws the *get* and (right) the wife catches it.

wife's wishes. This ban (known as *herem de-rabbenu Gershom,* "the ban of our teacher Gershom") was accepted in the Ashkenazi world, and in Israel today it is the law for Sephardim as well. The result is that as the law has developed there is equality between men and women with regard to divorce, and the consent of both parties is required (except in instances such as those mentioned above). However, the equality is not entirely complete. In certain circumstances (where the wife becomes incurably insane, for instance), a dispensation of the *herem* can be granted to the husband by 100 Rabbis residing in three different countries, while such a remedy is not open to the wife (since for her to marry again without a *get* is adultery, whereas for the husband it is only an offense against the ban). In practice this meas that in Jewish law there is divorce by mutual consent, though the Rabbinic court will only arrange for the *get* to be delivered after they have exhausted every attempt at reconciling husband and wife.

It is important to appreciate a point that has unfortunately eluded many critics of Rabbinic Judaism—that the statements in the Mishnah (*Gittin* 9:10) about the grounds for divorce are in the nature of legal decisions and not moral advice. (In any event, even from the purely legal point of view, we have seen that eventually the consent of the wife is required, so that the rulings in the Mishnah have no force even in law.) The School of Shammai, in the Mishnah, prohibits divorce unless the wife is unfaithful. The School of Hillel, on the other hand, permits a husband to divorce his wife "even if she spoiled a dish for him" while R. Akiva permits it "even if he found another fairer than she." This is a purely legal debate on what grounds are necessary for a divorce to be allowed. The School of Shammai permits divorce only on grounds of unfaithfulness, the School of Hillel even on other grounds which disturb the harmony of the home, while R. Akiva does not require any "grounds" at all. For Akiva, once the marriage has fallen apart, for whatever reason, a divorce is allowed.

As far as the moral attitude is concerned, it is clear that in the Jewish tradition a marriage is contracted for life. It is true that there are no marriage "vows" but the intent is for the couple who marry to live together as man and wife and not to contemplate divorce. That is why "making peace between husband and wife" is considered a high religious duty and why a Rabbinic court will do its utmost to bring about a reconciliation between a couple applying for a divorce. In fact, in this matter, the courts have acted as marriage counsellors as well as judges in their efforts to help a marriage to succeed. Tractate *Gittin*, in which the laws of divorce are described in great detail, concludes, in the Babylonian Talmud (90b), with the following passage:

> *R. Eleazar said: If a man divorces his first wife, even the altar sheds tears, as it is said: "And this further ye do, ye cover the altar with tears, with weeping and with sighing, insomuch that He regardeth not the offering any more, neither receiveth it with good will at your hand. Yet ye say, Wherefore? Because the Lord hath been witness between thee and the wife of thy youth, against whom thou hast dealt treacherously, though she is thy companion and the wife of thy covenant" (Malachi 2:13–14).*

The very fact that in Biblical passages the relationship between God and Israel is described in terms of the marriage relationship demonstrates both that marriage is held in high esteem and that divorce is severely frowned upon if it can be avoided. There is a Ḥasidic saying according to which this is the reason why R. Gershom of Mainz is known as *Me'or ha-Golah,* "Light of the Exile." R. Gershom's ban on polygamy and on divorcing a wife against her will has given new hope and illumination to the Jews in exile. For God must obey the law and however displeased He is with His people He cannot take another people to be His nor can He divorce Israel. A pleasant piece of fancy but one that throws light, too, on the way Jewish teachers have looked upon divorce.

Drugs

While there are references in the classical Jewish sources to the use of drugs as medicine or painkillers there are no references to the taking of drugs for what is nowadays called psychedelic effects. It is known that in some ancient religious systems drug-taking was part of the ritual, but there is not the slightest trace of anything like this in the Bible or the Talmudic literature. The attempts that have been made, on alleged philological grounds, to prove that the "sacred mushroom" was used in ancient Jewish worship are completely unfounded and have been dismissed by all the competent scholars in the field. Apart from the total lack of any evidence in the texts, plants producing psychedelic effects did not grow in the part of the world in which the Bible was compiled.

This applies also to the Jewish mystics. Nowhere do we find that they resorted to drugs in order to "expand the limits of perception." The nearest we get to artificially induced states in the mystics is the use of alcohol by the Ḥasidim. Recently, Yaffa Eliach[1] has, however, argued that the famous *lulke* ("pipe") smoked by the Ba'al Shem Tov, the founder of the Ḥasidic movement, contained something rather more potent than tobacco. But the evidence for this is flimsy and leaves unsolved the question of where and how something like "pot" could have been available in Volhynia and Podolia in the eighteenth century. Moreover, it is unlikely that, if the Ba'al Shem had really used drugs with a religious motive, none of his followers should have adopted the practice or even referred to it.

In "hippie" culture, it is frequently claimed that states similar to, or identical with, those experienced by the great mystics can be attained by such artificial means as the taking of drugs, such as LSD. Aldous

---

[1] *Proceedings of the American Academy for Jewish Research,* Vol. 36, pp. 57–83, 1968.

Huxley believed that the mystical states he describes in *The Perennial Philosophy*[1] could also be attained through mescalin.[2] Huxley describes his own experiments with mescalin, and his books, published in paperback form, have had a broad influence. Arthur Koestler has said that the mystic and the drug-taker both reach the same peak, but one climbs there laboriously by foot while the other uses the cable-car. If this were really so the Puritan might retort that shortcuts to sainthood were not for him, while those out for kicks of the more intense kind might argue that, provided one reaches the peak, the way of ascent matters little. But is it, in fact, the same peak that is reached? In a learned book[3] Professor R. C. Zaehner argues that the very quality of the experience of the mystic who sees God is different from the nature-mystic's experience. Zaehner's thesis is that it is incorrect to consider, as some scholars have done, all mystical experiences as being of the same order. It would follow, says Zaehner, from the argument of those who say that the experiences are the same, that not only can "mystical" experience be obtained artificially by taking drugs but it is also natural to the manic, since if one goes by superficial descriptions the hallucination of the lunatic is "one and the same" as the vision of God by the mystical saint. Some would be prepared to say precisely this, but if one does believe in God and the possibility of rare souls having a vision of Him even in this life it is hard to accept the facile identification of the two states.

In this connection, the acute analysis of mystical states by Dov Baer of Lubavitch, the second leader of Ḥabad Ḥasidism, is directly relevant.[4] After first distinguishing between authentic and sham ecstasy (in the latter case a person is sufficiently disengaged to be able to watch himself enjoying his raptures), Dov Baer makes a further distinction between "divine ecstasy" (*hitpa'alut ha-elohut*) and "ecstasy of the fleshly life" (*hitpa'alut ḥayei basar*). Divine ecstasy is an authentic experience of God in which the divine spark in man leaps in rapture to meet its source. It is purely spiritual, the meeting of like and like, whereas the other sort, even when authentic, is semi-physical, owing much—though,

---

[1] London, 1946.

[2] *The Dawn of Perception and Heaven and Hell,* London, 1959.

[3] *Mysticism, Sacred and Profane,* Oxford, 1957.

[4] *Kunteros ha-Hitpa'alut,* Warsaw, 1868; translated under the title *Tract on Ecstasy,* London, 1963.

of course, Dov Baer does not put it in quite these terms—to the metabolism of the body.

Dov Baer is not quoted to clinch the argument. After all, one can disagree with Dov Baer's analysis, even though by all accounts he was a genuine theistic mystic who knew what he was talking about. But from Dov Baer's remarks on the subject, one can see that, while the Ḥasidim were certainly not averse to using artificial stimulants (the dance, music, and alcohol) to assist them in the attainment of ecstasy, they believed that ultimately the really authentic kind was the result of deep contemplation and arduous moral effort and that there are no shortcuts. Their views on the subject are supported by the kind of testimonies from Christian and Muslim mystics quoted by Zaehner and others.

It is clear from the above that there are hardly any references in the Jewish sources to the use of drugs for the attainment of ecstatic states. We are on much surer ground when we consider what Judaism has to say on the harmful effects of drug-taking. In the Jewish tradition, any act that is harmful to body or mind is strictly forbidden. The dangers of a "bad trip" are too well known to require elaboration, to say nothing of the real possibilities of psychological, if not physical, addiction even in the case of "soft" drugs. The damage done by the "hard" drugs such as heroin is so severe that civilized countries have treated drug-trafficking as a heinous crime to be prosecuted with the full rigor of the law. According to the Rabbis, anything that is dangerous to life and limb must be avoided. In eastern climes, where there was a chance that snakes might inject their venom into drink, it was forbidden to drink any liquid left uncovered (Mishnah, *Terumot* 8:4). The law in Deuteronomy (22:8) states: "When thou buildest a new house, then thou shalt make a parapet for thy roof, that thou bring not blood upon thy house, if any man fall from thence." The Rabbis extended this to prohibit a man from keeping a mean dog or an unstable ladder in his house (*Ketubbot* 41b). The story is told of a Rabbi who refused to enter the house of another Rabbi because he kept dangerous mules in his stable. "The angel of death is in this man's house and shall I accept his hospitality?" (*Ḥullin* 7b). Maimonides (*Yad, Rozeaḥ* 11:5) sums up the Rabbinic view: "There are many things forbidden by the sages because they are dangerous. Whoever does them, saying: 'If I wish to risk my life what business is it of others?' or 'I do not mind taking the risk'—he is to be flogged." The *Shulḥan Arukh* (*Yoreh Deah* 116:5) rules that it is a worse offense to endanger one's life than to eat forbidden food, so that even though in certain cases, where the risk of it being forbidden is remote, food may be eaten, even a remote risk of danger should be avoided—walking under an unsafe wall, for example. From all that has been said it is obvious that drug-taking (except under medical supervision) is forbidden according to the Jewish tradition.

Ecology

The Midrash (*Ecclesiastes Rabbah* to 7:13) tells how God took Adam around the Garden of Eden, showing him all its beauty, and then He said to him: "See how lovely and how worthy of praise are My works. They have all been created for your sake. Take care not to spoil or destroy My world." This would serve as an admirable text for a discussion of the problem which is now agitating a large number of thoughtful people—the problem of ecology. There are three essays in English on the Jewish attitude to the problem, all of which repay study: "Ecology in Jewish Law and Theology" by Norman Lamm[1]; "Ecology and the Jewish Tradition" by Eric G. Freudenstein[2]; and "Ecology and the Jewish Tradition: A Postscript" by Jonathan I. Helfand.[3]

The problem is essentially a new one, caused by the proliferation of vast industries; by the succesful fight against disease which has created the danger of overpopulation; by the invention of the diesel engine; by global wars; by the use of nuclear energy; and by building activities on a scale unimagined in the past. It is futile, therefore, to expect any direct guidance from the Jewish tradition. Nor is it relevant to quote: "And replenish the earth, and subdue it; and have dominion over the fish of the sea, and over the fowl of the air, and over every living thing that creepeth upon the earth" (Genesis 1:28). When this verse was recorded there was no problem of ecology. Quite the contrary, at that time man's problem was how to master the environment. This is apart from the fact that Jewish interpretations of the verse have never understood it to mean that man's right and duty to conquer nature is unlimited. What one can do is to examine the principles found in the classical sources and try to apply them to our situation. When this

---

[1] *Faith in Doubt*, New York, 1971, pp. 162–185.
[2] *Judaism*, Vol. 19, Fall 1970, pp. 406–414.
[3] *Judaism*, Vol. 20, Summer 1971, pp. 330–335.

indirect method is pursued it becomes clear that Jewish teaching certainly disapproves of man's exercising the kind of uncontrolled exploitation of nature that, if persisted in, will eventually destroy the world and man himself. But it must be repeated that the lesson to be derived from the sources is only an indirect one. These sources do not deal with the problem on a global scale, where the cooperation of many nations is required, but with the more limited problem of how city dwellers are to cope with their environment and how the individual Jew is to avoid wasting nature's resources.

Waste disposal, for instance, was a major problem in Rabbinic times. Care was to be taken that bits of broken glass should not be scattered on public land where they cause injury. We are told that saintly men would bury their broken glassware deep down in their own fields (*Bava Kama* 30a). Other rubbish could be deposited on public land, but only during the winter months when in any event the roads were a morass of mud due to the rains (*Bava Kama* 30a). The following rules from the Mishnah in the second chapter of *Bava Batra* demonstrate how Rabbinic concern for a peaceful and clean environment expressed itself in law. A dovecot must not be kept within fifty cubits of a town and no one may keep a dovecot on his own property unless his land extends fifty cubits in every direction around it. The reason is to prevent the doves from consuming the seeds sown in the neighboring fields. Since a city is more attractive with a wide open space around it, no trees may be planted within a distance of twenty-five cubits from the city. If the trees were there before the city was built they can be cut down, but the owner must be compensated for them. Carcasses, graves, and tanneries must be kept at a distance of at least fifty cubits from the city. A tannery must not be set up in such a way that the prevailing winds can waft the unpleasant odor to the town. Because of the damage they might cause to young plants, the Mishnah (*Bava Kama* 7:7) rules that goats or sheep must not be raised in the cultivated areas of the Land of Israel. There is little doubt, historically considered, that this is a measure that was introduced to encourage renewed agricultural growth after the devastations to the land caused by the wars with Rome.

Relevant further to the theme is the prohibition against destroying anything of value. This is known in Rabbinic traditions as *bal tashḥit* ("do not destroy") and is based on the Biblical prohibition (Deuteronomy 20:19) against destroying fruit-bearing trees but extended by the Rabbis to include all cases of wasting things that can be used. Thus, while it is the practice to rend the garment on hearing of the death of a near relative, to tear too much or too many garments violates this principle (*Bava Kama* 91b). Maimonides (*Yad, Melakhim* 6:10) summarizes the Rabbinic view when he writes:

> *It is not only forbidden to destroy fruit-bearing trees but whoever breaks vessels, tears clothes, demolishes a building, stops up a fountain or wastes food, in a destructive way, offends against the law of "thou shalt not destroy."*

It is forbidden to destroy animals (*Hullin* 7b) or even to cause the oil in a lamp to burn too quickly (*Shabbat* 67b), The prohibition of *bal tashhit* does not apply, however, if the thing is destroyed for constructive purposes. This is the meaning of Maimonides' qualification "in a destructive way." If, for instance, a fruit-bearing tree causes damage to other trees or the value of its wood for fuel is greater than the value of the fruit it produces, it may be cut down (*Bava Kama* 91b–92a). However, even if the tree is needed for building purposes it is better to use other wood. The Midrash (*Exodus Rabbah* 34) observes that the reason the wood used for the Tabernacle in the wilderness was not from fruit-bearing trees was to teach us that our own houses should be built with wood from other than fruit-bearing trees.

The problem today can only be tackled with the help of experts who can advise how to exercise sufficient control over what we do so as not to impoverish the world. Obviously, Judaism cannot have anything to say about how these experts should go about achieving their aims or even whether all their dire warnings are justified. But it is clear that Judaism affirms without reservation that the world is God's creation and that whoever helps to preserve it is doing God's work.

Ecumenism

This term refers to a pronounced movement among Christians towards greater unity and closer cooperation between Catholics and Protestants, Anglicans and Methodists, in the belief that for all the different practices and doctrines there is a unifying ground of common faith. It is an old saying that *Wie es Christelt sich so Jüdelt sich*, that is, that Jews are not infrequently influenced by their Christian neighbors. Since ecumenism is in the air, Jews have begun to ask themselves whether there is room for ecumenism in the Jewish community, chiefly among the different religious trends of Orthodox, Reform, and Conservative Judaism. Basically, the problem for Jews is quite different than for Christians. The division between Orthodoxy and Reform is not really a denominational one in the Christian sense. All Jews belong to *Kelal Yisrael*, the Community of Israel, so that the divisions which ecumenism is supposed to heal do not exist for Jews in the first place.

It is true that in some Orthodox circles a tendency is to be observed toward greater polarization between the different groups. And it is still rare to find Orthodox Rabbis occupying Reform pulpits and *vice versa*. There is a view that Reform Judaism is virtually a different religion from Orthodox Judaism and that, therefore, in the religious sphere at least there is no possibility of any kind of fraternization. But side by side with all this is the opposite tendency—reinforced by the fact that Hitler and the Nazis made no distinctions between Jews—towards a greater measure of cooperation between the groups for the sake of those many things they hold in common.

Reference should be made in this connection to a statement that has become a classic expression of the unity of *Kelal Yisrael*. Speaking at a dedication ceremony at the Reform Hebrew Union College in 1913, Solomon Schechter of the Conservative Jewish Theological Seminary used the interesting illustration of the British Parliament, in which the governing party is known as His Majesty's Government and the opposition as His Majesty's Opposition. Schechter continued[1]:

> *This sounds like a paradox, yet it contains a deep truth, implying as it does that both His Majesty's Government as well as His Majesty's Opposition form one large community, working for the welfare of the country and the prosperity of the nation. The same principle may also be applied to theology, there being, under Providence, room also for the opposition party, which has its purpose and mission assigned to it by history. Of course, there are exceptions, but generally there is hardly any phenomenon in Judaism in the way of sect or movement which has not served a certain purpose in the divine economy of our history. For opposition there must be, owing to the difference of temper and temperament, the difference of training, the difference of surroundings which no process of schooling can entirely obliterate, and the difference of opportunity. Of course, it will always be a question as to which is which; we Conservatives maintaining that we are His Majesty's Government and you His Majesty's Opposition. But this is one of the differences. For reduce your differences as much as you want, and, indeed, I hope and pray that the difference of aims is not as deep as we sometimes think, the fact remains that we are unfortunately divided both in questions of doctrines —at least certain doctrines—and even more in practice. But, thank God, there are still a great many things and aims for which both parties can work in perfect harmony and peace, and unite us.*

Differences are important. It is both unrealistic and undesirable to imagine that thinking men will lightly give up their cherished opinions for the sake of uniformity. The aim of a Jewish ecumenical movement should not be a colorless uniformity but the unity of men holding differing views who can still cooperate in furthering the ideals they hold in common as members of *Kelal Yisrael*.

---

[1] Published in his *Seminary Addresses* (2nd edition, pp. 239–244, New York, 1959) under the title "His Majesty's Opposition."

Environment

The influence of environment on character is frequently affirmed in the Jewish tradition. A Rabbinic comment (*Sanhedrin* 108a) on the Biblical statement (Genesis 6:9) that Noah was a righteous man "in his generations" understands this to mean that even in a corrupt age Noah managed to remain uncontaminated but that if he had lived in the generation of Abraham he would have been even more righteous. A saying in *Avot* (1:7) reads: "Keep away from a bad neighbor and have no associations with the wicked," upon which a later Rabbi comments: "even for the purpose of studying the Torah." The first Psalm (which some scholars see as an introduction to the Book of Psalms) declares:

> *Happy is the man that hath not walked in the counsel of the wicked, nor stood in the way of sinners, nor sat in the seat of the scornful, but his delight is in the law of the Lord, and in His law doth he meditate day and night.*

Maimonides (*Yad, Deot* 6:1–2), basing himself on Rabbinic teachings, summarizes it as follows:

> *Man has been so created that he is influenced in his thought and action by his friends and associates and he follows the customs of his countrymen. Therefore, a man should associate with righteous men and sit always among the wise in order to learn from them how to behave. And he should keep himself far away from the wicked who walk in darkness in order not to learn from them. That is why Solomon says: "He that walketh with wise men shall be wise; but the companion of fools shall smart for it" (Proverbs 13:20). And it is said further: "Happy is the man that hath not walked in the counsel of the wicked" (Psalms 1:1). So if he lives*

in a land the customs of which are evil and whose inhabitants do not behave uprightly he should go away from there to a place whose inhabitants are righteous and conduct themselves properly. If, however, all the lands he knows or of which he has heard follow a path that is not good, as in our day, or if he is unable to go to a land with worthy practices because of the movements of armies or because of sickness, then he should live in solitude, after the manner of the verse: "Let him sit alone and keep silence" (Lamentations 3:28). If they are so wicked that they do not allow him to stay in the land unless he associates with them and follows their evil ways, then he should go out to the caves and the place of thorns and the desert rather than behave as do the wicked, as it is said: "Oh that I were in the wilderness, in a lodging-place of wayfaring men" (Jeremiah 9:1).

It is a positive command of the Torah for a man to cleave to the sages and their disciples in order to learn from their ways, as it is said: "And to Him shalt thou cleave" (Deuteronomy 10:20). Is it possible for man to cleave to the Divine Presence? Therefore the sages explain this verse to mean: "Cleave to the sages and their disciples." Consequently, a man should strive to marry the daughter of a scholar, to marry his daughter to a scholar, to eat and drink together with scholars, to assist a scholar in his business activities, and to associate with scholars in every possible way, as it is said: "And to cleave unto Him" (Deuteronomy 11:22).

Escapism

Escapism in today's usage generally has a pejorative connotation, suggesting an indulgence in dreams, a refusal to face responsibility, an unwillingness to grapple with life's problems. The reference is not to harmless diversions like films or theater performances that have no message but are meant to provide pure entertainment.

Judaism is opposed to man's shirking his duties by attempting to live in an unreal world of his own devising. This is the burden of a great deal of Jewish teaching. A man has *mitzvot* to perform. He must be aware of the darker side of existence, that there are mourners to be comforted, the sick to be visited, the poor to be helped, war and hatred to be fought, truth to be upheld against error, anger and envy to be shunned. It has rightly been said that one of the aims of religion is to comfort the troubled and trouble the comfortable.

Maimonides (*Yad, Teshuvah* 3:4) reads this idea into the command to blow the *shofar* on Rosh ha-Shanah. Discussing the meaning of repentance, he writes:

> *Although it is a divine decree that we blow the shofar on Rosh ha-Shanah, a hint at the following idea is contained in the command. It is as if to say: "Awake from your slumbers, ye who have fallen asleep in life, and reflect on your deeds. Remember your Creator. Be not of those who miss reality in the pursuit of shadows, and waste their years in seeking after vain things which neither profit nor deliver. Look well to your souls, and let there be betterment in your acts. Forsake each of you your evil ways and thoughts."*

The idea is expressed cogently in a well-known Ḥasidic tale. In Jewish mystical writings there are references to a world of illusion. In that world there are great cities, many people, fine buildings, roads and carts and ships, just as in the real world, but there they are only an illusion. The

Ḥasidim tell of a boy who, on hearing of this, asked his father: "How do we know that we are living in the real world and not in the world of illusion?" There are two versions of the father's reply. The first is that he replied: "Those who live in the world of illusion are not aware that there is a world of illusion." In the second version the father replied: "No one is ever called to the reading of the Torah in the world of illusion." The two versions explain themselves. To know that man can be deluded is itself the beginning of a realistic approach to life. If one knows that there is a world of illusion he is not living in it. Furthermore, there are no Torah readings in the world of illusion. For the Torah exists in order to awaken man to his duties and responsibilities as a free creature of God in whose image he is created to share with Him the task of producing light out of darkness.

Euthanasia

Jewish law strictly forbids any attempt at cutting short the life of even a dying man. To take away even a few moments of human life is treated as an act of murder. When a man is on his deathbed it is forbidden, for example, to move his limbs if this will have the effect of speeding his death. It is, however, permitted to remove any external cause, such as the noise of a hammer, which prevents the departure of the soul (*Shulḥan Arukh, Yoreh Deah* 339:1). Basically, then, a direct act which brings death nearer is forbidden even if the person to whom it is done will die soon in any event.

But there are instances in Jewish law of an act otherwise forbidden being allowed where certain circumstances warrant it. The question to be considered is whether there are any circumstances that would warrant the act of hastening the end. Would it be permitted if the person would otherwise suffer severe pain and then die in any event? The Midrash (*Genesis Rabbah* to Genesis 9:5) refers to the case of King Saul, who threw himself on his sword because he knew that the Philistines would capture him and torture him to death (I Samuel 31:4–6). The Midrash states that Saul did not act illegally and was not, therefore, treated as a suicide. This opinion is also recorded in the *Shulḥan Arukh* (*Yoreh Deah* 345:3). The medieval authorities also discuss whether it is permitted to pray for someone suffering from an incurable disease and in great agony to be released mercifully from his suffering by death. The Talmud (*Ketubbot* 104a) tells of the maidservant of Rabbi Judah the Prince who prayed for him to die when she saw that he was in great pain. R. Nissim Gerondi (fourteenth century) the *Ran* (commentary to *Nedarim* 40a) cites this tale as proof that it is permitted to pray for an extremely sick person in great pain to be released from his suffering. Indeed, the *Ran* declares that it is obligatory to do so. However, there is an obvious difference between prayers for a person to die and any physical act to put him out of his misery. The case of Saul, in which physical torture would have been his lot and where the honor of the king was involved, is again in a different category.

Rabbinic authorities at the present are opposed to doctors shortening life by such physical intervention as the injection of a drug with the express intention of speeding the end. But it is generally held that a sufferer in agony can be given injections of pain-killing drugs even though these will have the eventual effect of cutting his life short. It is also generally agreed that doctors are not obliged to resort to artificial means of keeping an incurable and greatly suffering patient alive if without these means nature will take its course and he will die.

The Evil Eye

Belief in malevolent powers residing in the eye is widespread in human culture. There are many references to the evil eye—Hebrew *ayin ha-ra* —in Jewish sources. It is interesting, however, that in the early sources the *ayin ha-ra* denotes simply envy of the good fortune of others and has no occult significance. A good example of this earlier usage is to be found in the Book of Proverbs (28:22):

> *He that hath an evil eye hasteneth*
> *after riches,*
> *And knoweth not that want shall*
> *come upon him.*

The evil effects here are not on the victim of envy but on the envious man himself. Similarly the references in *Ethics of the Fathers* to the evil eye (*Avot* 2:9 and 11; 5:13 and 19) all have to do with envy and lack of generosity which have harmful effects on the character of the man given to these traits.

In a later period, however, belief in the evil eye in the magic sense is found even among the Rabbis. Of the numerous instances recorded in the Talmudic literature a few examples can be given. The famous Babylonian teacher Rav is said to have remarked when he visited a cemetery that 99 out of 100 persons buried there had died through the evil eye (*Bava Meẓia* 107b). It was believed that the evil eye could not harm a descendant of Joseph, hence the curious incantation found in the Talmud (*Berakhot* 55b) to ward off the evil eye: "Take the thumb of the right hand in the left hand and the thumb of the left hand in the right hand, and say: 'I, so-and-so, am of the seed of Joseph over which the evil eye has no power.'" A report tells of the Palestinian teacher R. Johanan who was very handsome and would allow women to gaze at him so that they would have handsome children. When he was asked why he was not afraid that the evil eye might harm him he replied that he was descended from Joseph, over whom it had no power (*Berakhot* 20a). In another passage it is said that people whose occupation is such as to give the impression of success will never see any blessing in it because of the evil eye that others cast on it (*Pesaḥim* 50b).

Belief in the evil eye has persisted among many Jews down to the present day. The popular expression *kenanhora* is an abbreviated form of the Hebrew for "let there be no evil eye." It is still widely used when praising someone. Various amulets, charms and spells to ward off the evil eye are also known and used by some.

If it is asked what Judaism has to say about all this, one can only point to the great theological difficulties which arise if these and other superstitious beliefs are entertained. Although it is true that many of the great Rabbis of the past did not succeed in eradicating superstition and some of them even entertained superstitious opinions themselves,

North African parchment "hand" amulet. The hand is supposed to ward off the "evil eye."

it is still hard to see how superstition can be reconciled with belief in the one God whose power is unlimited. Maimonides enters the most notable protest against the belief in magic and superstition. Although in his gigantic Code the *Mishneh Torah*, Maimonides faithfully records all the opinions found in the Rabbinic literature, he makes an exception in refusing to record any superstitions found there or any practices based on these. The anti-magical view is stated with power in the Talmud itself (*Hullin* 76b). When a woman attempted to cast a spell over R. Hanina he said to her: "Try as you will, you will not succeed, for it is written: 'There is none else beside Him' (Deuteronomy 4:35)."

Evolution

There have been various evolutionary theories since ancient times but by evolution most people understand the Darwinian theory according to which higher forms of life have developed from lower forms by the process of natural selection. Man is included in the process. When Darwin first published his views they were attacked by representatives of the Christian religion on the grounds that they deprived man of his unique status and in fact contradicted the Biblical account of man's origins in the Book of Genesis. According to the theory of evolution, the long, slow climb from the amoeba to man took place over a period of millions of years. According to the literal meaning of Genesis, all things were created in six days less than six thousand years ago and man was created specially from the "dust of the earth."

Some Jews still feel obliged to reject the theory of evolution and all theories which postulate a vast age for the earth because they are contradicted by the Bible. A representative teacher holding this view is the present Rabbi of Lubavitch in Brooklyn who has repeatedly stressed that the believing Jew is bound to accept as true the literal meaning of Genesis. According to this view, God placed the fossils in the earth, as it were, when He created the world. Stated baldly, the idea seems ridiculous, but in fairness to its proponents what it really means is that God's creation bears the marks of gradual growth even though in reality it was spontaneous. Trees, for example, were created with the rings which give the appearance of growth over hundreds of years not because they really did grow over a long period but because this is what they would have to look like in order to be trees. There used to be a discussion on whether Adam was created with a navel!

Other Orthodox Jewish thinkers have been prepared to accept the evidence for evolution and have consequently interpreted Genesis in a non-literal fashion. An early interpretation following this line was published by Rabbi Israel Lipschutz (1782–1860) in his famed commentary to the Mishnah entitled *Tiferet Yisrael.*[1] Lipschutz relies on theories found among some of the Kabbalists that there are cycles of creation, i.e. that the creation of our world as described in Genesis was not the first creation but the beginning of a new cycle. The dinosaurs and the skeletons of primitive men and so forth are the remains of creatures which existed in a previous cycle.

An enthusiastic Orthodox evolutionist was Rabbi A. I. Kook (1865–1935). In his work *Orot ha-Kodesh*[2] Rabbi Kook declares that the theory of evolution is in full accordance with the Kabbalah, of which he was a devotee, in that it sees the whole of creation as striving to express itself in ever higher forms leading eventually to God. (The parallel with the views of Teilhard de Chardin is remarkable.) According to Rabbi Kook, the Biblical difficulty is non-existent since everyone acknowledges that the creation narrative belongs to the "secrets of the Torah," i.e., must not be understood literally. Rabbi Kook writes:

> *The theory of evolution, now so well-known as a result of recent scientific researches, has revolutionized our thought patterns. This does not apply to the elite, who approach matters logically and reasonably for they always tended to see things in terms of development, even the spiritual side of existence which is less tangible. For them it is not at all strange to understand by analogy that the material substance of the physical universe proceeds by the same method of development as the spiritual. It is natural for the physical universe to follow the course of development of the spiritual universe, in which no stage is by-passed or left unfulfilled. But the masses have not yet succeeded in understanding evolution as a consistent and comprehensive theory and have been unable to connect it with their spiritual lives. It is not the difficulty of reconciling certain statements in the Bible or in other traditional sources with the theory of evolution which encourages the masses to remain indifferent. It is easy enough to see how the two can be reconciled. Everyone knows that these topics, which belong to life's mystery, are always dominated by metaphor, riddle*

[1] Vilna, 1892, end of Order *Nezikin*, pp. 562–3.
[2] Part V, 19–22.

and hint. Even the ear of the masses is attuned to hearing
the brief formula that this or that verse or statement belongs
to the secrets of the Torah which are on a higher plane than
the simple meaning would suggest.

Rabbi Kook was so enamored of the theory of evolution that he applied
it to the moral sphere as well. In his view man's moral nature has improved and evolved so that today the conflict is far less marked than
in former times between the lofty ethical demands of the Torah and
man's natural strivings and desires. It is doubtful whether Rabbi Kook
would have written quite so optimistically after two global wars, the
Nazis, and the concentration camps.

Another Orthodox thinker who accepted evolution was the British
Chief Rabbi, Dr. J. H Hertz (1872–1946). Hertz[1] argues that in the face
of the great diversity of views among earlier Jewish teachers on how the
creation narrative in Genesis is to be interpreted, there is nothing in-
herently un-Jewish in the evolutionary view of the origin and growth of
forms of existence from the simple to the complex, and from the lowest
to the highest. Dr. Hertz concludes:

God the Creator and Lord of the Universe, which is the work
of His goodness and wisdom; and Man, made in His image, who
is to hallow his week-day labors by the blessedness of Sabbath-
rest—such are the teachings of the Creation chapter. Its
purpose is to reveal these teachings to the children of men—and
not to serve as a text book of astronomy, geology or anthropol-
ogy. Its object is not to teach scientific facts; but to proclaim
highest religious truths respecting God, Man, and the Universe.
The "conflict" between the fundamental realities of Religion
and the established facts of Science, is seen to be unreal as
soon as Religion and Science each recognizes the true border
of its dominion.

A more modern, though less Orthodox, view would see the Genesis
narrative as the work of inspired men who had a tremendous insight
into eternal truth but who, so far as their picture of the physical universe
was concerned, had only the knowledge of their day. It seems almost
certain that the prophets, for example, like all the men of their time,

[1] *Pentateuch and Haftorahs*, 2nd ed., pp. 193–195, London, 1960.

thought that the earth was flat and had no knowledge of the vastness of the universe as revealed by modern astronomy (how could they have had except by a miracle?). This in no way affects the truth and enduring ethical and religious value of their message. Seen in this way, all attempts at "reconciling" the Biblical texts with the scientific picture are misguided. The two are irreconcilable and the Biblical picture of man's origins is unscientific. But no one goes to the Bible for science. People go to the Bible for its sublime teachings about religion and ethics.

There is no need for the religious believer to worry that if the theory of evolution is true man is degraded. Even if man is descended from the lower animals he is still different from them not only in degree but in kind. In the language of the Bible this is expressed by saying that man is created in God's image. Man is a rational animal, he has the power to think and to express his thoughts in speech, he has a soul which can reach out towards his Creator. Man can feel humble that his origins are so lowly. Humility is a virtue. But at the same time he can be proud of his uniqueness as the culmination of the evolutionary process until now. As the Psalmist puts it (Psalms 8:5–6):

> *What is man, that Thou art mindful*
> *of him?*
> *And the son of man, that Thou thinkest*
> *of him?*
> *Yet Thou hast made him but little*
> *lower than the angels,*
> *And hast crowned him with glory and honor.*

In similar vein a Midrashic homily (*Leviticus Rabbah* 14:1) has it that man was created after all the animals, so that if he lives worthily man is the culmination of creation, but if he lives unworthily he is reminded that even the mosquito arrived on the scene before he did.

Scientists like Darwin put forward the evolutionary hypothesis as the best way of explaining the origin of species. To draw vast philosophical conclusions from the theory as to continuous evolution from lower to higher in such areas as history, literature, morals, and religion, a procedure that was popular in the last century, is, to say the least, precarious. Even Rabbi Kook was influenced by the *Zeitgeist* to apply, as we have seen, evolutionary theories to the moral life of man. Most thinkers today have come to appreciate that the history of human thought does not follow a neat pattern of gradual development in ascending degrees. More especially in this century the doctrine of the survival of the fittest was applied to Nazi theories regarding the *Herren-volk* with the horrible consequences with which we are all too familiar.

There is one final aspect of evolutionary theory that must be considered in a discussion on what Judaism has to say. The Darwinian theory accounts in a natural way for the emergence of diverse species, and some atheistic thinkers have seized on this as a colossal blow to the whole theistic idea of a designing Mind. But this, too, is an intrusion of science, or rather of philosophy masquerading as science, into the domain of religion. From the theistic point of view Darwinism tells us how God worked, as it were, in His creative activity. It is God who is responsible for the process as a whole, for, as has been said, the arrival as well as the survival of the fittest. If evolution is true it must follow that the picture of a succession of separate creations by divine fiat must go, but why should it offend the religious mind to discover that God performs His wondrous works in one way rather than another? To be sure the argument from design, if seen as the only indication that God exists, has become much weaker as a result of the Darwinian theory. But the man of faith is in no way prevented by new theories about how the physical universe operates from seeing the hand of the Maker in all His works.

Existentialism

Existentialism is more of a road than a philosophy. It is a way of looking looking at life, individualistic, intense, personal. There are many varieties of existentialism. What they have in common is the idea of "true for me." Kierkegaard, generally acknowledged as the first truly existentialist thinker, is critical of Hegel, for instance, because this philosopher manages to construct a vast philosophic system in which an explanation is offered of the whole universe by a man who seems to stand outside the universe to observe it all in a detached manner. But Hegel is himself part of the universe he examines. He is a human being with fears and frustrations, hopes and desires. His needs and ambitions are important to him and they are bound to color his picture of what life means. How, then, can he pretend to get out of his skin to practice detachment as a philosopher? Vast systems constructed by thinkers tell us nothing about life as it really is, the existentialists argue. What really matters is the response of the whole human being, not only his mind, to life's challenges. The important thing, that which makes a man truly human, is his individual choice to see life in a certain way. The true picture of the universe apart from the way in which the individual man sees it is beyond the capacity of man to comprehend. It is the "true for me" that is alone significant.

Existentialism is easier to grasp among its atheistic exponents. Sartre, for example, has said that existence precedes essence. This means that man has no essence to which he is bound to conform. He creates his own values, which is to say he determines his own essence through his existence and not the other way around. The man who allows others to determine his way of life is being false to himself if he simply acquiesces in it. He must make his individual choice in order to be truly himself. The atheistic premise maintains that there is no God to create man and the pattern of his existence. But even the religious existentialists place great emphasis on man's free choice. The choice comes first. The essence or pattern provided by theistic belief is here because the individual has freely chosen to embrace the theistic way. Indeed, for thinkers like Kierkegaard religious faith is not something that one can achieve once and for all. The tensions created between belief and unbelief are ever present as part of man's situation. Again and again he must opt for faith, grasping it as a freely choosing human being just when it seems most elusive. This is the significance of Kierkegaard's famous "leap of faith."

It follows that religious existentialists are very suspicious of the classical "proofs" for God's existence. According to the existentialist view, religious faith is not in the nature of a series of propositions about God but a meeting or dialogue with God. If this meeting takes place, to prove that God exists is futility and an impertinence, much, in Kierkegaard's metaphor, as it would be if a man conversing with a king were to break off in the middle in order to prove that the king is really present. On the other hand, if the meeting does not take place, proofs or arguments for God's existence are mere intellectual exercises; at the most they can succeed in winning assent to the purely intellectual proposition that God exists, with none of the warmth and passion by which real religious faith is characterized.

The importance of personal choice is stressed by the two best-known Jewish existentialists, Martin Buber and Franz Rosenzweig. The two differ in their attitude to the Halakhah, the legal side of Judaism. Buber sometimes writes as if submission to the precepts of the Torah as laws imposed from without is a betrayal of the personal choice that must be present, for him, at the heart of religion. He does not, however, preclude the acceptance of the precepts, or some of them, as part of the individual's free choice. Rosenzweig's attitude is much more traditional. Eventually, Rosenzweig became a traditional and observant Jew. But even of Rosenzweig the oft-repeated remark is made that at one stage in his life he was asked whether he wore *tefillin*. His reply was: "I have not reached *tefillin* yet!"

Buber stresses particularly the life of dialogue. A man gets to know his fellows not by talking about them or using them for his own ends or by seeing them in a detached way but by meeting them as persons in their own right. He has an "I-Thou" relationship with them not an "I-It" relationship. Through the particular "Thous" he meets man comes face to face with God who is the *Thou* behind all particular "Thous." Buber's interpretation of the golden rule is: "Thou shalt love thy neighbor (who is a person, not a thing, and is therefore) as thyself." "As thyself" does not qualify "Thou shalt love" but "thy neighbor." It might be observed that according to many Biblical scholars something of this nature really does belong to the actual meaning of the verse according to its syntactical form.

It is in the area of personal choice that even religious existentialism is in conflict with traditional views of Judaism. According to traditional Judaism man has to accept "the yoke of the kingdom of Heaven" and "the yoke of the precepts." These exist prior to man's acceptance of them. For traditional Judaism there is a divinely ordained pattern which man is obliged to follow. There are philosophical difficulties, too, in the extreme subjective approach of the existentialists. Caution must consequently be exercised by the Jew against swallowing existentialism whole. But undoubtedly some of the insights provided by the existentialists are in full accord with the Jewish approach. Judaism does believe that there is freedom of choice as it believes in the value of the individual soul in the eyes of God. And it has often been remarked that speculative system building is foreign both to the Bible and Rabbinic Judaism, in both of which God is to be met and experienced rather than thought about or discussed.

A helpful work by a Jewish thinker on the problem of existentialism is Eugene B. Borowitz's *A Layman's Introduction to Religious Existentialism* (1965).

Extra-Sensory Perception (ESP)

The term ESP is generally used to denote extra-sensory perception, including telepathy, clairvoyance, and other parapsychological phenomena. If there is such a thing as ESP it means that minds can communicate with one another directly without the aid of the physical senses.

There is no doubt that in former times there seemed nothing particularly strange in such forms of communication. The prophet was a "seer" who had psychic powers. In the first book of Samuel, chapter 9, the prophet is able to tell Saul where to find the asses that had been lost, though the passage does suggest that this kind of clairvoyance belonged to an earlier stage in the history of prophecy:

> *Beforetime in Israel, when a man went to inquire of God, thus he said: "Come and let us go to the seer"—for he that is now called a prophet was beforetimes called a seer (I Samuel 9:9).*

The many references in the later literature to *ruah ha-kodesh*, "the holy spirit," frequently include the power to see into the future or to be aware of events that were taking place at a distance. In a Talmudic passage (*Bava Batra* 12a–b) it is suggested that the sage who hits upon a new idea which corresponds exactly to something said by another sage does so by means of the prophetic faculty which, even though it has been taken from the prophets, has not been taken away from the sages. In Ḥasidic and mystic lore there are numerous tales of holy men gifted with a sixth sense. The Ḥasidic master R. Jacob Isaac (d. 1815) of Lublin was called the "Seer" because of his clairvoyant powers.

Of course, all this belongs to the formulations of a prescientific age in which anything could happen. Since the legendary element in miraculous tales was communicated from mouth to mouth, and since there were no reliable eyewitnesses and the texts in which the tales are recorded were compiled long after the events they describe took place, it is precarious, to say the least, to build on the basis of the accounts a theory that ESP is really possible. The new feature in the situation is that scientific investigations into parapsychology have been undertaken by unbiased observers, including those working in university departments of a high order of scientific respectability. Rhine's experiments with cards is the best-known example. Under conditions of the most rigorous control, some people were not only able to state which cards were being turned up in another room but to state which cards were about to be turned up! To be sure, the whole matter still awaits further study and experiment, but the evidence so far is very convincing that there is something in it. The odds against some of the phenomena that have been noted occurring by pure coincidence are overwhelming, unless all those who have participated in the experiments have been engaged in a colossal conspiracy to defraud or have been guilty of self-deception. At this stage of the investigations great caution must be exercised before drawing any definite conclusions, but it would be thoroughly unscientific to dismiss the possibility of ESP entirely.

What has Judaism to say about it? The question is not a very significant one. If ESP becomes conclusively established all it means from the Jewish point of view is that more is known about the order of nature as God has ordained it. The non-believer will not be converted into a believer by the establishment of the truth of ESP. He will not argue that the supernatural is real but only that the scope of the "natural" has been enlarged. However, in one area of thought the establishment of the truth of ESP does have religious implications. Materialistic philosophies are opposed to theistic faith. But if there is such a thing as ESP, it cannot be explained on the basis of materialism. If minds can engage in communication without the mediation of sense perception it must follow that any philosophy which holds that matter is all there is must be false. In this respect the question of ESP is relevant to religion and hence to Judaism. Judaism, which affirms that there is a supreme Mind in control of the universe, will not be astonished to learn that even finite minds have powers, granted to them by that Mind, over and above sensory experience.

Faith Healing

Generally speaking, the traditional Jew, influenced by the many Biblical injunctions, such as those of Deuteronomy 18:10–11, against resorting to witchcraft, divination, and other magical practices, has tended to view with suspicion anything of real or imaginary supernatural origin beyond the horizon of normal Jewish life. His own life was so saturated with religion that its spiritual content had become familiar, almost commonplace, to him. Any new attempts to gain contact with the spiritual world was mistrusted as an attack on the sobriety and sanity of his faith. Small wonder, then, that faith healing has found few exponents among Orthodox Jews. The traditional Jew tends naturally to reject the idea that all human ills are illusory. He heartily subscribes to the common-sense repudiation of this fantastic doctrine expressed in the limerick:

> *There was a faith healer of Deal,*
> *Who taught that all pain is not real,*
> *When I sit on a pin,*
> *And puncture my skin*
> *I dislike what I fancy I feel.*

During the first decades of the twentieth century a number of influential Jews became attracted to the Christian Science movement. As an antidote, in the year 1922, a graduate of the Hebrew Union College, Morris Lichtenstein, founded a similar movement, with the imitative name of *Jewish* Science, which, he claimed, was fully in accord with Jewish tradition. Joshua Loth Liebman's bestseller *Peace of Mind* similarly advocates the helpfulness of a Jewish religious outlook in curing disorders, especially mental instability. The Central Conference of American [Reform] Rabbis[1] discussed the question of "spiritual healing" and issued a report reaffirming belief in the healing powers

---

[1] *Yearbook* for 1927 and 1928.

of the synagogue but disapproving of cults that deny reality to all human ailments. Orthodox Jewish authorities have had little to say on the subject, but reference should be made to a Responsum of Rabbi David Hoffmann (1843–1921) in which the author permits a pregnant woman to follow the custom of hanging amulets in her room, because of their psychological effect.[1]

In the earlier sources there is hardly any reference to the question but it is tempting to understand the Talmudic accounts of certain sages taking the hand of a sick person and raising him from his sickbed as examples of "faith healing" (*Berakhot* 5b). We are told that the third century Palestinian teacher R. Johanan performed this service for R. Ḥiyya bar Abba and for R. Eleazar b. Pedat. When R. Johanan was himself sick, we are told, this service was performed for him, R. Johanan being unable to raise himself because "a prisoner cannot free himself from the prison house." It is well known that the pre-Ḥasidic *ba'alei shem* (wonderworkers) and many of the Ḥasidic masters were supposed to possess great powers of healing the sick. Allowing for the numerous legendary embellishments, the evidence is still too strong to be lightly dismissed. There appears to be no valid reason for doubting the effect of deep faith and strong will-power on the body and its disorders, a judgment amply supported by the modern emphasis on psychosomatic illness and its cure.

Possibly the most helpful Jewish approach to the question of faith healing is to make a distinction between Rabbis or others cooperating with doctors to apply the healing powers of faith as an aid to recovery, an activity that is surely beneficial, and faith healing as a cult or even a rival religion to Judaism. This kind of distinction is behind a Ḥasidic tale told of the Ḥasidic master R. Simḥah Bunam of Pzhysha (d. 1827). This master, who suffered from bad eyesight, was once advised, after doctors had declared themselves powerless to help, to consult a faith healer. R. Simḥah Bunam is said to have retorted that the Torah advises us to consult doctors who heal by natural means. But if the healer invokes faith then it is wrong to go for a cure to one who does not accept Judaism; one should rather go for this to a Jewish master of prayer.

---

[1] *Melammed le-Ho'il,* Vol. I, No. 63.

Friendship

The two extreme examples of friendship in the Bible are to be found in the story of David and Jonathan (I Samuel 20) and the story of Ruth and Naomi (Ruth 1). In both these instances one of the friends (Jonathan and Ruth) is ready to sacrifice everything out of loyalty to the bond of friendship. In both instances the friendship is between persons of the same sex. No doubt this is because close friendships between men and women were exceedingly rare, on the grounds of sexual morality, so that "friendship" between a man and a woman was expressed in marriage. To conclude, as some have done, that there is a homosexual element in the friendship of David and Jonathan or Ruth and Naomi is belied by the narrative and is a thoroughly perverse notion. The Rabbis (*Avot* 5:16) hold up the friendship of David and Jonathan as an illustration of how love that does not depend on any ulterior motive is everlasting. ("Love" here is used in the sense of affection and deep friendship.)

Christians have often quoted the verse in the Gospel of John (15:13): "Greater love hath no man than this, that a man lay down his life for his friends." Christian, and many Jewish, thinkers look upon the verse as a typical Christian statement. The truth is, rather, that the verse assumes that the sentiment expressed is axiomatic and would have been accepted by the *Jews* of the time. It is not presented as a special Christian doctrine and if any conclusions at all can be drawn from it then they are that this sentiment was considered self-evident by the Jews at the time when the Gospel of John was written. It is only the attribution of the saying to Jesus and the special application to him that are colored by the Christian tendency of the book, not the sentiment itself.

The value of friendship is mentioned not infrequently in the Rabbinic literature. R. Joshua, when asked by his teacher to discover the best and worst thing in a man's striving towards self-improvement, replied that the best thing is to have a good friend and the worst to have a bad

The friendship of David and Jonathan (bottom left) in the illuminated manuscript *Somme le Roi*, France, late 13th century. On the right, Saul threatens
David with a spear. The dove and hawk in the upper register symbolize, res-
pectively, love and hate.

friend (*Avot* 2:9). A very early teacher is reported as advising a man to get himself a teacher and acquire a friend (*Avot* 1:6). The editor of the Mishnah, R. Judah the Prince, is reported as saying: "Much have I learned from my teachers, more from my friends, and most of all from my pupils" (*Makkot* 10a). In these and similar sayings, however, it is to be noted that the friendships referred to were among colleagues who associated for the purpose of studying the Torah. In a Talmudic legend told of the miracle-worker Honi the Circle-Drawer (*Ta'anit* 23a) it is said that this man slept for 70 years. When he awoke he was given the cold shoulder by those who frequented the House of Study, as he had very little in common with them because of the "generation gap." When Honi saw this he prayed to be released from his agony by death. The story quotes in this connection the saying of the fourth century Babylonian teacher, Rava: "Either friendship or death."

Among the Hasidim friendship was encouraged, especially among adherents of the same Hasidic master, these having, in Hasidic parlance, the same "soul-root." The early Hasidic master R. Elimelech of Lyzhansk advises his followers to have a true friend to whom they could confess their failings and who would help them to tread the road to self-perfection (*Tzettil Katan*).[1]

In modern Hebrew the terms used for a friend are *haver* ("associate") and *yedid* ("dear companion").

---

[1] Printed at the end of *Noam Elimelekh* in various editions.

Funerals

To accompany the dead to their final resting place is considered a high religious obligation. The famous remark of the great eleventh century French commentator is a good indication of the Jewish attitude. Rashi comments on the command of Jacob to his son Joseph to bury him: "Deal kindly and truly with me" (Genesis 47:29). Why "kindly and truly" (*hesed ve-emet*)? Rashi's explanation is that all other forms of kindness may be in anticipation of reciprocal kindness in the future from the beneficiary. At the back of the mind of the donor there may be a self-seeking motive so that his "kindness" is not "true," i.e., completely sincere. But kindness performed for the dead must in the nature of the case be sincere. The dead cannot reciprocate. In most Jewish communities in the past there were special societies, the members of which attended to the burial of the dead. These were called Society of Kindness and Truth (as above) or the Holy Society (*Hevra kaddisha*) because theirs was a sacred task. Membership was open only to the most distinguished persons of the community and to be elected as a member was held to be a great honor. This practice persists in some communities to the present day.

In the Rabbinic view respect for the dead is incumbent upon the living for the same reason that the rich are obliged to help the poor. There is none so helpless as a dead man. To the corpse the Rabbis apply the verse: "He that mocketh the poor blasphemeth his Maker" (Proverbs 17:3). Especially the dead are "poor" in that they can no longer carry out the precepts of the Torah. Hence the Rabbis (*Berakhot* 18a) forbid the recitation of the *Shema* or the performance of any other precepts in the presence of a corpse and they apply the verse in Proverbs to anyone who does these things. For this reason the duty of attending a funeral was so important to the Rabbis as the supreme example of disinterested service. The following passage (*Berakhot* 18a) speaks for itself:

Cut-glass goblet of the Mlada Boleslav *ḥevra kaddisha*, with a scene of a hearse preceded by members of the burial society and followed by the family and mourners, 1838.

> *Whoever sees a corpse on the way to burial and does not*
> *accompany it is referred to in the verse: "He that mocketh*
> *the poor blasphemeth his Maker." But if he does accompany*
> *it, what is his reward? R. Assi says: To him apply the verses:*
> *"He that is gracious unto the poor lendeth unto the Lord"*
> *(Proverbs 19:17), and "He that is gracious unto the needy*
> *honoreth Him" (Proverbs 14:31).*

It would appear that out of respect for the dead, funerals were at one time quite lavish, the shrouds being of silk or other costly material. There is no doubt historical truth, however, behind the Talmudic account of how this attitude changed. The Talmud (*Ketubbot* 8b) observes that funerals had become so expensive that the financial burden borne by the bereaved family was a heavier burden than the death itself and that families would shirk their responsibility of burying the dead. Rabban Gamaliel, therefore, decreed in his will that, prince of his people though he was, he was to be buried in simple shrouds of linen. The example set by him was so beneficial that at houses of mourning a special cup of wine was raised to his memory. Allowing for the element of hyperbole in this passage, the Rabbinic attitude to costly funerals emerges clearly. In the same passage, R. Papa, the Babylonian teacher of the late fourth century, said that "nowadays we bury the dead in a shroud made of canvas costing no more than a *zuz* [a small coin]."

The approach which developed and was followed in Jewish life consisted of a blend of proper respect for the dead and the avoidance of waste and ostentation. In the light of this it is not difficult to conclude that Judaism does not approve of expensive funerals. Many a Rabbi has argued that if a family has money to spare, a better way of honoring the dead is to donate a sum of money in the name of the departed to some worthy cause.

Gambling

There are no references in the Bible to gambling but one must be cautious in drawing any conclusions from this as to the absence of gambling habits among the Hebrews. After all, the Biblical literature is comparatively small and it is possible that none of the Biblical writers had occasion to refer to gambling (though one is justified in concluding that gambling cannot have been indulged in to the extent that it became a social evil, otherwise we would have expected some expression of disapproval somewhere in the Biblical writings). The casting of lots, however, is frequently mentioned in the Bible and was often resorted to. Lots were cast to determine which of the two goats was to be offered up to God and which sent to Azazel (Leviticus 16:8–10); in the affair of Jonathan (I Samuel 14:42–43); and to divide up the land (Numbers 26:55 and Joshua 15). The sailors in the Book of Jonah cast lots in order to determine who was responsible for their evil condition (Jonah 1:7) as did Haman to determine the most suitable month in which to realize his nefarious plot (Esther 3:7). The German Halakhist Jair Ḥayyim Bacharach (1639–1702) even goes so far as to conclude, on the basis of these Biblical passages, that a raffle is a legitimate means of allowing God's providence to operate in favor of the winner (Responsa *Ḥavvot Yair* No. 61). He quotes the verse: "The lot is cast into the lap; but the whole disposing thereof is of the Lord" (Proverbs 16:33).

It might also be mentioned that in Rabbinic law the element of chance enters into the widely applied law of *ruba* ("majority"). If, for example, nine shops in a town sold kosher meat and one *terefah*, meat found in a street of the town would be kosher; it being assumed that it came from a kosher shop (*Pesaḥim* 9b; *Ḥullin* 11a). The famous yeshivah head, R. Simeon Skopf (1860–1940), in his work *Sha'arei Yosher* (Sha'ar 3), uses, in his discussion of this law, the illustration of the higher price paid for two or more lottery tickets than for one, and goes on to consider the whole theory of mathematical probability.

151

Engraving of a Ḥanukkah celebration with children playing games and adults gambling. From Kirchner, *Juedisches Ceremoniel*, Nuremberg, 1734.

To turn to the actual question of gambling, this is dealt with in the Mishnah (*Rosh ha-Shanah* 1:8; *Sanhedrin* 3:3), where it is stated that two types of gambler are disqualified from acting as witnesses in a Jewish court of law. These are the dice-player—"playing with *kubya*" (from the Greek *kubeia*, "dice")—and the man who bets on pigeon-racing. On this the Talmud (*Sanhedrin* 24b) quotes two opinions. Rami bar Ḥama understands the Mishnah to refer even to the occasional gambler. He is disqualified, argues this Rabbi, because he commits the crime of theft by accepting his winnings, seeing that in Jewish law, according to him, the winner of a bet has no claim on the loser. R. Sheshet disputes this. In his view it is only the habitual gambler, who has no other trade, who is disqualified, not because he is a thief but because he plays no part in the betterment of society. Maimonides in his comment to the Mishnah, follows R. Sheshet. The Tosafists to *Sanhedrin* 26a allow games of chance where the stakes are placed on the table, but where there is only a promise to pay they forbid them, for here the winner has no legal claim on the loser and it would be theft for the winnings to be collected. It is interesting to find that the legal question revolves around the problem of whether the winnings constitute theft. There is no suggestion that gambling is wrong on the grounds that the winner gets something without really working for it—an argument often to be heard in non-Jewish circles when gambling is discussed. The *Shulḥan Arukh*, the final court of appeal, refers to the prevalent custom of occasional gambling and permits it (*Ḥoshen Mishpat*, 207:13 and 370).

It would thus appear that there is no legal objection to a Jew indulging in a "mild flutter" or to his buying a ticket in a lottery or sweepstake. In fact, in Eastern Europe, many devout Jews not only did this but if they won considered the winnings to be God's special gift to them, His way of enabling them to earn a living. Occasionally some Ḥasidic communities organized lotteries of their own, the proceeds going to charity.

Against this, the Jewish moralists have generally been fierce opponents of gambling as a frivolous pursuit evincing a lack of faith in God and a "get-rich-quick" attitude and opening the door to financial ruin. Everyone knows of the distress suffered by the wives and children of men addicted to gambling. As early as the thirteenth century the preacher Jacob Anatoli, though he admitted that gambling was not legally forbidden, frowned upon the amusements of the gambling-table. Leon de Modena in 1584, at the age of 14(!), wrote a treatise on the evils of gambling, though, by a strange twist of fate, in later life he developed a passion for the vice he had so eloquently condemned in his youth. Various medieval communities introduced repressive measures to combat the evils of gambling.[1]

While gambling in a mild form is not forbidden in Jewish law it is hardly an ideal occupation, even in this form, for the devout Jew.

[1] S. Baron, *The Jewish Community*, Vol. 2, p. 316 and notes.

Gurus

The word guru (from the Sanskrit, meaning "dignified") signifies a Hindu spiritual leader but is used today to denote any charismatic personality who acts as a spiritual guide. Is there anything akin to this in Judaism?

The Rabbis of the Talmud had their disciples, though these did not normally look upon their masters as spiritual guides in the guru sense but as teachers of the Torah. The references in the Talmud to "ministering to the Sages" (*shimmush talmidei ḥakhamim*) seems to mean that over and above the actual teaching the disciples learned a good deal from the way in which the teacher conducted himself in accordance with the demands of Jewish law. Thus when certain disciples were challenged for their audacity in hiding themselves in their master's bed-chamber or in the privy in order to see how the master behaved, their reply was: "It is Torah and I have to learn." The practices they suggest emulating were the ones laid down by Jewish law and not the personal practices of the master which were derived from his particular spiritual insights (*Berakhot* 62b).

In the moralistic literature, on the other hand, we find numerous examples of individual practices (*hanhagut*), lists of which were drawn up and no doubt followed by chosen disciples.

But the nearest we get to the guru idea in Judaism is in the Ḥasidic movement. The Ḥasidic *Ẕaddik* teaches his followers how to pray, how to have God in their thoughts, how to live a life of purity and holiness. The Hasidim confide in the *Ẕaddik* their innermost thoughts, their fears and hopes, their spiritual ambitions and their failure to realize them. In addition, they scrutinize closely his every word and movement to see how the holy man behaves in God's presence. One of the disciples of the Great Maggid of Mezhirech, the leader of Ḥasidism, said that he did not journey to the Maggid to learn Torah from him but to see how he ties his shoelaces. It was precisely this prominence

154

given to the role of the *Zaddik* that aroused the ire of the *Mitnaggedim*, the opponents of Hasidism who looked upon the whole institution of Zaddikism as thoroughly un-Jewish. They argued that the *Zaddik* tends to become an intermediary between God and man whereas the Jew traditionally approaches his God directly. For the *Mitnaggedim*, the new type of spiritual leader represented by the *Zaddik*, or *Rebbe*, as he is generally called, represents a usurpation of the role of the Rabbi whose duty it is to teach the Torah and nothing else, or, better, nothing else requires to be taught.

As a reaction to the Hasidic challenge the *Mitnaggedim* produced guru types of their own in the leaders of the Musar movement of nineteenth century Lithuania, though the more conservative Rabbis looked upon this innovation, too, as superfluous. But the Musar teacher allows greater individual freedom to his followers than the Hasidic *Zaddik*. The idea, found among the Hasidim, that the Hasid "annihilates" himself before the Rabbi is not found among the Musarists. The founder of the Musar movement, R. Israel Salanter, is reported to have said that both the Hasidim and the *Mitnaggedim* are in error: the Hasidim in imagining that they have a *Rebbe*, the *Mitnaggedim* in imagining that they do not need a *Rebbe!*

Happiness

A number of moralists have tried to demonstrate that the citadel of happiness cannot be taken by storm and have seen the failure of many to achieve happiness as being due to the very determination to achieve it. Happiness cannot be consciously striven for, these thinkers have argued, since happiness involves the satisfaction of needs and once these have been satisfied there appears to be something in man which makes him restless for more. That is why some of the greatest thinkers have prescribed as a recipe for happiness the pursuit of a high aim for its own sake. In the process of pursuing this aim man finds happiness or, rather, he becomes so absorbed that he forgets to ask himself whether he is miserable. This is what Shaw, for example, referred to when he spoke of being used by the Life Force as the key to happiness.

Judaism does not speak of being used by the Life Force but of being used by God. In following the Torah and walking in its ways man finds happiness. This thought is expressed by the Rabbis in their description of the hard life that is the lot of the dedicated Torah student (*Avot* 6:4):

> *This is the way of the Torah. Eat bread with salt, drink water by measure, sleep on the ground and live a life of pain while you toil in the Torah. If you do this then: "Happy shalt thou be and it shall be well with thee" (Psalms 128:2).* Happy shalt thou be - *in this world;* and it shall be well with thee - *in the world to come.*

It is illuminating in this connection to study the biblical application of the term *ashre* ("happy is he" or "happy are they"). Among the many instances of the use of this term the following illustrations can be quoted. Those who support the "tree of life" that is wisdom are happy (Proverbs 3:18). Those who trust in God are happy (Psalms 2:12) and those whom God chastises (Job 5:17). The man who does not sin is

156

happy (Psalms 32:2) as well as the man who does not associate with sinners (Psalms 1:1). Those who dwell in God's house are happy (Psalms 84:5) as are those who fear Him (Psalms 112:1). Men who practice justice are happy (Psalms 106:3) and men who consider the poor (Psalms 41:2). The man who keeps the Sabbath is happy (Isaiah 56:2) and the man who earns his living by honest toil (Psalms 128:2). These and similar verses constitute a valid program for the contemporary Jew who wishes, as all men do, to find happiness and at the same time give full expression to his capabilities.

The Hereafter

Belief in an afterlife, however little pronounced in the early Biblical period, came to assume a prominent place in Jewish faith. Basically there were two ideas, originally quite separate, that had been combined by the time of the Rabbis: the resurrection of the dead (*tehiyat ha-metim*) and the immortality of the soul. According to the original resurrection doctrine, when a man dies he is truly dead. His "soul," too, is "dead," until, after the Messianic Age, it is reunited with his body when the latter is raised from the grave. According to the doctrine of the immortality of the soul, in its original form, the body dies and is permanently lost but the soul lives on for ever after the death of the body. Eventually, when the two were combined, the doctrine ran that when a man dies his soul lives on in Heaven until the time of the resurrection when soul and body are reunited. This explains the ambiguities to be found in this matter in the Rabbinic literature. The term for the Hereafter, found with great frequency in that literature, is *Olam ha-Ba*, "the world to come." But does this refer to the resurrection (as Nahmanides has it in the Middle Ages) or to the immortality of the soul (as Maimonides has it)?

Orthodox Judaism still accepts the combined beliefs. Thus there are prayers in the traditional liturgy both for the repose of the souls of the departed "under the wings of the Divine Presence" and references in the prayers to the resurrection of the dead. The Sabbath morning hymn[1] expresses the Orthodox view:

> *There is none to be compared unto Thee, neither is there any beside Thee; there is none but Thee: who is like unto Thee? There is none to be compared unto Thee, O Lord our God, in this world, neither is there any beside Thee, O Our*

---

[1] *Singer's Prayer Book*, p. 177.

King, for the life of the world to come; there is none but Thee,
O our Redeemer, for the days of the Messiah, neither is
there any like unto Thee, O our Saviour, for the resurrection
of the dead.

Here the term "the world to come" clearly refers to the immortality of the soul. On the other hand, the prayer recited during grace and after meals[1]: "May the All-merciful make us worthy of the days of the Messiah, and of the life of the world to come" can only refer to the resurrection of the dead. As Naḥmanides remarks when discussing this question, the one who recites the Grace is hardly expected to look forward to his own demise.

Reform Judaism, on the other hand, rejects the doctrine of the resurrection of the dead and accepts only the belief in the immortality of the soul. This was the view of Philo in ancient times and in the Middle Ages Maimonides, too, seems to emphasize the spiritual bliss of the soul in the afterlife. Although toward the end of his life Maimonides did write an essay *Ma'amar ha-Teḥiyah (Treatise on the Resurrection)* in which he accepts the belief in the resurrection of the dead, it is clear that this doctrine is not central to his thought. Indeed, in this same essay Maimonides argues that the resurrection will be only a temporal one. Eventually the resurrected dead will return to dust and the soul alone will remain immortal. Some modern thinkers have adopted the doctrine of the resurrection in a modified form, arguing that the immortality of the soul is a Greek belief in a kind of vague survival, whereas what survives is the whole personality of man. But these thinkers, too, reject a biological resurrection.[2] In the Reform Pittsburgh Platform the passage regarding belief in the Hereafter reads:

We reassert the doctrine of Judaism that the soul is immor-
tal, grounding this belief in the divine nature of the human
spirit, which forever finds bliss in righteousness and misery
in wickedness. We reject, as ideas not rooted in Judaism,
the beliefs both in bodily resurrection and in Gehinnom and
Eden (Hell and Paradise) as abodes for everlasting punish-
ment and reward.

[1] Singer's Prayer Book, p. 383.
[2] For this view see, e.g., Will Herberg, *Judaism and Modern Man*, p. 229, New York, 1959.

The righteous in a state of beatitude in Paradise. Full-page miniature from the
Hebrew *Ambrosian Bible*, S. Germany, 1236–38. The animal heads, a sign of
holiness in the Middle Ages, were adopted by the 13th-century south German
school of Jewish illumination as a means of avoiding the depiction of human
figures. The top frame depicts the fare on which the righteous will feast: the
mythical ox, the leviathan, and the bird *ziz*.

A few short passages from Maimonides' account of spiritual bliss in the Hereafter would not be out of place here. These passages are part of Maimonides' treatment in his Code (*Yad, Teshuvah* 8):

> There are neither bodies nor bodily forms in the world to come but only the disembodied souls of the righteous who have become like the ministering angels. Since there are no bodies there is no eating or drinking there nor is there anything which the human body needs in this world. Nor does there occur there any of the events which occur to the human body in this world such as sitting, standing, sleep, death, distress, laughter, and so forth. The ancient sages say: "In the world to come there is no eating or drinking or procreation but the righteous sit with their crowns on their heads and bask in the radiance of the Divine Presence."
>
> You may despise this kind of goodness, imagining that the only worthwhile reward for keeping the commandments and for a man being perfect in the ways of truth is for him to eat and drink well and have beautiful women and wear garments of fine linen and embroidery and live in marble palaces and have vessels of silver and gold and so forth as hold the stupid and perverse Arabs who are immersed in lewdness. But the sages and intellectuals know that these things are vain and nonsensical and have no value and are only great goods for us in this world where we have bodies and bodily form. All these things have to do with the needs of the body. The soul only longs for them because the body requires them if it is to remain healthy and perform its functions. But all these things cease when there is no longer a body in existence. There is no way at all for us in this world to know or comprehend the great goodness which the soul experiences in the world to come, for in this world we know only of material pleasures and it is these we desire. That good is exceedingly great and can only be compared to the good of this world by analogy, but in reality there can be no way of comparing the good of the soul in the world to come with the physical goods of food and drink in this world. That good is great beyond all our understanding and incomparable beyond all our imagination.

Maimonides refers here to analogy. In Jewish sources a number of analogies are, in fact, given for the nature of bliss in the Hereafter, e.g., that of Sabbath delight and that of the delight the student of the Torah derives from his studies. In Rabbinic literature the Hereafter is spoken of both as the "day that is all Sabbath" and as the "Heavenly Academy" in which the righteous are taught the Torah by God himself.

The Jewish mystics speak a great deal about spiritual bliss in the Hereafter. They develop the doctrine of "bread of shame." Man's firm independence of mind refuses to allow him to be permanently satisfied with unearned gifts. To eat unearned bread given to him as a gift is to eat "bread of shame." God in His goodness wishes man to earn his spiritual bliss. Consequently, man was placed here on earth where he has a choice of good and evil. By freely choosing the good he makes it his own and comes nearer to God. He can then enjoy God for all eternity and enjoy Him, moreover, by right—a right which he has earned by pursuing the good in his life. The mystics speak, too, of eternity not as endless duration in time but as outside time altogether. Eternity is a state, not a place. One should not speak of the good man going to Heaven but becoming Heaven.

The celebrated eighteenth century mystic and moralist R. Moses Hayyim Luzzatto in his *Path of the Upright* (pp. 1–19) observes that the Rabbis teach that the whole purpose of man's creation is to "earn his keep" in the Hereafter. True perfection, says Luzzatto, lies only in communion with God. But only by arduous effort can man earn that good, only through the performance of God's will as revealed in the *mitzvot*, the precepts of the Torah. Luzzatto writes:

> *The Holy One, blessed be He, has placed man in a world where there are many things that keep him aloof from God. If a man follows the promptings of his physical desires, he gradually departs from the true good, and soon finds himself engaged in a desperate battle . . . Tempted both by prosperity and by adversity, man is in a sore predicament. If he is valorous and conquers his enemies, he becomes the perfect man who earns the privilege of communing with his Creator. Then he will pass from the vestibule of this world into the palace to enjoy the Light of Life. To the extent that a man subdues his evil inclinations, keeps aloof from the things that prevent him from attaining the good, and endeavors to*

*commune with God, to that extent is he certain to achieve
the true life and to rejoice in it.*

In the above quotations from Maimonides and Luzzatto there breathes
a pure spirituality. Of course there are to be found in Jewish writings
much cruder notions: rivers of balsam, marble halls, beautiful trees,
the enjoyment of a great banquet and the like as well as detailed descriptions of the geography of Heaven. But these belong to speculation
and folklore and are in no way anything like an official Jewish view. The
most refined Jewish thinkers have refused to take such statements literally
and have emphasized the purely spiritual nature of existence in the Hereafter.

In modern times there has been a reaction to the other-worldly
emphasis so prevalent in medieval writings. It has been argued convincingly that while the Talmudic Rabbis certainly believed in the Hereafter, they did not hold that this life was only of value as a school for
eternity. This life, as a gift from God, would be of value even if there
were no afterlife. It is said that in a famous yeshivah in Eastern Europe
a devout student said after immersing himself in Luzzatto's *Path of
the Upright*: "All very true! But this world is also a world!" Yet unless
we are to deprive life of its spiritual quality the hope of spiritual bliss
for all eternity will not cease to exercise its fascination for us. Keats's
line: "This world is a vale of soul-making" still has power for moderns.

It has been objected, however, that human survival after death is
impossible, since obviously man's mind is dependent on his brain.
When the brain is damaged man's mind cannot function. When the
brain grows old man becomes senile. How, then, is survival possible
when the brain is no more? But all the scientific evidence does is to
demonstrate that in this life the mind needs the brain. From the evidence
there is nothing to deny that the mind might be using the brain as its
only instrument in the physical world. If the doctrine of immortality
is true there may be other ways by which the mind or soul functions
in the Hereafter. Speculation here is extremely precarious, but perhaps
we can use the analogy of a moon traveler. While on the moon he is
totally dependent on his space suit. If it is damaged he will die. But once
he returns to earth he can dispense with his space suit and throw off
its restrictions to move about as he pleases.

Is Judaism, then, a this-worldly or an other-worldly religion? The
correct answer is that it is both. The paradox here was never expressed

more vividly than in the remarkable saying of the second century teacher R. Jacob (*Avot* 4:17): "Better is one hour of repentance and good deeds in this world than the whole life of the world to come; yet better is one hour of blissfulness of spirit in the world to come than the whole life of this world."

Heredity

The prolific writer on Rabbinic themes Rabbi S.J. Zevin is the author of the only study (to which this essay is heavily indebted) on heredity in Jewish thought.[1] Zevin deals chiefly with the legal aspects of the question, for example whether Jewish law recognizes blood tests as evidence of paternity, but from the sources he quotes in his essay it appears certain that in the Rabbinic literature, at least, the idea is prominent that heredity is an important factor in determining the character of a person. The good man, it was believed, is likely to transmit some of his goodness to his children. While the Rabbinic doctrine of *zekhut avot*, "the merit of the fathers," is sometimes understood as a kind of divine guarantee that their offspring will be worthy, it also means frequently that righteous parents are more likely to have righteous children because in some measure children inherit the character traits of their parents.[2] The Ḥasidim have the mystical notion that the holy man, by means of his purity of thought when he is with his wife, can succeed in bringing down to the child which is conceived at that time an especially lofty soul. This is the reason for the hereditary dynasties in Ḥasidism. The son of the *ẓaddik* is endowed from birth with special qualities.

The Mishnah (*Eduyot* 2:9) informs us that R. Akiva said: "A father endows his son with handsomeness, strength, riches, wisdom, and length of years." The fifteenth century commentator R. Obadiah of Bertinoro quotes two interpretations of the Mishnah that were evidently current in the Middle Ages. One interpretation understands the Mishnah to mean that as a reward for the father's piety God blesses him with sons who have the qualities mentioned. But the other interpretation

---

[1] *Le-Or ha-Halakhah,* pp. 147–158, Jerusalem, 1946.
[2] Solomon Schechter has a chapter on the doctrine of *zekhut avot* in his *Aspects of Rabbinic Theology,* pp. 170–198, New York, 1961.

has it that the reference in the Mishnah is to the transmission by a natural hereditary process. If the father is handsome, strong, wise, and lives long the likelihood is that his children will have the same qualities. (Biologists today are still discussing the whole question of the extent to which such characteristics are transmitted in the genes.) As for riches, this interpretation understands it simply to mean that a wealthy father will normally leave a sizeable inheritance to his children.

Particularly with regard to Torah learning it was held that the hereditary principle works. In the name of a third century Palestinian teacher it is said that if a man is a scholar, and his son is a scholar, and so is the son's son, the Torah will not depart from that family. As it was put: the Torah henceforth seeks to visit the home in which it is afforded hospitality (*Bava Mezia* 85a). Jewish history knows, in fact, of generations of Rabbis in one family. Against this another Rabbi said (*Nedarim* 81a) that the reason why scholars do not usually have scholarly sons lies in divine decree in order that people should not imagine that the Torah is the legacy of the scholars.

Because of the significance of heredity the Rabbis advise the choice of a marriage partner who comes from a good family. It was especially believed that a child normally takes after his mother's brothers (*Bava Batra* 109b–110a). The *Shulḥan Arukh (Even ha-Ezer* 2) contains detailed rules on the importance of marrying into a good family. Following passages in the Talmud, the rule is also given that it is a special merit for an uncle to marry his niece. But interestingly enough many Rabbis have recently argued in the Israeli Halakhic periodical *Noam* that because of the dangers we now know to be present in the marriages of near relatives such as uncle and niece and first cousin, if the family has a history of hereditary illness the rule should be disregarded.

Hijacking

That Judaism condemns hijacking, a threat to civilization involving the terrorization of innocent people and leading frequently to murder, goes without saying. It needs only to be said that the Pentateuchal legislation treats the kidnaping of even a single individual as a capital offense: "He who kidnaps a man—whether he has sold him or is still holding him—shall be put to death" (Exodus 21:16).

The problem Judaism does have to face is that of the attitude to be adopted when hijackers, with their victims held as hostages, present their demands. Should terms such as the release of terrorists or the payment of large sums of money be met in order to save innocent lives or should they be resisted even at the risk that the threats will be carried out? It is a frightening decision to have to make, but the thrust of Jewish thinking is in favor of resisting the hijackers, the risk to life in the process being the terrible price to be paid if it is to be brought home to those with murderous intent that their schemes will never pay off. The few are to be placed in jeopardy for the sake of the many who would otherwise find themselves in the same position. Such a decision runs counter to all natural feelings of compassion but experience has shown that this is the only way to defeat terrorism.

The problem is not, in fact, entirely new. During the Rabbinic period it was laid down that to ransom Jews held by bandits was a supreme religious obligation. The duty of "ransoming captives" (*pidyon shevuyim*) was called by the Rabbis "a great *mitzvah*" (*Bava Batra* 8a-b). It was considered axiomatic by the French medieval commentators (Tosafists to *Bava Batra* 8b) that a Scroll of the Law could be sold in order to raise the money to ransom captives. Yet the Rabbinic teachers were fully aware of the dangers inherent in a situation in which bandits would be encouraged to kidnap Jews, knowing full well that the Jewish community will stop at nothing to secure their release. Consequently, the ruling was given (Mishnah, *Gittin* 4:6) that it is forbidden to pay more than the usual ransom money to secure the release of Jewish captives. The term used is "for the sake of order in society" (*tikkun ha-olam*, lit. "improvement of the world"), i.e., new legislation must be introduced if the law as it stands tends to encourage practices harmful to society as a whole. Reference should be made to the case of Rabbi Meir of Rothenburg (c. 1215–1293), some of the details of which are somewhat obscure but which has substantially been authenticated. This famous teacher was held in prison by the emperor Rudolph I in order to force the Jews to pay the kind of discriminatory taxes that would brand them as slaves. Rabbi Meir refused to permit the community to ransom him on these terms. He died eventually in prison where his body remained until it was redeemed many years later by Alexander Wimpfen and buried at Worms.

To be sure, in such delicate matters, and having regard for the highest value which Judaism places on each individual human life, there are many reservations and qualifications, as one can see from the way these laws developed (*Shulḥan Arukh, Yoreh Deah* 252 and commentaries), but there is little doubt that, as we have suggested, the whole tendency of Jewish teaching is to resist the threats of the hijackers.

Hinduism

Until comparatively recent times Hinduism and the other Far Eastern religions were unknown to Jews. There are, consequently, no references to Hinduism in the classical Jewish sources. There are, of course, aspects of Hinduism which are quite incompatible with the Jewish faith, for example, the belief in, and worship of, many gods, which Judaism looks upon as idolatry (*avodah zarah*). In this connection reference can be made to a question addressed to the distinguished Jerusalem Rabbi Pesaḥ Ẓevi Frank, the reply to which is given in his Responsa collection.[1] The question was whether it is permitted to drink milk obtained from a "sacred cow" since the animal is worshiped as a god. The learned Rabbi replies that according to Rabbinic law an animal that is worshiped is only forbidden to be offered as a sacrifice in the Temple but it may be eaten. Consequently, he rules that the milk of a "sacred cow" can be drunk. Another prominent feature of the Hindu way of life is the caste system. Needless to say there is no parallel in the Jewish sources.

However, it would be altogether too narrow a view that would dismiss Hinduism completely as alien to Judaism. There is a deep spirituality in Hindu thought that is bound to win the admiration of religious people. Bhavagadgita is justly renowned as a great religious work. While in some of the Upanishads ultimate reality, Brahman, is thought of in impersonal terms, in others Brahman is close to a personal deity. The idea that there is something in man, his transcendent self, which corresponds to Brahman—Atman is Brahman or, in the famous saying, *tat tvam asi*, "That is thou"—is certainly very unconventional in Jewish thought, yet in some versions of Ḥasidism it is not unknown. In Ḥabad thought, for instance, deep in the recesses of the human psyche there is a "divine spark," so that man finds God by transcending the selfish ego to meet the real self that is divine. To be sure, ideas such as these

[1] *Har Ẓevi*, Jerusalem, pp. 106–7, 1964, No. 118.

were dubbed heretical by most Jewish teachers but they are present nonetheless in Ḥabad thought. Since Judaism believes in the One God, Creator of the Universe, it would seem to follow that He is revealed to those of His children who are without the Torah—the Hindus, for example—in their own scriptures insofar as these do not contradict Jewish monotheism.

Homosexuality

Homosexual conduct between males is mentioned much more frequently and more heavily condemned in the traditional Jewish sources than such conduct between females. The emphasis is on the sexual act between males rather than mental homosexual tendencies, as in Leviticus 19:22: "Thou shalt not lie with mankind, as with womankind; it is an abomination" and in Leviticus 20:13: "And if a man lie with mankind, as with womankind, both of them have committed abomination; they shall surely be put to death; their blood shall be upon them." Some scholars have suggested (though it is not certain that they are right) that the "price of a dog" in Deuteronomy 23:19 ("Thou shalt not bring the hire of a harlot, or the price of a dog, into the house of the Lord thy God for any vow; for even both of these are an abomination unto the Lord thy God") refers to the hire of a man by a man for sexual purposes. While the men of Sodom (Genesis 19:5) wished to abuse the two men who stayed with Lot, the main sin of Sodom, according to the Jewish tradition (see Ezekiel 16:49), was its injustice and cruelty, so that a term like "sodomy" for homosexual acts between males is not found in the Jewish sources. The term *kadesh* in Deuteronomy 23:18 is rendered in some English versions as a "sodomite" but the New English Bible renders the verse more accurately as: "No Israelite woman shall become a temple-prostitute, and no Israelite man shall prostitute himself in this way."

A debate dating from the second half of the second century is recorded in the Mishnah (*Kiddushin* 4:14). R. Judah here forbids two unmarried males to sleep together, while the Sages permit it. The reason given (*Kiddushin* 82a) for the ruling of the Sages is that Jews are not suspected of engaging in homosexual practices. The *Shulḥan Arukh* (*Even ha-Ezer* 24), however, though recording the opinion of the Sages as the law, continues: "But in these times when there are many loose persons about one should avoid being alone with another male." The

171

Polish commentators to the *Shulḥan Arukh* (*Ḥelkat Meḥokek* and *Bet Shemuel*) argue that the author of the *Shulḥan Arukh* was speaking of his own milieu but "in our lands" it is only a special act of piety to refuse to be alone with another male. Nonetheless, they say, two males should not sleep together in the same bed.

According to the Rabbis, gentiles, too, are commanded by the Torah to abstain from homosexual practices. This belongs to the special Torah laws for gentiles—the "seven laws of the sons of Noah." It is said that even those gentiles who indulge in these practices at least have the decency not to draw up a formal marriage contract between two males (*Ḥullin* 92a–b). In Rabbinic legend Nebuchadnezzar used to submit the kings he had conquered to sexual abuse (*Shabbat* 149b).

Female homosexuality is referred to in the comment of the *Sifra* on the verse: "After the doings of the land of Egypt, wherein ye dwelt, shall ye not do; and after the doings of the land of Canaan, whither I bring you, shall ye not do; neither shall ye walk in their statutes" (Leviticus 18:3). The *Sifra* observes that this does not mean that one must not copy the architectural styles, for instance, of Egypt and Canaan but refers only to their sexual practices. "What did they do? They allowed a man to marry a man and a woman a woman." The Babylonian teacher R. Huna said (*Shabbat* 65a–b) that if a woman performs a sex act with another woman they are no longer considered to be virgins and could not, therefore, marry a High Priest, who must only marry a virgin (Leviticus 21:13). From the discussion it emerges that the concern is not with whether they may marry a High Priest (in any event the High Priesthood had ceased long before the third century when R. Huna lived), but with the immorality of the practice. This is Rashi's explanation of the passage in question but, in fact, the term used is "for the priesthood" and not for "the High Priesthood," so that the Tosafists understood R. Huna to mean that women who indulge in these practices are treated as harlots who are forbidden to the priests (Leviticus 21:7). However, elsewhere in the Talmud (*Yevamot* 76a) it is said that R. Huna's ruling is not followed. The women would not be treated as harlots but as indulging in obscene practices.

Maimonides (*Yad, Issurei Biah* 21:8) rules, on the basis of the above, that lesbian practices are forbidden but a married woman who is guilty of them does not thereby become automatically forbidden to her husband. Maimonides continues that a husband should object to his wife's indulging in such practices and should furthermore prevent his wife from associating with women who are known to be addicted to such practices.

It is clear, then, from the above sources that homosexual practices are severely frowned upon but that female homosexuality is treated less severely than male homosexuality. Why this should be so is not stated in the sources but would appear to be due to the fact that in the nature of the case the possibility of physical contact is less in the former instance. The sources, moreover, do not seem to recognize either male homosexuals or lesbians as distinct groups, or in any event there is reference only to practices and not to some men or women having homosexual natures.

Humanism

Humanism as a movement tends to decry religion as a hindrance to man's fulfillment, arguing that the dos and don'ts in every religious system frustrate man's desire for individual self-expression. Judaism replies that man has a need for God, so that to ignore the religious dimension of human life is itself a thwarting of man's development. To stifle man's spiritual longings is as much an interference with the human personality as to prevent any other aspect of his growth. It is for this reason that one can speak without contradiction of a religious humanism. While there are undoubtedly tendencies in some Jewish teachings of an anti-humanist character there is enough in the works of some of the most respected Jewish teachers to support the claim that human strivings are given their full weight in the Jewish traditions.

It is a commonplace of the Rabbinic tradition that the precepts of the Torah are divided into two categories—those between man and God (*ben adam la-makom*) and those between man and his fellows (*ben adam la-ḥavero*). The Day of Atonement, we are informed (Mishnah, *Yoma* 8:9), only brings pardon to offenses against God. Offenses against one's neighbor are not pardoned unless the wrong done has been rectified. A number of Jewish teachers have gone so far as to suggest that if a man loves his neighbor only because God has commanded him to do so he has not fulfilled the command, which demands the cultivation of regard for others until it becomes so spontaneous that it no longer requires the spur of religious obligation. The founder of the nineteenth century Musar movement, R. Israel Salanter, once said that concern for one's neighbor's material well-being is not a material thing at all but belongs to the spiritual. In the well-known tale about Hillel and the proselyte (*Shabbat* 31a), Hillel declares: "That which is hateful unto thee do not do unto thy neighbor. This is the whole of the Torah. The rest is commentary. Go and learn." To be sure the commentators are puzzled by the absence of any reference to man's religious obligations

174

(in one version, Rashi understands "unto thy neighbor" as referring to God!) but the way in which the tale is told and Hillel's maxim formulated suggest that, indeed, the emphasis is on the purely human side of the religious outlook. Naturally, too extreme conclusions must not be drawn from homiletical passages and it would not be difficult to find other passages in which the purely religious aspects are stressed. Nevertheless, it is true to say that one need not look far to discover the strongly humanistic mood in Jewish teaching.

There is a saying of the Ḥasidic teacher R. Mendel of Kotzk. On the verse: "And ye shall be holy men unto Me" (Exodus 22:30) he commented: "Be holy but be a *mensch*." Martin Buber used this saying for his idea of the "humanly holy." It would be a gross distortion of Judaism to equate it with secular humanism. But it would be as great a distortion to think of Judaism as limited to prayer and worship in the narrow sense. The Jewish ideal is to be humanly holy, or, as William Temple has said, God is interested in many things besides religion.

Humility

Humility is among the highest of the Jewish virtues. Moses, the greatest of men, is praised for his humility: "Now the man Moses was very meek, above all the men that were upon the face of the earth" (Numbers 12:3). Although Maimonides, for example, advocates the golden mean in character training and the avoidance of extremes, in connection with humility he stresses that the middle way should not be followed and that every form of pride should be rejected (*Yad, Deot*, 2:3). Maimonides writes:

> *It is wrong for a man to follow the middle way in connection with some character traits but he should go to extremes. The reference is to pride. It is not a good way that a man should merely be humble but he should be lowly of spirit and his spirit exceedingly humble. That is why it is said of Moses our teacher "very meek" and it does not simply say that he was "meek." That is why the Sages declare (Avot 4:4): "Be exceedingly lowly of spirit" The Sages say further (Sotah 4b) that whoever is proud in his heart denies the basic principle of faith, as it is said: "Then thy heart be lifted up, and thou forget the Lord thy God" (Deuteronomy 8:14). And they said further (Sotah 5a): "One who is proud of spirit is placed under a ban."*

One of the most significant biblical passages in praise of humility is the rule (Deuteronomy 17:20) that the king was to read the scroll of the law in order "that his heart be not lifted up above his brethren."

When Saul is chosen as the first king of Israel he is discovered "hid among the baggage" (I Samuel 10:22), a phrase which became current in Jewish speech for the man who shuns the limelight. A Midrashic comment on the strange plural form in the creation narrative: "Let *us* make man" (Genesis 1:26) is that God took counsel with the angels

176

before creating man to teach man the virtue of humility, of consulting others before embarking on any major undertaking (*Genesis Rabbah* 8:8). The Torah, say the Rabbis (*Ta'anit* 7a), is compared to water, for just as water runs downhill and not uphill the word of God can only be found in the heart of a humble man.

The obvious forms of pride are easily recognized for what they are, but the Jewish moralists are not slow to point out the more insidious forms in which pride masquerades as humility. In Moses Hayyim Luzzatto's *Path of the Upright* (p. 104ff.) the different types of mock modesty are penetratingly discussed. Luzzatto writes:

> *Another imagines that he is so great and so deserving of honor that no one can deprive him of the usual signs of respect. And to prove this, he behaves as though he were humble and goes to extremes in displaying boundless modesty and infinite humility. But in his heart he is proud, saying to himself, "I am so exalted, and so deserving of honor, that I need not have any one do me honor. I can well afford to forgo marks of respect." Another is the coxcomb, who wants to be noted for his superior qualities and to be singled out for his behavior. He is not satisfied with having every one praise him for the superior traits which he thinks he possesses, but he wants them also to include in their praise that he is the most humble of men. He thus takes pride in his humility, and wishes to be honored because he pretends to flee from honor. Such a prig usually goes so far as to put himself below those who are much inferior to him, even below the meanest, thinking that in this way he displays the utmost humility. He refuses all titles of greatness and declines promotion in rank, but in his heart, he thinks, "There is no one in all the world as wise and as humble as I." Conceited people of this type, though they pretend mightily to be humble, cannot escape some mishap which causes their pride to burst forth, like a flame out of a heap of litter . . .*

Luzzatto might have added the man who is proud of not indulging in mock modesty and who thinks of himself as superior to others in this respect.

It is generally assumed that pride is the particular temptation of great men. This is not necessarily so. The man with an "inferiority complex" is especially tempted to overcompensate. A Hasidic tale tells of the disciples of the Kotzker Rabbi who paid great deference to a man whom they held to be humble. "Is he a scholar?" they were asked. "No," was the reply. "Is he a rich man?" "No." "Is he of good family?" "No." "Then what has he to be proud about?" But when the Kotzker heard of it he declared: "If the man is no scholar, is poor and of bad family, and yet manages to be humble his is, indeed, a great achievement!"

On the deeper level, humility consists not so much of a man thinking little of himself but of him not thinking of himself at all. In Hasidic thought the ideal of *shiflut* ("lowliness") is associated with the Hasidic doctrine of "self-annihilation" (*bittul ha-yesh*), i.e., of transcending the ego so that all that matters is that God's will be done and a man's own achievements can be seen in as detached a way as if they were those of another. It is clear that there are many subtleties in this whole question of humility. The Hasidim implied that self-forgetfulness is the real ideal and that its attainment is hampered rather than encouraged if a man is too preoccupied with the question of his own humility.

Humor

Examples of Jewish humor abound through all periods of Jewish history. In spite of claims made to the contrary, there is not much humor in the Bible, but Elijah's taunt of the prophets of Baal has often been quoted as a superb illustration of Biblical irony (I Kings 18:27):

> And it came to pass at noon, that Elijah mocked them, and said: "Cry aloud; for he is a god; either he is musing, or he has gone aside, or he is in a journey, or peradventure he sleepeth, and must be awakened."

Another Biblical example is that of the prophet (Isaiah 44:13–17) mocking the idolator who carves a god for himself, out of part of a block of wood, the other half of which he uses for fuel:

> The carpenter stretcheth out a line; he marketh it out with a pencil; he fitteth it out with planes, and he marketh it out with the compasses, and maketh it after the figure of a man according to the beauty of a man, to dwell in the house. He heweth him down cedars, and taketh the ilex and the oak, and strengtheneth for himself one among the trees of the forest; he planteth a bay-tree, and the rain doth nourish it. Then a man useth it for fuel; and he taketh thereof, and warmeth himself; yea, he kindleth it, and baketh bread; yea, he maketh a god, and worshipeth it; he maketh it a graven image, and falleth down thereto. He burneth the half thereof in the fire; with the half thereof he eateth flesh; he roasteth roast and is satisfied; yea, he warmeth himself, and saith: "Aha, I am warm, I have seen the fire." And the residue thereof he maketh a god, even his graven image; he falleth down unto it and worshipeth, and prayeth to it. And saith: "Deliver me, for thou art my god."

179

The Rabbis, sensing an apparent contradiction between passages such as this and the injunction against scoffing (Psalms 1:1), remark that while to scoff is normally wrong it is permitted, as in these passages, to mock idols and idolatry (*Megillah* 25b). However, in the Talmudic passage quoted the reference is to obscene jests directed against idolatry. The Rabbis had a keen sense of humor, as is evident from numerous witty sayings in the Talmudic and Midrashic literature. The fourth century Babylonian teacher Rabbah gave his lectures in a serious frame of mind but would always preface them with a joke or witticism, believing that by making his pupils smile he would help them to appreciate better the difficult subjects he intended to expound to them (*Shabbat* 30b).

A Talmudic legend tells (*Ta'anit* 22a) of Elijah pointing out to a Rabbi two men in the market place who were assured of a place in Paradise. When the Rabbi asked them the nature of their occupation they said that they were comedians who brought cheer into the lives of sufferers by amusing them with their witticisms. In many Talmudic arguments humor is introduced in order to support a case.

During the Middle Ages parodies of various kinds were written, especially for use on Purim. In the famous tractate *Purim* the Talmudic rules regarding the search for leaven before Passover are parodied. The search is not for leaven but for water which must be entirely removed from the home before Purim; wine alone is to be kept there to gladden men's hearts. Later Rabbis were renowned for their humor. There are a number of collections of humorous Rabbinic tales and sayings.

Hochzeit—Spa machers Tanz

A *badhan* dancing at a Galician wedding. A postcard from Cracow, 1902.

The folk-humor of Eastern European Jews is too well known to require attention being called to it. The psychological value of all this is fairly obvious. If the Jew had not had the courage to laugh at his misfortunes and at himself, the crushing burden of his existence would have proved too much for him. To the question "Why does the Jew always answer a question with a question?" the traditional answer is: "Why not?"

Hunting

The Bible refers to hunting for food (for example in Leviticus 17:13) and sees no objection to it. The principle, as established by the Rabbis, is that although cruelty to animals is strictly forbidden, it is permitted to kill animals for food or for their skins and the same would apply to hunting animals for this purpose. Nevertheless, the only two persons mentioned in the Bible as hunters are Nimrod (Genesis 10:9) and Esau (Genesis 25:27), neither of whom is held up for admiration in the Jewish tradition. The whole of the Biblical and Rabbinic literature does not even refer to hunting for sport.

There are, however, two frequently quoted Responsa on the question of hunting for sport. The first is by the Italian Rabbi Isaac Lampronti (1679–1756). This author discusses in his encyclopedia of Jewish Law (*Pahad Yitzhak*, *s.v. zedah*) whether it is permitted to hunt animals and kill them. Lampronti forbids it on the grounds of wastefulness (*bal tashhit*). The second Responsum is by Rabbi Ezekiel Landau (1713–1793) of Prague (*Noda bi-Yehudah, Tinyana, Yoreh Deah*, No. 10). This Rabbi argues that hunting animals for sport is forbidden, in addition to the reasons given by Lampronti, on the grounds of unnecessary cruelty to animals and the danger to human life in the chase. Landau points out that the Talmudic discussion on the duty of killing wild animals even on the Sabbath (*Shabbat* 121b) only applies to wild animals that come among men and are dangerous and not to pursuing them in their own haunts. Walter Rathenau's remark has also been frequently quoted in this connection: "When a Jew says he's going hunting to amuse himself, he lies."

There is no logical reason for distinguishing between hunting animals and catching fish, yet some Jews who would not hunt animals see no harm in fishing as a hobby. Perhaps they hold that the fish caught will be eaten and fishing is therefore not purely for sport or perhaps they believe that fish feel less pain than animals.

Hypnotism

Rabbi Ẓevi Hirsh Spira of Munkacs (d. 1913) in his compendium of laws to the *Shulḥan Arukh, Yoreh Deah,* sees fit to discuss the question of whether hypnotism is a legitimate form of healing, in the section of the Code dealing with the prohibition of magical practices (*Darkhei Teshuvah* 179:6). Natural methods of healing are acceptable, but is hypnotism supernatural so that its use might fall under the heading of these practices? Spira quotes the Responsum on this topic by the German authority Rabbi Jacob Ettlinger (1798–1871). A pious Jew had fallen ill and was advised by his doctors to resort to hypnotic cure (more specifically to "magnetism"). Ettlinger replies that he consulted the experts and received contradictory answers from them. Some of the experts dismissed the whole method as charlatanism but others were less skeptical. Ettlinger permits it on the grounds that those who practice it believe that it is a purely natural form of healing. Since Ettlinger's day hypnotism has been widely used by reputable physicians, especially in treating various kinds of mental illness, so that there is no reason nowadays to forbid a pious Jewish patient from submitting to hypnotism.

More recent authorities have discussed whether an act performed by a person who has been hypnotized can be considered an intentional act in Jewish law.[1]

---

[1] For this see Solomon B. Freehof, *The Responsa Literature,* pp. 259–261, Philadelphia, 1959.

The Individual

The idea of peoplehood, of the Jewish group or community, is so frequently stressed that the importance of the individual in the Jewish scheme is sometimes overlooked. One of the momentous truths taught by Judaism is that the individual counts, that he matters to God, that what he does with his life is of eternal significance. This teaching is especially reassuring in an age when over wide areas of the globe the totalitarian view prevails in which the State reigns supreme, with the individual a mere cog in the machine. He *belongs* to the State and the latter has every right to ride roughshod over his interests.

Judaism raises its voice in protest against this inhuman attitude. The teaching that the individual matters is to be found in numerous passages in the great classics of the Jewish faith but nowhere more specifically and with greater emphasis than in the Mishnah, which discusses the procedure to be adopted by the ancient Court of Law in emphasizing the sacredness of human life to witnesses in cases involving capital crimes (*Sanhedrin* 4:5). When a man was on trial for his life, though it was their duty to testify against him if he was guilty, witnesses must not do so without being fully aware of the enormity of destroying an innocent life. They were to be referred, says the Mishnah, to the Genesis story of Adam and Eve, in which all mankind is descended from one human couple. If Adam had been destroyed there would have been no humankind; so it follows, argues the Mishnah, that each individual is potentially a whole world. This is how the Mishnah puts it:

> *Therefore but a single man was created in the world, to teach that if any man has caused a single soul to perish Scripture imputes it to him as though he had caused a whole world to perish; and if any man saves alive a single soul Scripture imputes it to him as though he had saved alive a whole world. Again (but a single man was created) for the sake of peace*

184

> *among mankind, that none should say to his fellow: "My father was greater than thy father"; also that the heretics should not say, "There are many ruling powers in heaven." Again (but a single man was created) to proclaim the greatness of the Holy One, blessed be He; for man stamps many coins with the one seal and they are all like one another; but the King of kings, the Holy One, blessed be He, has stamped every man with the seal of the first man, yet not one of them is like his fellow. Therefore every one must say, For my sake was the world created.*

No two men are alike, the birth of a single man is the birth of a whole world, therefore every man must say, "For my sake was the world created." What clearer evidence is required that although Judaism is a religion that centers round a *people*, it considers the *individual* to be of supreme importance? The argument is not, of course, made less valid by the fact that nowadays we do not normally take the story of Adam and Eve literally. In the narrative at least mankind is descended from one man and one woman and the great teachers of the Mishnah did stress the supreme value of the individual. The Jew is encouraged to look upon himself both as a member of the covenant people consecrated to God's service and as a person of value in his own right in the sight of God, with a contribution that only he can make. This dual function of the individual is possibly expressed in the *Shema*, the Jewish declaration of faith. The second paragraph of the *Shema* (Deuteronomy 11:13–21) is in the plural, it is addressed to the *community* of Israel: "And it shall come to pass, if *ye* shall hearken diligently unto My commandments which I command *you* this day . . . " But the first paragraph (Deuteronomy 6:4–9) speaks directly to the individual as he is in himself: "And *thou* shalt love the Lord thy God with all *thy* heart, and with all *thy* soul, and with all *thy* might."

In another Talmudic passage (*Berakhot* 58a) it is said that a special benediction is to be recited when a huge crowd of Israelites is observed. The benediction is: "Blessed is He who discerneth secrets." The interpretation given for the wording is that God alone knows the secret character of each individual, "for the mind of each is different from that of the other, just as the face of each is different from that of the other." No two human faces are exactly alike (nowadays we might also say that no two persons have identical fingerprints), and no two minds are exactly alike. The implication is that each individual possesses a fraction of the divine light which only he can reveal. In a similar vein the Midrash (*Exodus Rabbah* 5:9) comments on the verse: "The voice of the Lord is with power" (Psalms 29:4) that the meaning is "according to the power [i.e. capacity] of each person to receive it." That is to say, the voice of Sinai is adopted to the capacity of each person; no two persons hear exactly the same voice. There is a clearly defined pattern of Jewish life for all, but within that pattern there is room for individual response and creativity.

Since God is the Father of all mankind it must follow that each individual human being is important. Against the accusation of Jewish exclusiveness stands the frequently quoted late Midrash (*Yalkut* to Judges 4:4 from *Tanna de-vei Eliyahu*): "I bring heaven and earth to witness that the Holy Spirit dwells upon a non-Jew as well as upon a Jew, upon a woman as well as upon a man, upon maid-servant as well as man-servant. All depends on the deeds of the particular individual!" Here speaks the authentic voice of Judaism. "All depends on the deeds of the particular individual." None is insignificant. God cares for each and the destiny of each is in His hand so that each can live worthily, recognizing God's truth and fulfilling God's purpose in his or her own way.

It can hardly be denied that there have been times in the long history of the Jews when the role of the individual was played down, especially when the group as a whole was threatened. In recent years a thinker who called attention to the fact that the group is comprised of individuals, and that there is no mystical corpus of the group over and above its individual members, was Rabbi Abraham Chen (1878–1958). Chen wrote a number of essays over the years emphasizing the supreme value of the individual and that he must never be subordinated to the group. Chen's emphasis is too extreme for many but serves as a useful check to the opposite extreme of the modern form of idolatry that is worship of the group. Chen's essays were published posthumously in book form under the title *Be-Malkhut ha-Yahadut*.[1] In the preface to this volume Rabbi S. J. Zevin describes Chen's thought:

> *The conventional view is that the individual must give way to the group, not only in the sense of the one having priority*

[1] Jerusalem, 1959.

over the other but also in the sense of either/or. The individual is to be sacrificed to the community, literally sacrificed, his flesh and blood But there Rabbi Chen stood out as an individual in the public domain. He argued that the whole distinction in number between one and more than one only applies to things that are a means to an end, to objects, to articles which "belong" to others, which have owners. Things that are ends in themselves—not objects belonging to anyone—are excluded right from the beginning from the concept of number. He who has no owner apart from himself is himself in his own being his own master and one cannot make of him and his life a total of two or three or more. Man is sui generis. *He is an end in himself and is not a means to an end. He is unique and not merely a unit. Every man belongs in the category of "there is none else" and "there is none beside him." Man is created in the image of God and His eternity.*

Infallibility

There is obviously nothing in Judaism to correspond with the Catholic doctrine of Papal Infallibility, since, among other reasons, Judaism has no institution similar to the Papacy. Even the most outstanding and widely recognized Rabbis enjoy only the authority of the Torah they interpret and can be subject to error in their interpretations. The history of Jewish law knows of countless debates in which the decisions of great teachers are challenged by other teachers on the grounds that the arguments presented for a given ruling are untenable. No Rabbi is entitled to state dogmatically that the law is such and such. All he can do is to say that from his examination of the sources it emerges that the law is such and such. He must quote chapter and verse and defend the accuracy of his reading of the sources. While there is a marked tendency among post-*Shulḥan Arukh* authorities to accept the decisions of the *Shulḥan Arukh* and the pre-*Shulḥan Arukh* authorities (the *rishonim*) as binding, scholars such as the Gaon of Vilna have not hesitated to depart from the rulings of even these early authorities if they appear to be misconceived.

It is only in comparatively recent times that the concept of an infallible teacher has managed to gain a foothold in some Jewish circles. Thus it is not unusual today for the ideas of a *Gadol ha-Dor* ("Great One of his Generation") to be accepted as infallible truths even when they do not concern law but politics and social conduct generally. This is a radical departure from the traditional Jewish attitude. It is true that among the 48 requisites for the acquisition of the Torah (*Avot* 6:5) one is *emunat hakhamim* ("faith in the sages"), but in the context this means no more than that a disciple must have confidence in his teachers if he is to learn from them. The concept is now frequently expanded to mean that one must have implicit faith that every opinion of the distinguished Rabbinic authorities of the day is *da'at Torah* ("the opinion of the Torah"), i.e., the infallible view of what it is that

188

the Torah would have the Jew do. A typical illustration of this attitude is put forward in a defense of the Neturei Karta sect[1] as follows:

> *A* Godoil be-Yisrael [sic] *in the true sense of the term must have been born to fulfill his role. "Before I formed thee in the womb, I knew thee" (Jeremiah 1). The effort of a Jew to acquire a knowledge of* Torah, *and to approach the higher degrees of personal holiness, can achieve only as much as the individual in question is* equipped *to achieve* . . . *The words and decisions of the genuine* Godoil be-Yisrael, *are not only binding with regard to matters of direct* Torah *concern; they affect everything to which the assumption of an attitude is demanded. The true* Godoil *does* not *need to support his words* with proof *or argument. For he* himself *is so closely identified with* Torah *that even his thoughts constitute* Torah *and his views unconsciously and effortlessly reflect the loftiest source of wisdom.* [Author's emphasis.]

It would be difficult to find anything like this kind of attitude in the classical sources of Judaism, but it is an attitude held today by a not inconsiderable number of traditional Jews.

Among the Ḥasidim, too, the Ḥasidic *Ẓaddik* is a charismatic personality whose views, for his own followers at least, are conveyed to him by the holy spirit and are hence infallible. This infallibliity is also extended to the early Ḥasidic leaders such as the Ba'al Shem Tov and to the "holy books," i. e., the writings of the great Rabbis of the past, especially when these treat of mystical and general religious topics. The celebrated Ḥasidic master R. Ḥayyim Halberstam (1793–1876) rules (*Divrei Ḥayyim*, II, *Yoreh Deah*, No. 105) that the parents were right when they took their children away from a teacher who had denied that the work *Or ha-Ḥayyim* by R. Ḥayyim Ibn Attar (1696–1743) was written by the holy spirit.

All this concerns the post-Talmudic authorities. Until modern times there was a consensus of opinion, albeit with certain qualifications which we shall note, that the opinions of the Talmudic Rabbis are infallible. Maimonides[2] states that the Talmud, once it had been completed, is the final and infallible authority "to which nothing must be

---

[1] I. Domb, *The Transformation*, pp. 73–74, London, 1958.
[2] *Commentary to the Mishnah*, Introduction.

added and from which nothing must be subtracted." Yet while this consensus obtained in connection with the laws of the Talmud, in other matters some teachers held that the Talmudic Rabbis could be in error. Maimonides himself disregards, even in his Code of Law, all Talmudic rules based on a belief in the efficacy of magic or in demons or astrology. In matters of science Maimonides does not hold the Talmudic Sages to have infallible knowledge (*Guide* II,8), remarking that these Sages themselves acknowledged that the views of the "Sages of the Nations" were more accurate in the science of astronomy. Maimonides and later teachers do not recoil on occasion from interpreting the Mishnah differently from the interpretations given in the Gemara, though they qualify this by stating that the law must be based on the Gemara's interpretation.[1] The Renaissance scholar Azariah de Rossi (d. 1578) held that the Talmudic Rabbis were sometimes in error on matters of history.[2] For his pains his work was threatened with burning by the more conservative Rabbis of his day.

Modern critical scholarship has tended more and more to see the ideas contained in the Talmudic literature as subject to the same patterns of development to be observed in all human culture, with a consequent skepticism in regard to claims of infallibility. For this reason, to a large extent, infallibility is denied even to the Bible, especially in its picture of the age of the earth and the nature of the physical universe. The result has been that most Conservative thinkers as well as a few of the Orthodox, when they accept the binding character of Jewish law based on the Talmud, do so not because of the infallibility of the Talmudic Rabbis but because of the acceptance of the law by the historical Jewish community. Conservative thinkers such as Zacharias Frankel (1801–1875) come close, in fact, to a substitution of the infallibility of the Jewish people for the infallibility of the Talmudic Rabbis. A favorite quotation by Frankel was the Talmudic saying that if the Jews are not prophets they are the children of prophets, i.e., there is a kind of built-in guarantee that Jewish law always develops in the right direction. Other thinkers who accept the law do so on less mystical grounds. It is not so much a question of infallibility as of the law as historically developed *being* binding on Jews. Reform thinkers, on the other hand, tend to see the Talmud as offering guidance rather than the final word in any matter.

---

[1] See the discussion in I. H. Weiss's *Dor Dor ve-Dorshav*, Part III, Chapter 18.
[2] *Me'or Einayim, Imrei Binah*, Chapter 27.

Islam

Since the rise of this faith as a "daughter religion" of Judaism the resemblances and differences between the two religions have been noted by the adherents of both. With the establishment of the State of Israel, there has been renewed interest among Jews in the religion of the Arab and in some circles there has even been interest in a "dialogue" between Judaism and Islam. Indicative of this new interest is the fact that the journal *Judaism* devoted a whole issue[1] to a symposium on Judaism and Islam in which a number of distinguished scholars took part. This symposium has little reference, however, to Islam as a religion in conflict on basic issues with the Jewish religion.

The resemblances between Judaism and Islam are obvious. Both have systems of religious law; both have daily prayers and dietary laws; above all both are purely monotheistic faiths. The general opinion among the medieval Jewish teachers was that the Talmudic laws governing relations between Jews and idolatry (that it was forbidden, for instance, for a Jew to have business dealings with a pagan three days before any of the latter's religious feasts) could be relaxed in Islamic lands since Muslims were not idolaters. Some medieval authorities even went so far as to rule that a Jew compelled to embrace Islam is not obliged to suffer martyrdom rather than accept the Islamic faith as he would be obliged to do if compelled to worship idols. Maimonides[2] sides with the convert to Judaism from Islam, Obadiah by name, who had argued that Muslims were not idolaters. Obadiah's teacher had chided him for this opinion, calling him a fool. Maimonides declares that the teacher was wrong and Obadiah right. Although certain practices reputed to take place at Mecca may have had their origin in pre-Islamic idolatry, Muslims have banished all idolatrous associations

[1] Vol. 17, No. 4., Fall, 1968.
[2] *Responsa,* ed. J. Blau, Jerusalem, 1960, No. 488, Vol. II, pp. 725–728.

from their worship and are pure monotheists. This became the accepted Jewish view.

The major difference between Judaism and Islam is that Islam, like Christianity, while accepting God's revelation to Israel, believes that the Torah has been superseded. Mohammed is for Islam the true prophet and the Koran the new sacred book. Judaism retorts that the Torah is true for all time and has not been nor ever will be substituted by another faith. In the Middle Ages the Muslims accused the Jews of falsifying the Hebrew Scriptures by adding passages and deleting references to Mohammed. According to this view the Torah still contains hints about Mohammed's life and, for instance, it was Abraham's son Ishmael, the ancestor of the Arabs, who Abraham bound on the altar, and not Isaac. Jews have rejected all this as totally unfounded. It was probably in reaction to the role of Mohammed in Islam that Jewish teachers in the Middle Ages tended to magnify the personality of Moses. For Maimonides, Moses is a superhuman figure (though in no way, of course, divine) and the seventh principle of Maimonides' Creed—that Moses is the greatest of the prophets—is almost certainly a formulation aimed against Islam. Under Islamic influence, and in reaction to it, the medieval Jewish writers sometimes refer to Moses as "The Prophet."

The indebtedness of Jews in the Middle Ages to Islamic thought was considerable. It was through Arabic translations that the works of the Greek philosophers were known to the Jewish thinkers and many of their philosophical discussions were conducted against an Islamic cultural background. It is no accident that Saadiah, Bahya Ibn Paquda, Judah Halevi, and Maimonides wrote their philosophical works in Arabic. It has also been suggested that the systematic presentation to be observed in Jewish legal works, of which Maimonides' great Code is the foremost example, owes much to Islamic models. Medieval Jewish poetry, including religious verse, borrowed much in style from the patterns of Arabic verse. Islamic theologians and saints were even admired as religious teachers with influence on Jewish thought. It has long been recognized that Bahya's *Duties of the Heart* was strongly influenced by the Sufi asceticism of his day.

For all that it is clear that Judaism rejects totally the religion of Islam as a false religion. Yet, as we have seen, this does not mean that Jews are incapable of learning from Islamic teachers. Nor does it mean that in the Jewish view Muslims are doomed because they live in doctrinal error. The Rabbinic doctrine of the righteous of the nations, who keep

A miniature from *Zubdat al-Tāwarīkh* by Luqmān-i-Ashūrī, Turkey, c. 1583.
The lower register shows Abraham about to sacrifice Ishmael, and underneath
is a genealogy of the children of Ishmael. In the top register Abraham is shown
in Nimrod's fiery furnace (Gen. R. 38:19).

the seven laws of the sons of Noah (aimed against theft and murder, for instance) and who have a share in the world to come, certainly applies to Muslims. If Muslims live up to the highest demands of their own faith they belong among the righteous of the nations. But the Jew who embraces Islam is considered to be a *meshummad*, a renegade, who has forsaken the truth and has been disloyal to its bearers, the people of Israel.

Justice

Aḥad Ha-Am attacked Claude Montefiore for suggesting that some aspects of the Christian ethic can profitably be combined with the Jewish ethic. Aḥad Ha-Am roundly declares that, without going into the question of value, there can be no combination of an ethic based on justice and one based on love. The Jewish ethic is based on justice and justice demands that a man be fair to himself as well as to others. Consequently, the Christian ethic, based on love, sees it as an act of great merit when a man sacrifices his life for his friends, but Judaism would deny a man the right to sacrifice his life for others. In a justice-based ethic altruism is only inverted egotism. This is a highly dubious thesis. There have been examples of Jews sacrificing their lives for others and their action was approved by the Jewish teachers. The truth is that such neat distinctions between the two faiths on the ethical side are far too simplistic. Judaism knows much of love as well as justice. Repudiating as we must Aḥad Ha-Am's generalization, it remains true, however, that there is a very strong emphasis on justice in the Jewish tradition.

The evidence is so powerful that it seems unnecessary to present it in any detail. What are the great codes of law, from the Pentateuch to the Mishnah to Maimonides and the *Shulḥan Arukh*, if not a great celebration of the demands of justice in human affairs? Abraham pleads with God himself to practice justice: "That be far from Thee to do after this manner, to slay the righteous with the wicked, that so the righteous should be as the wicked; that be far from Thee; shall not the judge of all the earth do justly?" (Genesis 18:25). In the Pentateuchal laws justice is demanded for the slave (Exodus 21:26–27); for the stranger (Exodus 22:20); for the widow and the orphan (Exodus

---

[1] *Essays, Letters, Memoirs—Ahad Ha-Am,* translated by Leon Simon, East and West Library, pp. 128f, London, 1946.

195

22 :21); for the poor (Exodus 22 :24–26); even for animals (Exodus 22 :29; Deuteronomy 22 :6–7; 25 :4); and even for Israel's enemies (Deuteronomy 23:8–9). The introduction to the code of laws in Deuteronomy (16:18–20) states:

> Judges and officers shalt thou make thee in all thy gates, which the Lord thy God giveth thee, tribe by tribe; and they shall judge the people with righteous judgement. Thou shalt not wrest judgement; thou shalt not respect persons; neither shalt thou take a gift, for a gift doth blind the eyes of the wise, and pervert the words of the righteous. Justice, justice shalt thou follow, that thou mayest live, and inherit the land which the Lord thy God giveth thee.

The remarkable repetition of the word "justice" in the last verse, especially since it is in a sober legal context, supports the view that the Hebrews had a passion for justice. Rabbi A. I. Kook, speaking of the way the law was loved and adorned by generation after generation of Jews so as to become a sublime work of art, once remarked that just as there are laws of poetry there is poetry in laws.

The prophetic writings continually inculcate the need to practice justice. It is clear that Isaiah sees the good life in terms of justice (1 :17–27):

> Learn to do well—seek justice, relieve the oppressed, judge the fatherless, plead for the widow . . . . Thy princes are rebellious, and companions of thieves; every one loveth bribes, and followeth after rewards; they judge not the fatherless, neither doth the cause of the widow come unto them . . . . Zion shall be redeemed with justice, and they that return of her with righteousness.

In the eighteenth chapter of the Book of Ezekiel the prophet considers idolatry and acts of injustice the particular offenses to be utterly rejected. In the name of justice he refuses to believe that a righteous son will be punished for the sins of the father:

> Now, lo, if he begat a son, that seeth all his father's sins, which he hath done, and considereth, and doeth not such like, that hath not eaten upon the mountains, neither hath lifted up his eyes to the idols of the house of Israel, hath not defiled his neighbor's wife, neither hath wronged any, hath

not taken aught to pledge, neither hath taken by robbery,
but hath given his bread to the hungry, and hath covered
the naked with a garment, that hath withdrawn his hand from
the poor, that hath not received interest nor increase, hath
executed Mine ordinances, hath walked in My statutes;
he shall not die for the iniquity of his father, he shall surely
live.

Micah's prescription has often been quoted as the highest demands of prophetic religion (6:8):

It hath been told thee, O man,
what is good,
And what the Lord doth require of thee:
Only to do justly, and to love mercy,
and to walk humbly with thy God.

The prophet Amos warns the people that God wants none of their worship if they practice injustice (5:23-24):

Take away from Me the noise of
thy songs;
And let Me not hear the melody
of thy psalteries.
But let justice well up as waters,
And righteousness as a mighty stream

Passages such as these are found again and again throughout the prophets, so that the term "prophetic Judaism" has been used in modern times as a synonym for a Judaism which preaches justice.

The Scottish divine Dr. Davidson was a non-Jewish Hebrew scholar and the author of one of the best grammars of classical Hebrew. In his introduction to this work, Davidson points out that if the principles of the language are understood it can be seen that there are very few irregularities in its structure. Davidson refers to the principle of "compensation." For example, the root *nafal* ("to fall") should be, in the imperfect, *yinpol* ("he will fall"). But since it is somewhat difficult to pronounce the "n" and the "p" together the letter *nun* ("n") is deleted and the word becomes *yipol*. But the lost *nun* is compensated for by adding another *pei* ("p"), hence *yippol*. It is as if the Hebrews were sorry for the poor *nun* that is lost and requires compensation. Davidson, and he may well be right, sees in this the Hebraic passion for justice carried over even into their language!

The Rabbi of Lublin, R. Meir Schapiro (1887–1934), is reported to have describbed thus the difference between the Hasid and the *Mitnagged* in their approach to Talmudic studies. The Talmud tells of Jonathan b. Uzziel, disciple of Hillel, that his was such a holy life that if a bird flew over his head while he was studying the Torah it would be burnt to a cinder. The Hasid, when he reads this passage, waxes eloquent over Jonathan's great sanctity. How wonderful for a man to be so holy! The *Mitnagged*, when he reads the passage, wants to know whether Jonathan would be responsible in law for the destruction of the bird! Who is to say which attitude is the more deeply religious? Enthusiasts for religion have a useful role to play, but the more usual Jewish approach is the approach of the *Mitnagged*—sober, matter-of-fact, but sublime in a different way—whose main concern is with justice, with the rights and wrongs of a case, with how the righteousness which God demands of man is to be expressed in daily living among men and women of flesh and blood.

R. Jacob b. Asher (d. 1340) was the author of one of the most important codes of law, the *Tur*, the divisions and pattern of which is followed by the *Shulhan Arukh*. In the first chapter of the section dealing with law proper (*Hoshen Mishpat*) the *Tur* summarizes the Jewish attitude to justice and its administration:

> *Abraham our father was only known by God and called His friend because he walked in the way of justice and trained his sons therein, as it is written (Genesis 18:19): "For I have known him, to the end that he may command his children and his household after him, that they may keep the way of the Lord, to do righteousness and justice,"*
>
> *And Moses our teacher, on whom be peace, master of all the prophets, took the advice of Jethro (Exodus 18) regarding justice, to set up judges who would warn the people of Israel and command them to practice justice and God gave His consent. Joshua, after making a covenant between God and Israel, concluded his speech with reference to justice, as it is written (Joshua 24:26): "So Joshua made a covenant with the people that day, and set them a statute and a judgement in Shechem." For justice is the foundation and a great*

principle in the service of God . . . And the King Messiah, too, may he come speedily in our days, is praised by scripture in connection with justice, as it is written (Isaiah 1:4): "But with righteousness shall he judge the poor, and decide with equity for the meek of the land . . . "

It is easy to understand, therefore, why the Jew has seen the practice of justice as a divine imperative, why in modern times many Jews have been in the forefront of movements working for social justice, and why the Biblical teachings have been the most powerful force for justice in the whole history of civilization.

Leadership

Leadership is generally thought of in the Jewish tradition as an unenviable role, fraught with the dangers of ambition, lust for power and self-seeking at the expense of those who are led. The ideal attitude is for the leader to express sincere unwillingness to assume the onerous position and to accept it only after much persuasion. Even in the instance of the comparatively mild form of social prominence, that of prayer-leader, a man should only accept the position, say the Rabbis (*Berakhot* 34a), after first refusing its awesome responsibilities. The supreme example in the Bible is that of Moses at the beginning of his mission who declares repeatedly that he is unfit for the great task until God compels him to accept it (Exodus 3:11–4:17). Moses, as a true leader, is ready to sacrifice himself for his people (Exodus 32:32). He leads them with complete devotion to their interests "as a nursing-father carrieth the sucking child" (Numbers 11:12). The Talmud (*Yoma* 86b) speaks of Moses and David as the two good leaders that God raised up for the people. In another passage (*Ta'anit* 9a) it is said that God raised up for Israel three good leaders, Moses, Aaron, and Miriam. In one early Rabbinic passage (*Avot* 1:10) a man is even advised to "hate lordship" and in another Talmudic passage (*Pesaḥim* 87b) "lord-ship" is described as "burying" those who attain to it. It is said (*Eruvin* 13b) that the reason the rulings of the School of Hillel are followed is because its members were not ambitious, "to teach you that whoever tries to achieve authority it eludes him but whoever runs away from authority it pursues him." Yet it is recognized that there may be tasks of leadership and authority for which a man is particularly suited and which he should not therefore refuse. When Aaron was diffident about accepting his role as High Priest, say the Rabbis (*Sifra* to Leviticus 9:7), Moses urged him to be proud enough and self-confident enough to accept the high office for which God had chosen him. The same sentiment is probably behind the saying attributed to Hillel (*Avot* 2:5): "Where there are no men strive to be a man."

From Rabbinic times onwards the leader of the Jewish community, the person especially responsible for its welfare, was known as *parnas*. There is a debate (*Arakhin* 17a) whether "the generation is according to the *parnas* or the *parnas* according to the generation," i.e., whether the great leader molds the character of his followers or whether they produce the leader they require. This is perhaps the Rabbinic way of stating that each community gets the leader it deserves. The *parnas* is not a spiritual leader but an administrator. He is especially warned against abusing his power. God weeps, as it were, over a *parnas* who lords it over his community (*Ḥagigah* 5b). On the other hand, a *parnas* who leads his community with gentleness will have the honor of leading them in the world to come (*Sanhedrin* 92a). Indicative of the abuses to which the office of *parnas* could be put is the saying (*Yoma* 22b) that only a man with a box of vermin behind him should be appointed as a *parnas*, so that if he assumes haughty airs he can be told to look behind him. In all probability the "box of vermin" refers to base elements in his ancestry.

As far as we can tell, the community leaders in the Middle Ages were conscientious and served their people well, though human nature being what it is we find complaints against unscrupulous leaders hungry for wealth and power. There was certainly a social element, for instance, in the struggle of the Ḥasidim in the eighteenth century to achieve independence of the hegemony of the *Kahal*, the official communal leadership, which was accused of neglecting the poorer classes in favor of the rich and the scholar. An insight into the heavy burdens that were sometimes the lot of the communal leader is the letter of Maimonides (who, in addition to his scholarly activities and his work as a physician, was the leader of his community) to Samuel Ibn Tibbon in 1199. Ibn Tibbon had asked Maimonides if he could pay him a visit, but Maimonides informs him that every moment of his day is so taken up with his work and communal business that he has no time to spare in which to receive visitors. So busy is he, Maimonides writes, that he is only able to partake of one meal a day.

Leadership of the community has taken different forms throughout the long history of the Jewish community. In Biblical times (a very long period, so that allowances have to be made for many institutional changes) the leaders were the king, the prophet, the priest, the judge, and the sage. The prophet brought a message to the people in the name of God, so that he was not an elected leader, though some modern scholars

view the prophets as cult functionaries. The priest was the custodian
and interpreter of the laws (Deuteronomy 17:8–13; Malachi 2:7)
and he appears to have combined at times the office of judge with his
functions in the Temple. The "sage" (hakham) was the giver of the kind
of moral counsel and prudent advice found, for instance, in the Book
of Proverbs. There are references also to the "mighty man" and to the
wealthy as occupying positions of importance in the community.
This explains Jeremiah's plea (Jeremiah 9:22–23):

> Thus saith the Lord:
> Let not the wise man glory
> in his wisdom;
> Neither let the mighty man
> glory in his might,
> Let not the rich man glory in
> his riches;
> But let him that glorieth
> glory in this;
> That he understandeth, and
> knoweth Me,
> That I am the Lord who exercise mercy,
> Justice, and righteousness, in the earth;
> For in these things I delight,
> Saith the Lord."

The question of leadership in Rabbinic times is extremely complicated
because of the difficulty in determining which of the many sources
describe actual conditions. In Palestine the leader of the whole community was the Nasi but there are reports of his leadership being challenged. The narrative regarding the deposition of Rabban Gamaliel
because of his autocratic behavior as Nasi is very late and partly legendary
but it no doubt contains echoes of the conflicts around the position
of Nasi. In the narrative Rabban Gamaliel visited R. Joshua, who was
a poor smith, and expressed surprise when he learned of this. R. Joshua
retorted: "Woe to the generation of which you are the leader, for you
do not know how the scholars earn their living with difficulty"
(Berakhot 28a).

In more recent times leadership of the community was in the hands
of the Rabbis and the Parnasim. The Hasidic movement produced
a new type of spiritual leader, the Zaddik, who taught his followers

how to worship God, advised them in their daily affairs, and prayed for their welfare. Although the leadership of the *Zaddik* was a matter of voluntary acceptance by his followers, his powers were considerable. To this day, among some Hasidic groups, the followers of the *Zaddik* accept his every wish as a command to be obeyed without question. The leadership of the modern Rabbi is expressed through teaching Judaism, preaching, and pastoral work. The attempt by a few modern Rabbis to compare their role to that of the ancient prophet is not received very kindly and has little for support it.

Literature

One has only to note the immense literature produced in the course of Jewish history to see that literature and literary pursuits are highly regarded in Judaism. The Bible, apart from its religious value, belongs among the very greatest literary works of mankind. Much of the Apocryphal and the Pseudepigraphical works are hardly to be classed as great literature, but the same cannot be said of the works of Philo and Josephus and the unique Talmudic and Midrashic works. In the Middle Ages Jews wrote responsa, commentaries, philosophical works, grammars, poetry, histories, mystical works, legends, works on science and medicine, moralistic treatises, and even parodies. The bulk of this material is religious and semi-religious. The Haskalah movement in the nineteenth century gave the impetus to the production of a secular literature —novels, poetry, criticism, polemics, essays, philosophy, science, works of scholarship, and translations of the literary classics of the world into Hebrew. In addition to Hebrew, Jews wrote in Greek, Arabic, and all the European languages. With the invention of printing, books of all kinds were published by the great Jewish presses. In one corner of Jewish life and thought, the Ḥasidic movement, it has been estimated that no fewer than 3,000 books were produced by the Ḥasidim, to say nothing of the many works on and about Ḥasidism. It has also been estimated that the State of Israel has a larger proportion of buyers of books than any other country in the world.

It is nevertheless worthy of note that among religious writers there is to be observed a determined effort to play down the literary quality of the Bible. It is not only that we do not find anywhere in the classical works any praise of the Bible as literature but it is implicit in a number of passages that to see the Bible as literature is to denigrate its divine character and religious message. To hail the Bible as a work of literary art is, it seems to have been held, to look upon it as a human work; to say, for example, that the Bible has a fine literary quality seemed

A scene at the annual Hebrew Book Fair in Tel Aviv.

as absurd as to say that God writes well. For the Jewish mystics the Bible is a series of mystical texts whose literal meaning is secondary, and to read the Bible as literature would tend to call attention to this literal meaning and divert the reader from the divine mysteries that are its real truth. The extreme statement of this position is found in the Zohar (III, 152a):

> *Rabbi Simeon said: woe to the man who says that the Torah merely tells us tales in general and speaks of ordinary matters. If this were so we could make up even nowadays a Torah dealing with ordinary matters and an even better one at that. If all the Torah does is to tell us about worldly things there are far superior things told in worldly books so let us copy them and make up a Torah of them. But the truth is that all the words of the Torah have to do with lofty themes and high mysteries.*

Of course, the Bible is great literature and Jews today appreciate the significance of its literary art far more than the medieval teachers. Yet it is not difficult to see that there can be a conflict between Judaism studied as religious precept and studied purely as literature. Indeed, the problem of Torah versus culture is all the more acute and far more complicated precisely because today there is on the one hand a greater appreciation of general literature and, on the other hand, an awareness that the Bible and the other sacred works are in many respects like other literature, so that their literary forms can be studied and they can be enjoyed purely as literature.

The problem was, in fact, stated in the Talmud. The Babylonian teacher Rava was asked why David was punished in the story of Uzziah (II Samuel 6:6–8), i.e., why was David to blame for failing to prevent Uzziah from trying to keep the ark from slipping? Rava replies (*Sotah* 35a) that David was blameworthy because in the Book of Psalms he had referred to the words of the Torah as "songs"—"Thy statutes have been my songs in the house of my pilgrimage" (Psalms 119:54). Rava comments: "The Holy One, blessed be He, said to David: 'Words of Torah, of which it is written: *Wilt thou set thine eyes upon it? It is gone* (Proverbs 23:5) thou recitest as songs! I will cause thee to stumble in a matter which even schoolchildren know.' For it is written: 'But unto the sons of Kohath he gave none, because the service of the sanctuary . . .' (Numbers 7:9); and yet David brought it in a wagon."

Rava's meaning is clear. Every schoolchild knows that the ark—the symbol of the Torah—was not to be carried in a wagon but on the shoulders of the priests. The Torah needs no assistance. In the words of the Rabbis, it carries those who carry it. To place the ark in a wagon is a direct result of calling the words of the Torah "songs." Both are evidence of lack of comprehension as to the true nature of the Torah, far beyond all human productions as a sacred light from the divine. There is no doubt that the treatment of the Jewish classics as literature, while it has heightened appreciation for them from one point of view, has weakened their effect as sacred literature. One of the great problems of the Jew today is to try to preserve the sacred character of the Torah while being fully aware of its human side as a great work of literature capable of literary analysis and accurate philological and historical investigation.

Love

In few areas of Jewish life has apologetic motivation succeeded in clouding the issue more than in discussions concerning the role of love in Judaism. Both Christians and Jews have stated dogmatically that Christianity speaks of love while Judaism prefers to remain silent. Christians have seen this as evidence for the superiority of their faith. Jews have proudly accepted it as evidence of the more sober, unemotional approach that is typical of Judaism. The truth is that the distinction is totally unfounded and can only have arisen as a result of religious controversy in which the facts are sacrificed to the need to score over opponents. The love of God and the neighbor are basic to Judaism. Where else did Christianity find this love if not in Judaism? No one who has studied the sources of Judaism can imagine for one moment that love is relegated to a secondary role in this faith. Even one who has never studied Judaism seriously ought to be aware that "Thou shalt love thy neighbor as thyself" occurs in the Book of Leviticus (19:18) and that the devout Jew recites the *Shema* twice daily in which the verse occurs (Deuteronomy 6:5): "And thou shalt love the Lord thy God with all thy heart, and with all thy soul, and with all thy might."

The Rabbinic explanation of this latter verse (Mishnah, *Berakhot* 9:5) became authoritative in Jewish practice, so that throughout subsequent ages pious Jews tried to live up to its lofty standards. "With all thy heart" means, in this explanation, "with the *two* inclinations, the good and the evil." (There is a play on the word for "heart" (*levav*), with the letter *bet* doubled.) Serving God with the "evil inclination" seems to mean the subordination of man's propensity for evil to the will of God, which is that he should embrace the good. "With all thy soul" means "even if He takes thy soul from thee," i.e., that if necessary the Jew must suffer martyrdom rather than be false to his faith. In Jewish law martyrdom is rarely demanded—only if the Jew is compelled to worship idols or commit murder or adultery or incest. But where

A decorated opening from the "Book of Love [of God]" in the *Jerusalem Mishneh Torah*. The illustration shows one man hugging the Scroll of the Law and another man reciting the *Shema* before going to bed. Written in Spain and partially illuminated, probably by Mateo di Ser Cambio. Perugia, c. 1400.

martyrdom is demanded, the good Jew must be prepared to suffer it out of love for God. The history of Jewish martyrdom demonstrates that this was not treated as merely a theoretical preachment. "With all thy might" means "with all thy wealth," i.e., that the Jew must sacrifice all his hard-earned wealth if his faith demands it. Another interpretation of "with all thy might" is that the Jew must give thanks to God even for the hardship and sorrows he meets within his life. In the *Sifra* (Deuteronomy 32) another explanation of "Thou shalt love the Lord thy God" is given. It is taken to mean that a man should cause others to love God as did Abraham, who converted people to the pure monotheistic faith and "brought them under the wings of the divine presence."

All this represents one tendency in Jewish thought, namely that which places the emphasis on action. The above passages speak of righteous actions which are themselves the expression of man's love for God. But another tendency is to be observed in which the love of God is understood in a mystical sense, the heart of man longing for the nearness of the Creator. For instance, a Midrash (*Numbers Rabbah* 3:1) comments that the righteous are compared to a palm tree (Psalms 92:13) because just as the palm tree longs, as it were, to be grafted to another palm so do the righteous long for God. The medieval Jewish thinkers in particular dwell eloquently on the mystical love of God. The French scholar Georges Vajda[1] has examined the view of these thinkers in great detail and has shown how the love of God burned in the souls of even the great rationalists among the medieval Jewish thinkers. Bahya Ibn Paquda, for instance, in his *Duties of the Heart*,[2] defines the love of God as "the soul's longing of her own accord for the Creator, to cleave to His supernal light." When man reflects on God's power and greatness, says Bahya, he bows in dread before His sublime majesty until God stills the soul's dread so that the fear and love of God are awakened in the soul. Such a God-lover has no interest in anything other than God's service and gives no thought to it. No limb of his body moves unless it be for the purpose of worship or to do God's will. He has complete faith and trust in God and accepts all his sufferings patiently and with love. Bahya quotes the saint who used to rise at night to proclaim: "My God, Thou hast made me hungry and left

[1] *L'amour de Dieu dans la Theologie Juive du Moyen Age,* Paris, 1957.
[2] Gate 10, Chapter 1.

me naked. Thou hast caused me to dwell in night's darkness and hast shown me Thy power and might. Yet even if Thou wouldst burn me in fire I would continue only to love Thee and rejoice in Thee." Maimonides (*Yad, Yesodei ha-Torah* 10) gives his idea of what the love of God means. The famous rationalistic philosopher, usually hailed as the outstanding advocate of the "supremacy of reason," emerges here as a mystic with his soul afire. Moreover, the passage does not occur in his philosophical writings but in his Code of Law, largely intended not for the elite alone but for all Jews. Maimonides writes:

> *When man loves God with a love that is fitting he automatically carries out all the precepts in love. What is the love that is fitting? It is that man should love God with an extraordinary powerful love to the extent that his soul becomes tied to the love of God and he longs for it all the time. It is as if he were love-sick, unable to get the woman he loves out of his mind, pining for her constantly when he sits or stands, when he eats and drinks. Even more than this is the love of God in the hearts of those who love Him and yearn constantly for Him, as He has commanded us: "With all thy heart and with all thy soul." Solomon expresses it in the form of a parable: "For I am love-sick" (Song of Songs 2:5). The whole of the Song of Songs is a parable to illustrate this topic.*

Of course, the mystical love of God in its higher reaches is only for rare souls. Both Baḥya and Maimonides declare that ultimately it is a gift of God received only after much arduous effort and training. The ordinary devout Jew may have some inkling of what it all can mean but in his daily life the love of God means, as the previous Rabbinic passages have it, complete submission in the daily round to the will of God. This is why the Jewish sources speak of the love of the Torah as an adjunct to the love of God. Nowhere has the love of the Torah been expressed more intensely and poetically than in the 119th Psalm:

> *Oh how I love Thy Torah!*
> *It is my meditation all the day.*
> *Thy commandments make me wiser*
> *than mine enemies;*
> *For they are ever with me.*

I have more understanding than all
my teachers;
For Thy testimonies are my meditation.
I understand more than mine elders,
Because I have kept Thy precepts.
I have refrained my feet from evil ways,
In order that I might observe Thy word.
I have not turned aside from Thine
ordinances;
For Thou hast instructed me.
How sweet are Thy words unto my palate!
Yea, sweeter than honey to my mouth!
From Thy precepts I get understanding,
Therefore I hate every false way.

Love of the neighbor is as much an imperative in Judaism as love of God. In the tradition, love of the neighbor includes love of humanity as a whole, referred to in the Rabbinic literature as *ahavat ha-beriot* ("love of [all God's] creatures"). Innumerable passages can be quoted to illustrate this but it is enough to quote from the little ethical work of the famous sixteenth century mystic of Safed, R. Moses Cordovero, entitled *Tomer Devorah* ("The Palm Tree of Deborah"). Cordovero (Chapter 2, end) writes:

> *A man should train himself to do two things: first to honor all creatures, in whom he recognizes the exalted nature of the Creator Who in wisdom created man. And so it is with regard to all creatures. In them is the wisdom of the Creator. He should see for himself that they are therefore exceedingly to be honored for the Creator of all, the most exalted Wise One, has busied Himself with them and if, God forfend, man despises them he touches upon the honor of their Creator . . .*
> *The second is to bring the love of his fellow-men into his heart, even loving the wicked as if they were his brothers and more so until the love of his fellow-men becomes firmly fixed in his heart. He should love in his heart even the wicked, saying: "Would that these were righteous, returning in repentance, so that they were all great men, acceptable to the Omnipresent; as the faithful lover of Israel [Moses]*

> *said: "Would that all the people of the Lord were prophets"*
> *(Numbers 11:29). How can he love them? By recalling*
> *in his thoughts the good qualities they possess, by covering*
> *their defects and refusing to look at their faults and only*
> *at their good qualities. He should say to himself: "If this*
> *loathsome beggar were very rich how much would I then*
> *rejoice in his company, as I rejoice in the company of some*
> *other. But if he were to don the splendid garments of some*
> *other there would be no difference between him and his supe-*
> *rior; why then should his honor be less in my eyes? Behold,*
> *in God's eyes he is superior to me for he is plagued with*
> *suffering and poverty and cleansed from sin and why should*
> *I hate one whom the Holy One, blessed be He, loves?" In*
> *this way man's heart will turn towards the good and he will*
> *accustom himself to ponder on all the good qualities we*
> *have mentioned.*

As for love between husband and wife, Dr. J. H. Hertz's comment, following Samson Raphael Hirsch,[1] is worthy of note. The comment is on the verse, "And Isaac brought her into his mother Sarah's tent, and took Rebekah, and she became his wife; and he loved her" (Genesis 24:67). Hertz writes:

> *The order of the words,* He took Rebekah, she became his wife, and he loved her *calls for comment. In modern life we would place "he loved her" first, and write: "He loved Rebekah, he took her, and she became his wife". But, however important it is that love shall precede marriage, it is far more important that it shall continue* after *marriage. The modern attitude lays all stress on the romance before marriage; the older Jewish view emphasizes the life-long devotion and affection after marriage (S. R. Hirsch).*

As a comment on the verse it is extremely doubtful whether this is any more than a pleasant exercise in homiletics. After all, in the story of Jacob, it is said that he loved Rachel before he married her (Genesis 29:18) and references to people "falling in love" are not unknown in the Jewish tradition. The Talmud (*Kiddushin* 41a) states that although the

[1] *Pentateuch and Haftorahs,* 2nd edition, p. 87, London, 1960.

law gives a father the right to marry off his daughter while she is a minor he should not do this but should wait until she is old enough to choose for herself the man with whom she is in love. But Hertz is surely right that Judaism sees it as a high ideal for the love of husband and wife to be permanent throughout their marriage. In a Talmudic passage (*Yevamot* 62b) a man is advised to love his wife as himself and to respect her more than himself. The Jewish ideal, expressed in one of the benedictions recited at the wedding ceremony, is that husband and wife should love one another and rejoice together as did Adam and Eve in Paradise:

> *O make these loved companions greatly to rejoice, even as of old thou didst gladden Thy creature in the garden of Eden. Blessed art Thou, O Lord, who makest bridegroom and bride to rejoice.*

No more powerful testimony to the significance of marital love and faithfulness in Judaism is required than the fact that the prophets of Israel use the love of husband and wife as a great parable for the relationship between God and Israel. In the exquisite description of Hosea (21:22):

> *And I will betroth thee unto Me for ever; Yea, I will betroth thee unto Me in righteousness, and in justice, And in loving kindness, and in compassion. And I will betroth thee unto Me in faithfulness, And thou shalt know the Lord.*

Marxism

How far the thought of Karl Marx was influenced by Jewish teaching is very uncertain. Some commentators on Marx have purported to see the heritage of the Hebrew prophets in his passionate concern for social justice. Others have tried to trace his dialectic not only to Hegel but to the Talmudic reasoning of his forebears, Marx being descended from Rabbinical families on both the paternal and maternal side. One thing, however, is certain. Marx's thinking on religion is utterly opposed to Jewish theism. Marx's followers to this day have fought bitterly against every religious interpretation of human life—Jewish, Christian, Muslim, Hindu and Buddhist. Orthodox Marxism is virulently atheistic and anti-religious.

Marx was born at Trier in Germany in 1818. He was born a Jew but his father embraced Christianity when the boy was only six years old. As soon as he grew to manhood Marx declared himself to be an atheist. Marx's doctoral thesis in 1841 was on the philosophy of Epicurus, the ancient Greek thinker who denied the power of the Greek gods. It is not without interest that in the Rabbinic literature the word formed from this Greek thinker's name—*epikoros*—became the term used to denote the unbeliever. Marx died in London in 1883. He was buried in Highgate cemetery in that city. To this day his grave, with its huge memorial stone surmounted by a bust of Marx, has become a place of pilgrimage for Marxists the world over. The quasi-religious elements of Marxism have been remarked on more than once. In addition to the solemn pilgrimage to his grave, there are the Marxist "Scriptures" with their commentaries, the battles around their interpretation and meaning, and the "heresies" of which Marxists have accused one another. For all its attacks on religion and for all its atheism, Marxism itself is a religion as much as it is a philosophy and a social program. Marxism resembles other religions, too, in having dogmas, which it is forbidden to question, and in its eschatological hopes.

It is important to distinguish between the atheism of Marx himself, which is derived almost entirely from the philosopher Feuerbach, and the full attack on theistic beliefs in the Communist philosophy as developed by Marx, Engels and Lenin. It is this latter that is understood today as Marxism and it is here that the opposition to Judaism becomes an out and out attack. In the Marxist scheme there is no room for God. But Marxism goes further, treating belief in God as positively harmful. Marxism holds that men adhere to theistic religion not because it is true but because it acts as a tool for the preservation of the economic and social *status quo*. This is particularly so since in the theistic faiths man's final bliss is not in this world at all but is reserved for him in the Hereafter. The priests of theism, it is argued, help those in power to exploit the poor by directing their hearts to an other-worldly existence in which they will find compensation for their misery here on earth. By turning men's eyes heavenwards theism encourages indifference to the economic struggle in the here and now. Religion is

The grave of Karl Marx in Highgate Cemetery, London.

thus "opium for the people." The strong appeal of religion, which cannot be doubted, is the appeal of any drug, providing contentment through vain dreams and producing a stupor from which man cannot awake to better himself. By dreaming of a God who helps him man is effectively prevented from helping himself.

The Marxist critique hits hard because Jews, together with other theists, recognize that it is not entirely without foundation. It is within the experience of most of us that some people do use their religion to further their own grasping ends, to still their social conscience, to act as a palliative against guilt feelings if they are exploiters, or as a tranquillizer if they are exploited. But the mistake of the Marxist is to imagine that all religious people use their religion in this way and to overlook the fact that theists have been at least as condemnatory as Marxism of the abuses to which religion can be subjected. The sweeping denunciation that one's philosophy of life is inexorably determined by one's economic needs can be turned only too easily against Marxism itself. It is incredible that some Marxists speak as if the Communist philosophy is never used to further injustice, selfishness, and greed.

It would be incorrect to suggest that social and economic exploitation in the name of religion is entirely unknown in the history of Judaism. But it is true to say that the demands of social justice figure prominently in Jewish teaching and that other-worldly tendencies, pronounced though they are in Rabbinic Judaism, have rarely been allowed to dominate Jewish thought to the extent of obscuring the need to improve human society in the here and now. The virtual silence on the whole question of the Hereafter among the great Hebrew prophets, and the prophetic demands for justice, righteousness, and compassion are too well known to require much reiteration. And, for all its other-worldliness, Rabbinic Judaism does not normally think of this life only as a "vale of soul-making," a mere preparation for the world to come, but as good in its own right, a precious gift from God. The ancient Rabbis were pioneers in the field of social justice, stressing the equality of men and protecting the worker against exploitation. The modern State of Israel, influenced by the Biblical and Rabbinic tradition, is making a mighty attempt to bring these teachings to bear in promoting social justice in the lives of its citizens.

As for the Marxist claim that the doctrine of the Hereafter is opposed to the need for social concern and responsibility in this life, it is difficult to see how Judaism is affected. The whole conception of a Hereafter occupies a very insignificant role in Biblical thought. It is certain that when the Hebrew prophets spoke in God's name their chief interest was with justice and righteousness in the here and now. Rabbinic Judaism, which does have a very strong other-worldly emphasis, is, nevertheless, an heir to the Biblical message; it could hardly have been anything else. For the Rabbis and their followers there is no contradiction between the claims of social justice and the longing of the individual for personal survival and spiritual bliss in the Hereafter. On the contrary, it is only through "good deeds," which largely embrace social and benevolent acts, that man can, for the Rabbis, attain to the state described by them as "basking in the radiance of the Divine Presence." One of the Rabbis characteristically stated (*Shabbat* 31a) that the first question a man is asked on Judgment Day is: "Did you conduct your business affairs honestly?" Another Rabbi gave expression to the paradox in this way (*Avot* 4:17): "Better is one hour of repentance and good deeds in this world than the whole life of the world to come; and better is one hour of bliss in the world to come than the whole of this world."

With very few, if any, exceptions, even the most determined other-worldly exponents of Judaism never forsook the Biblical insight. The mystic R. Moses Ḥayyim Luzzatto (1707–1747) in his *Path of the Up-right* bases his entire system of moral and spiritual advancement on firm belief in the Hereafter as the ultimate goal of man. In the very first chapter he writes:

> It is fundamentally necessary both for saintliness and for the perfect worship of God to realize clearly what constitutes man's duty in this world, and what goal is worthy of his endeavors throughout all the days of his life. Our Sages have taught us that man was created only to find delight in the Lord, and to bask in the radiance of His Presence, but the real place for such happiness is the World to Come, which has been created for that very purpose. The present world is only a path to that goal.

Though "only a path," this world is, for Luzzatto, the place where man acquires his immortality by engaging in good deeds, prominent among which are acts of justice and equity. One does not find in Luzzatto a fully developed system of applied social justice. But it remains true that he devotes three chapters of his work (10–12) to the acquisition of what he calls the trait of "cleanness," and, as he is at pains to point out, this embraces in large measure the need for sound social conduct based on the Biblical and Rabbinic ideal of justice.

Another eloquent refutation, by implication, of the Marxist view is the famous saying of the Hasidic master R. Jacob Isaac of Pzhysha (d. 1814), known as "the holy Jew." According to Hasidic teaching, there is nothing on earth without its good aspect, there are "holy sparks" in everything. In that case, asks R. Jacob Issac, what is the good in atheism? His answer is that in man's social duties and obligations he should behave as if he were an atheist, assuming that God did not exist to help the poor and needy, so that if he did not help them they would remain destitute. Faith is a virtue when applied to one's own life. It is wrong to have it on behalf of others. There is yet something of value in atheism, for even the believer has to be a small doubter when called upon to alleviate human suffering.[1]

Finally, it has to be said that Judaism has defended the claims of justice and has advocated the freedom of the individual as a God-created personality in other spheres of life. Precisely because Judaism is a freedom-loving and just faith it continues to protest against every form of slavery, including the denial of basic human rights in totalitarian systems.

---

[1] This view is recorded in the Hebrew biography *Rabbi Jacob Isaac of Pzhysha* by I. M. Rabbinowitz, pp. 59–60, Piotrkow, 1932.

Monasticism

Judaism, with its strong emphasis on social life and its demand that the will of God be performed in the normal affairs of men and women of flesh and blood, has not produced anything like the monastic orders of other faiths. Like all generalizations, however, this requires some qualification. We know very little about the sect of the Essenes, but it may be that they lived a monastic or semi-monastic life, as did, possibly, the members of the Qumran sect whose writings were discovered at the Dead Sea. The history of religion knows many examples of men, in times of national catastrophe and urban decline, fleeing to the desert to live as monks or hermits. At an earlier period, the Book of Jeremiah (Chapter 35) tells of the Rechabites who drank no wine, built no houses and planted no vineyards but dwelt in tents. The Rechabites, on the other hand, were not celibates. There is an explicit reference in Jeremiah to their wives and sons. Similarly, the medieval German movement known as the *Ḥasidei Ashkenaz* ("the Saints of Germany"), which flourished from around the year 1150 to 1250, and which, as scholars have noted, had strong resemblances to the Christian monasticism of the time, did not advocate celibacy. Ascetics in other matters, as Jewish mystics they observed faithfully the old Jewish law to "be fruitful and multiply." Maimonides (*Yad, Deot* 3:1) expressly forbids the Jew to live a celibate life, eating no meat and drinking no wine and refusing to marry "like the priests of idolatry." Yet Maimonides (*Yad, Deot* 6:1) advises the man whose fellow-citizens try to compel him to lead a dissolute life to "go out to a place of caves and thorns and into the desert," though this is, in all probability, hyperbolic and was not intended to be taken too seriously.

The nearest one comes to a Jewish form of monasticism in the Rabbinic literature is in the Talmudic story about the early second century teacher Ben Azzai (*Yevamot* 63b). In the story Ben Azzai delivers an eloquent sermon on the high religious duty of marrying and having

219

Aerial view of the excavated community at Qumran on the northwest shore of the Dead Sea.

children. Ben Azzai's colleagues rebuke him for not practicing what he preaches, since he was himself a bachelor, to which he retorts: "What can I do? My soul is in love with the Torah. The world will have to be populated by others." It is curious that the codifiers took the story of Ben Azzai not as an individual and highly unconventional viewpoint but as sober advice for any student of the Torah who was sincerely motivated. Maimonides (*Yad, Ishut* 15:3) states it as a rule:

> *Anyone whose soul is in love with the Torah and who is completely absorbed therein like Ben Azzai, who cleaves all his days to the Torah and never marries—such a man commits no sin, provided that his evil inclination does not get the better of him. But if his evil inclination is strong he is obliged to marry, even if he already has children, because otherwise he might be afflicted with sexual thoughts.*

The *Shulḥan Arukh* (*Even ha-Ezer* 1:4) follows Maimonides in giving the same ruling. It is notorious that in some of the great Lithuanian *yeshivot* a number of the students remained unmarried while they continued their studies into their thirties and more. The commentators are, however, divided on the meaning of Maimonides and the *Shulḥan Arukh*.[1] Some understand the expression "commits no sin" to mean that while no technical offense is involved it is nonetheless preferable even for such a devoted student of the Torah to marry. Others take it to mean that it is an admirable thing for him to remain single in his love for the Torah.

---

[1] *Oẓar ha-Posekim,* Vol. I, p. 8, n. 27, Jerusalem, 1947.

Music

The history of Jewish music has been studied extensively. Whole books and many articles have been written on the subject and there is no need to review their contents here except insofar as they have relevance to the more general theme of the Jewish attitude toward music.

The Biblical record is full of the idea that it is natural for man to burst spontaneously into song when he is especially moved by the wonders of God's creation or when God delivers him from harm. The various songs found in the Bible are all literary products of a highly contrived nature but they are introduced as if those who sing them are responding quite artlessly to the mood that has been evoked. They sing because the melody wells up within them and the words are ready at hand without effort. Moses and the people sing their song of deliverance by the sea (Exodus 15:1–19), as does Miriam accompanied by the womenfolk with timbrels (Exodus 15:20–21). The people sing the song of the well (Numbers 21:17–20) and Moses sings another song toward the end of his life (Deuteronomy 32:1–45). Deborah sings when her people are saved (Judges 5). David the "sweet singer of Israel" (II Samuel 23:1) sings thanks to God when he celebrates his personal deliverance from his enemies (II Samuel 22).

The Psalms are all songs and in all probability many of them were composed especially for liturgical use. In any event, there is no doubt that they were used in the Temple service as they were later used in the liturgy of the synagogue. Although the curious headings of some of the Psalms are still puzzling, it has been conjectured that they are musical notations, "to be set to the tune of . . ." It has also been conjectured that the word *la-menaẓe'aḥ*, prefixed to 55 of the Psalms, originally meant "to the chief musician," i.e., perhaps belonging to a special collection of psalms put together by this functionary. Similarly the mysterious word *Selah* (from a root meaning "to lift up") has been understood as a musical direction, for example, "lift up the voice" at this stage or "sing in a higher key" at this stage and the like. It must be said that despite the wide currency given to these theories they remain only guesswork and are unsupported by any real evidence. Nor, for that matter, do we really know the precise nature of ancient Hebrew music. It is likely that it resembled "oriental" musical patterns but we cannot tell for certain.

When the ark was brought back to its home there was dancing and singing accompanied by musical instruments (II Samuel 6:5). In the Temple the Levites sang and played their instruments to the glory of God (II Chronicles 5: 12–13; 29: 25–30). After the destruction of the Temple, however, musical instruments were used less and less except at weddings. It was only in recent times that Reform Judaism introduced organ accompaniment in the synagogue services as a permanent feature. There is a vast literature on the debate that this occasioned with the Orthodox, who accused the Reformers of aping Christian modes of worship. The *shofar*, the oldest musical instrument known to man, is naturally used everywhere in synagogues on Rosh ha-Shanah. Among the reasons given by the Jewish teachers for blowing the *shofar* is that the piercing notes of this primitive instrument awaken feelings of awe appropriate to the solemn season of the year.

The reading of the various Biblical books in the synagogue is traditionally done by cantillation. There is a special melody for the Pentateuch, another for the prophetic books, still another for the Book of Esther, a dirgelike tune for the Book of Lamentations and a different tune again for the Song of Songs, Ruth, and Ecclesiastes. Traditionally each part of the service has its own particular melody. The substitution, in some modern synagogues, of recitation for these traditional melodies, has been criticized as depriving the service of its warmth and color. Zangwill in his *Children of the Ghetto*[1] has effectively captured the atmosphere created by the melodies in his account of "the sons of the covenant," the members of a small conventicle in London's East End at the beginning of the century:

> *Their religious consciousness was largely a musical box:*
> *the thrill of the ram's horn, the cadenza of a psalmic phrase,*
> *the jubilance of a festival "Amen" and the sobriety of a*
> *workaday "Amen," the Passover melodies and the Penta-*

[1] London, 1909, pp. 155–6.

cost, the minor keys of Atonement and the hilarious rhap-
sodies of Rejoicing, the plain chant of the Law and the more
ornate intonation of the Prophets—all this was known and
loved, and was far more important than the meaning of it all,
or its relation to their real lives; for page upon page was
gabbled off at rates that could not be excelled by automata.
But if they did not always know what they were saying, they
always meant it. If the service had been more intelligible,
it would have been less emotional and edifying. There was
not a sentiment, however incomprehensible, for which they
were not ready to die or to damn.

The Ḥasidic movement, in particular, devoted a good deal of thought to the role of music in the religious life of the Jew. As mystics the Ḥasidim believed that the human heart has longings for God too deep to be expressed in words and for which melody is the only vehicle. A not untypical Ḥasidic description in mystical terms is that of R. Dov Baer of Lubavitch (1773–1827) in his manual of spiritual advice entitled *Kunteros ha-Hitpa'alut*.[1] Here the author develops the idea that the soul of Moses (the "Faithful Shepherd") embraced all the souls of his people, and since no two souls are exactly alike each person has his own particular melody by which he is drawn to the divine. R. Dov Baer writes:

What is the nature of melody? There is a well-known saying
that the Faithful Shepherd used to sing every kind of melody
in his prayer. For he included the six hundred thousand
souls of Israel and each soul can only ascend to the root
of the source whence she was hewn by means of song.

Some Ḥasidic thinkers have divided all melodies into three categories, corresponding to the three divine qualities of love, judgment, and harmony, i.e., sweet music represents God's love, powerful music God's sternness, and music in which there is a blend of both the harmonizing principle.

Music, for a very long period in Jewish history, was closely associated, like all other aspects of life, with religion. A good deal of the music enjoyed today is secular, whether classical, jazz, or "pop." The problems

---

[1] *Tract on Ecstasy*, Warsaw, 1868; English translation, pp. 76–77, London, 1963.

of Jewish attitudes toward secular culture are extremely complicated, chiefly because they are new. A Jewish appreciation of good music need not involve listening only to records of *Ḥazzanim* or attending concerts of Jewish folk-music and the like. Music-lovers have found elevation and inspiration in all forms of music. Religious Jews see the hand of God at work in whatever assists man to rise above his more restricted needs to a realm which not only mirrors this life and its anxieties but infuses it with a new spirit for the soul's enrichment.

Newspapers

One can only speak in this context of certain Jewish principles as they apply to the newspaper world. One of these is that Judaism does encourage its adherents to be aware of the world around them. Both the Biblical writers and the Rabbis of the Talmud were, judging by their works, thoroughly familiar with the political, social, and economic trends in their times, of the nations struggling for power and influence, of the cultural institutions of Egypt, Babylonia, Assyria, Persia, Greece, and Rome. According to the Mishnah (*Berakhot* 9:2) a special benediction has to be recited when one hears good news and thanks must be given to God for His concealed mercies even when one is the recipient of bad news. An alertness to the events around one seems to follow from a belief in God's providence as extending over all. The Rabbinic statement that the wise man is one who learns from all men (*Avot* 4:1) similarly implies that there is value in having an acquaintance with events and ideas as they present themselves. Nor is the entertainment and amusement value of newspaper reading to be dismissed. The *Shulḥan Arukh* (*Oraḥ Ḥayyim* 307:1) rules that while it is forbidden to talk of secular things on the Sabbath, people can tell one another the latest news if they enjoy it since then it belongs to the "Sabbath delight" (*oneg shabbat*) and hence is part of a religious obligation.

Journalistic ethics are determined by general ethical principles and standards and on these Judaism has much to say. Slander and malicious gossip are offenses whether they are committed in writing or by word of mouth. Obviously, the wide circulation of false information that modern newspapers are capable of makes the offense all the worse. Judaism has respect for the individual and his right to privacy and would strongly disapprove of journalistic invasions of privacy. Accuracy in the presentation of the facts would be demanded by Judaism as part of its demand for honesty, truth, and integrity. A Rabbinic saying has it that the seal of the Holy One, blessed is He, is truth. On the other hand editorial

comment has a right to be free and should be hard-hitting in the castiga-
tion of social evils. R. Israel Meir Kagan, known as the *Ḥafeẓ Ḥayyim*
(1835–1938), fought all his long life against *lashon ha-ra*, "the evil tongue,"
i.e., malicious talk against others, and wrote many works on the subject.
Yet he advocates strongly that a man should speak his mind where
failure so to do will result in harm being done to others. In this connection
he was fond of quoting the juxtaposition in the Biblical verse: "Thou
shalt not go up and down as a talebearer among thy people; neither
shalt thou stand idly by the blood of thy neighbor: I am the Lord"
(Leviticus 19:16). Talebearing is wrong but to stand idly by when there
is risk to another's life and limb is worse and to avoid the latter one
should speak out.

Nuclear Warfare

There has been no systematic treatment in the Jewish sources on the "just war," and this for a very good reason. For 2,000 years Jews had no State of their own, so that the whole question was academic. In the State of Israel much consideration has naturally been given to the problem. There are basic principles in Judaism which offer some guidance, although the problem is aggravated precisely because of the purely academic nature of discussions about warfare in the classical sources.

There is something obscene about any consideration of tolerating the horrible business of war in any circumstances. That every war is at best a necessary evil emerges clearly from the whole tendency of Jewish teaching. The Messianic dream of Isaiah (2:2–4) has become the ultimate ideal of all men; some of the words of the vision are engraved in the great hall of the United Nations building in New York:

And it shall come to pass in the end
of days,
That the mountain of the Lord's
house shall be established as the
top of the mountains.
And shall be exalted above the hills;
And all nations shall flow unto it.
And many peoples shall go up and say:
"Come ye, and let us go up to the
mountain of the Lord,
To the house of the God of Jacob;
And He will teach us of His ways,
And we will walk in His paths."
For out of Zion shall go forth the law,
And the word of the Lord from Jerusalem.
And he shall judge between the nations,

And shall decide for many peoples;
And they shall beat their swords
into plowshares,
And their spears into pruning-hooks;
Nation shall not lift up swords against
nation,
Neither shall they learn war any more.

This latter verse was quoted in the course of a debate recorded in the Mishnah (*Shabbat* 6:4). R. Eliezer ruled that since it is only forbidden to carry a "burden" in the public domain on the Sabbath and it is permitted to carry an "adornment," it is permitted to wear a sword, or other weapons, on the Sabbath. These, he argued, are an "adornment." Whereupon the Sages quoted the verse from Isaiah, declaring that weapons of war can never be looked upon by Jews as "adornments." King David was not granted the privilege of building the Temple because he had engaged in warfare (I Chronicles 22:8):

> *But the word of the Lord came to me, saying: "Thou hast shed blood abundantly, and hast made great wars; thou shalt not build a house unto My name, because thou hast shed much blood upon the earth in My sight."*

The Midrash (*Mekhilta* to Exodus 20:22) explains the law against using iron for the construction of the altar (Exodus 20:22) on the grounds that the altar stones were created to atone for man and prolong his life whereas iron, from which weapons of war are made, shortens man's life and it is not right to bring the two into contact with one another. The Midrash continues: "Now there is here an argument from the minor to the major. If the stones of the altar, which neither see nor hear nor speak, yet because they promote peace between Israel and their Father in Heaven, said that no iron must be lifted up on them, then how much more will he who promotes peace between city and city, nation and nation, government and government be saved from trouble!"

Yet Judaism does not adopt the complete pacifist attitude. Everything possible should be done to avoid war but if a nation is attacked a war of defense is not only permitted but obligatory. This is based on the stark principle laid down as axiomatic in the Talmud (*Sanhedrin* 72a): "If a person intends to kill you, be first to kill him." For this reason no Jewish teacher felt it to be anything but right for the free nations to declare war on Nazi Germany and for the State of Israel, desperately desiring peace but anxious for the lives of its citizens, to repel the attacks of the Arab states.

It must follow that if the sole justification of war is to defend life, if the result of the war will be the eventual destruction of the defenders themselves as well as the attackers, such a war would be forbidden. In the case of the individual, for example, the rule: "If a person intends to kill you, be first to kill him" can only apply if, as a result, the life of the intended victim will be spared. It is nowhere suggested that Samson's resolve in his tormented mind: "Let me die with the Philistines" (Judges 16:30) is a matter for emulation. Now if nations ever engaged in large-scale nuclear warfare it would be the end of civilization as we know it: millions of innocent human beings will be destroyed and the whole future of the human race placed in peril. In these circumstances there can be no justification for initiating nuclear warfare.

Nudism

The nudist movement believes that the wearing of clothes is unnatural and that it is healthier for men and women to move about unrestricted by garments, allowing the beneficial rays of the sun to get to the body. Nudists, or Naturalists, as they are sometimes called, arrange for camps in which they can give expression to their philosophy. It is only fair to say that Nudists are particular to exclude from their meetings people whose interest is prurient and they claim—though whether the claim is substantiated is another matter—that sexual excitement is virtually nil once the members have become accustomed to their new way of life.

Judaism sees the covering of the body as an important part of human dignity. The Jewish ideal is that of *tzeniut* ("modesty") in dress. It is true that such matters are affected by social attitudes—for a woman to wear short skirts, for example, in public during the nineteenth century would have been immodest simply because respectable women did not dress in this way at that time. Nowadays, the fact that fashion dictates the wearing of shorter skirts means that to follow fashion is not necessarily to offend against the ideal of *tzeniut*, though it must be said that Orthodox Jewish teachers still frown on short skirts and short sleeves as immodest dress for women. No responsible Jewish teacher has, however, advocated Nudism, and Jewish teachers of every group—Orthodox, Reform, or Conservative—see Nudism as a breach of the *tzeniut* ideal. In the Adam and Eve story it is only in the pristine innocence of Paradise that Adam and Eve are naked without feeling shame (Genesis 2:25). After they have sinned "the eyes of both of them were opened, and they knew that they were naked" (Genesis 3:7). The Rabbis forbid the recitation of the *Shema* or any other sacred text if a man's "heart sees his genitals," i.e., if he is naked from the waist down (*Berakhot* 25b).

The Rabbis urged their followers to be adequately dressed. The third

231

century Palestinian teacher R. Johanan used to call his clothes "my honorers" (*Bava Kama* 91b). David cut off the skirt of Saul's robe (I Samuel 24:5) and when David was old they covered him with garments but were unable to bring warmth to his aged body (I Kings 1:1), upon which the Rabbis remark that whoever despises clothes will be punished in that his clothes will not provide him with warmth (*Berakhot* 62b). If a man claims that he is poor and thus entitled to poor relief, the charity distributors are required to investigate whether he really is poor, but only if he demands food. If he demands clothes he should be provided with these without any prior investigation because otherwise he will be exposed to contempt (*Bava Batra* 9a). Commenting on the verse: "I will provoke them with a vile nation" (Deuteronomy 32:21), the Rabbis (*Yevamot* 63b) refer it to peoples who go about naked in the street "for nothing is more objectionable to God than the one who goes naked in the street." A Midrashic passage (*Megillah* 12b) understands the king's order to Vashti to appear before the princes wearing the royal crown (Esther 1:11) to mean with nothing else on, i.e., she was to appear naked, which is why she refused. Vashti was punished because it was her practice to strip Jewish girls naked and make them work for her. Nakedness is especially embarrassing to women. When clothes are distributed by the charity distributors women therefore take precedence over men (Mishnah, *Horayot* 3:7). Even when a woman criminal is being executed her sensitivity must be spared and she must be adequately covered (Mishnah, *Sanhedrin* 6:3).

It can be seen from the above passages that Nudism would not be frowned upon by Judaism on the grounds that the latter holds the body in contempt and therefore teaches that it should be concealed. On the contrary, the reason Judaism would be opposed to Nudism is because of its insistence on man's dignity. His body should be clothed as befits a human being and the wearing of clothes is one of the ways in which humans differ from animals.

Optimism

Optimism and pessimism are moods rather than permanent states. They vary not only from person to person but the same person is sometimes an optimist and at other times a pessimist. For this reason there is not much point in discussing whether Judaism is optimistic or pessimistic. The Messianic idea, which has frequently been produced as evidence of the optimistic nature of Judaism—one day the world will be perfected—is not really germane to the issue. That God "at the end of days" will usher in a new era of perfection has little relevance to the question of what attitude the individual takes to the problems of his life in the here and now. Nor does the Jewish doctrine of trust in God necessarily mean that a man should believe in the inevitability of the success of his efforts. In any sophisticated view, trust in God means that all is ordered by a divine providence the workings of which we cannot always discern. God's plan for the individual may be that he should suffer. Only in the sense that ultimately it will be well with him can the doctrine be said to be a cause for optimism. The well-being may be, as many of the Jewish teachers remark, in the Hereafter. The man who trusts in God that his striving for the good will not permanently be overlooked by God need not be optimistic about his immediate future. His faith provides him with the means to cope with the misfortunes which may come upon him. It does not provide him with a guarantee that his life will be free from misfortune. And, despite the arguments to the contrary on the part of some Jewish apologists, Judaism is not necessarily confident that man will always win out in his struggle with the evil within him. The Biblical statement that "the imagination of man's heart is evil from his youth" (Genesis 8:21) has frequently been accepted as man's normal estate in subsequent Jewish teaching. In a remarkable Talmudic passage (*Eruvin* 13b) it is said that the rival schools of Hillel and Shammai debated for two and a half years whether it would have been better for man if he had not been created. They came to the

233

conclusion that it would have been better, but now that he has been created he should examine his deeds.

The most optimistic of all Jewish movements is undoubtedly Ḥasidism, but it is important to appreciate that what Ḥasidic optimism entails is the Ḥasidic view that the world is infused with the divine. Ultimate reality is not the world of the senses but the spiritual realm by means of which it is sustained. It is in that other world that the Ḥasid seeks to live. He is indifferent to the troubles and sorrows which befall him because, for him, these are as unreal as the physical universe which is their background. Dubnow in his history of Ḥasidic views is in fact extremely critical of the Ḥasidic view as sheer "escapism." Even if we dissent from Dubnow and appreciate that Ḥasidism provided the vital impetus to go on living which the East European Jew desperately needed in an extremely hostile environment, it remains true that there is a paradox in Ḥasidic teaching. The Ḥasid is optimistic because basic-ally he entertains a world-negating philosophy.

There have been somber Jewish teachers as there have been Jewish teachers filled with the joy of living. There have been those who have dwelt on life's sorrows and others who have emphasized its delights. Both types have stressed that what matters from the religious point of view is the acknowledgment that man's status in life, whether his lot is fortunate or unfortunate, affords him the means of serving his God. If optimism means that one lives in a world in which God is the Father in Heaven in whom His children place their trust and pessimism means the bleak philosophy that man is the prey of blind forces and life has neither meaning nor purpose, then Judaism is optimistic. But if optimism means the hope that man's immediate needs will auto-matically be satisfied and pessimism that this is far from certain, then the problem is incapable of any neat solution. Dickens' Micawber fails to give expression to what the devout Jew has always understood by trust in God.

Patriotism

Love of one's country is a natural human tendency and a worthy one. For the Jew the country that is the object of love and loyalty is the Land of Israel, the ancestral home, but if he is born outside Israel the land that he loves is also the particular country of his birth or adoption.

The love for the Land of Israel is deeply rooted in the Jewish psyche. It is the land of the patriarchs and prophets, rich in associations with the most sacred ideas of Judaism. Longing for the return to the land of Israel pervades the traditional prayer-book. Now that the State of Israel is a reality there are few Jews who are not proud of its achievements and who do not feel a strong sense of involvement in its destiny. It is all largely emotional, but emotions are nothing to be ashamed of if, as this one is, they are reasonable and worthy.

As for the Jew born outside the Land of Israel, he has powerful natural ties to the land of his birth. Even when Jews had been carried away into captivity, the prophet Jeremiah urged them to seek the welfare of Babylon, where they had found a home (29:7):

> And seek the peace of the city whither I have caused you to be carried away captive, and pray unto the Lord for it; for in the peace thereof ye shall have peace.

There need be no conflict between the two kinds of patriotism. If historical circumstances occasion it, a man can love more than one country. People of Irish descent, for example, born in the United States, love the country of their birth and the Irish home of their ancestors. The dual love is especially possible for the Jew, in that the love of the Land of Israel has religious implications. It is perfectly natural for a Jew born in England, for example, to be fond of British institutions, the English countryside and way of life, while responding to the lure of the holy land as the center of his religious faith.

235

Nor need patriotism be an obstacle to the peace and well-being of mankind as a whole any more than love for one's own family necessarily involves a lack of concern for other families. A Talmudic saying (*Sotah* 47a) has it that there are three types of special charm: the charm of a city for those who live in it, the charm of a wife for her husband, and the charm of a purchase for the one who has bought it. A man's love for humanity is not impaired because he loves his wife. The two loves are quite different. Love of the more intense kind is always particularistic because it is based on acquaintance. The one is concrete, immediate, intense, the other more abstract, remote, and detached, though psychologically it is doubtful whether a man who has never known any particular love can be capable of any love at all, even of the more comprehensive kind.

That is why Judaism approves of patriotism while continuing to affirm its universalistic message. Of course, there are different shades of patriotism. Chauvinism or the attitude of "my country right or wrong" is incompatible with the Jewish ideals of justice and the brotherhood of all men.

Rabbi A. I. Kook (1865–1935), the first Chief Rabbi of Palestine, was an ardent patriot of the holy land, yet he finds no obstacle to writing[1]:

> *The love of all creatures comes before anything else, followed by the love of mankind which, in turn, is followed by the love of Israel. This latter really embraces the others since the people of Israel are destined to bring all creatures to perfection. All these types of love are of a practical nature, that is to say, the meaning is to love those mentioned, to help them and to bring about their elevation. Higher than all these is the love of God which is love in action, not for anything else but the very fact that the heart is full. It constitutes man's highest form of happiness.*

Rabbi Kook was writing in a mystical vein, but the truth he expresses must be obvious. To find a contradiction between particular and general love is to miss the nature of both.

---

[1] *Musar Avikha*, p. 92, Jerusalem, 1971.

Pedagogics

There is no mention of any school system in the Bible. It would appear that in Biblical times fathers taught their children at home—"and thou shalt teach them diligently unto thy children" (Deuteronomy 4:7). The statements in the Talmudic literature regarding the early date at which educational institutes were developed are in the main legendary, but there is clear evidence that there were organized schools for children in Palestine and Babylon in the third century C.E. and this pattern has persisted in all Jewish communities ever since then.[1]

The main subject taught to the children was, of course, the Torah, but a father was obliged, in addition, to teach his son a trade and, according to some, to teach him to swim (*Kiddushin* 29a). Studies were to be graded, the child beginning with easier topics and only being introduced to more difficult ones as his mental capacities became more mature. The Mishnah (*Avot* 5:21) gives the order as the age of five for the study of the Bible, ten for the study of the Mishnah and 15 for the study of Talmud (in this context the meaning is the study of the more elaborate discussions around the laws of the Torah). It is notorious that in Eastern Europe this reasonable approach was entirely neglected, to the scandal of many an educationalist. The Bible, apart from the Pentateuch, was neglected and the child was introduced to the most complicated Talmudic debates at an extremely early age. Many a child must have acquired a lasting distaste for study as a result of this system or lack of it.

R. Samuel b. Shilat was a famous skilled teacher in third century Babylon. The verse: "And they that turn many to righteousness are like the stars" (Daniel 12:3) was applied to schoolteachers, among whom R. Samuel b. Shilat was held up as the supreme example (*Bava Batra*

[1] A helpful book on the subject in English is *The Jewish School* by Nathan Morris, London, 1937.

8b). Rav is said to have advised R. Samuel b. Shilat not to accept any pupils before the age of six because their minds are too immature. But from the age of six they "should be stuffed with Torah like an ox" (*Bava Batra* 21a). A number of observations on teaching methods are reported in the name of the fourth century Babylonian leader Rava (*Bava Batra* 21a–b). A teacher, said Rava, should ideally not have more than 25 children in his class, but the number may be increased if there is no option. If, however, there are 40 children in the class an assistant must be appointed and if there are 50 children another teacher must be appointed. Rava further argued that if another teacher can be found who is more competent than the first, the first teacher should not be replaced because the second teacher may then become too confident and neglect his duties. But R. Dimi disagreed, arguing that on the contrary the second teacher will exert himself all the more. Although unfair competition was frowned upon by the Rabbis, schoolteachers were encouraged to compete with one another because "the jealousy of scribes increases wisdom." Another debate between Rava and R. Dimi concerns the matter of appointment of teachers. Is it better to appoint a slow teacher who never makes mistakes or a quick teacher

Young pupils introduced to the study of Torah on the festival of Shavuot, from the *Leipzig Maḥzor*, c. 1320. Left to right: a teacher giving honey to the children to show them the sweetness of the Torah; a father carrying his son, wrapped in a Torah binder, to the synagogue; children being taught that man without Torah is like fish without water.

who does? Rava argued that the quick teacher should be appointed since the mistakes will right themselves but R. Dimi held that the slow teacher is to be preferred. Once the children have accepted the mistakes as fact it will be extremely difficult for the errors to be eradicated. Rava rules, too, that an inefficient schoolteacher should be dismissed immediately, concern for the childrens' education taking precedence over compassion for the teacher.

The widely held nineteenth century view, exploded by Freud, that children were innocent little cherubs, was not shared by the Rabbis. On the contrary the child is born with his "evil inclination" and does not become possessed of the "good inclination" until he reaches the age of 13, when he is Bar Mitzvah (*Ecclesiastes Rabbah* to verse 4:13). But the child was not to be blamed for his nature. It was said that the world only endures for the sake of the breath of the schoolchildren, for the breath of grown-up scholars is "with sin" while that of children is "without sin" (*Shabbat* 119b). In the same passage it is said, no doubt with a degree of hyperbole, that schoolchildren must never be made to neglect their studies, not even for the building of the Temple.

The legend of the second century Palestinian teacher R. Ḥiyya (*Bava Meẓia* 85b) expresses, no doubt in exaggerated form, the extreme care to be taken in educating children. R. Ḥiyya is said to have seen to it that the Torah would not be forgotten in Israel. He would sew flax and fashion nets from the flax cords. With the nets he would trap deer, giving their meat to orphans and preparing scrolls from the deerskins upon which he would write the five books of Moses. He would then go to a town to teach the five books to five children and the six orders of the Mishnah (which were studied by heart) to six children, saying to them: "Until I return, teach each other the five books of Moses and the Mishnah."

The art of teaching was not, of course, confined to the education of little children. The Jew was expected to study the Torah all the days of his life. Especially in the great yeshivot, from Talmudic times, the Torah was taught to adolescents and grown-ups with unparalleled intensity. We have, in fact, a list of the 48 things by means of which the Torah is acquired, i.e. the methods the serious student must adopt in order to master his studies. The list (*Avot* 6:5) reads:

> *The Torah is acquired by the following 48 things: study,*
> *listening, rehearsing verbally, understanding, discerning, awe,*

reverence, humility, cheerfulness, attending the sages, consorting with other students, debating keenly with disciples; serene reflection, knowledge of the Scriptures and the Mishnah, sleeping little, engaging little in small talk, enjoying little pleasure, little jesting and engaging in business only in moderation; patience, a good heart, confidence in the Sages, acceptance of suffering, recognizing one's place and rejoicing in one's portion; making a fence round one's words and claiming no credit for oneself; being a popular person, loving God, loving God's creatures, loving acts of benevolence, loving rebukes, loving upright persons, keeping remote from fame, not feeling proud of one's learning and not taking delight in giving legal decisions; participating in the burdens of one's fellow, judging him generously, enabling him to see the truth and leading him to peace; considering well the topics studied, asking questions and answering them, listening to the topic studied and then adding to it; studying in order to teach and studying in order to practice; making one's master wiser and reporting teachings accurately and reporting a teaching in the name of its originator.

Maimonides (*Yad, Talmud Torah* 4) gives an excellent summary of Rabbinic ideas on teaching methods with additions of his own. The following contains some of Maimonides' rules for teaching the Torah:

One must only teach the Torah to a worthy student with good deeds to his credit or to one innocent of wrong-doing. But if a student walks in the wrong way he should first be restored to the good way and led into the paths of uprightness. His character should then be investigated and afterward he should be allowed to enter the House of Study to be taught there . . .

How is the teaching carried out. The teacher sits at the head with his disciples around him in a circle so that they can all see him and hear him. The teacher should not sit on a chair if his disciples sit on the ground. Either they should all sit on the ground or all on chairs . . .

If the students are unable to grasp the master's teaching he should not lose his temper and be angry with them but he should repeat the matter again and again until they grasp its profundity. Similarly, a student should not say "I understand" if he does not but he should ask his master to explain the matter again and again. If the master loses his temper with him he should say: "My master, it is the Torah and I wish to know it but my mental capacity is insufficient." A student should not feel embarrassed in that his fellow-students master the subject at the first or second attempt while he only manages to grasp it after many attempts. For if he is embarrassed in this way he will enter and leave the House of Study without ever learning anything at all . . . This applies only, however, to students who fail to grasp the subject because it is so difficult or because their mental capacity is inadequate. But if the master senses that the students fail to grasp the subject because they are indolent and easy-going, he is obliged to be angry with them and insult them in order to spur them on . . . Consequently, it is not proper for a master to behave frivolously in the presence of his students. He should neither jest in their presence nor eat and drink with them, in order that they might fear him and so learn quickly when he teaches them.

Questions should not be put to the master as soon as he enters the House of Study but he should be given time to settle down. The student, too, should have time to settle down before he puts his question. No two students should ask their questions at the same time. Questions should only be put on the topic being studied at the time and not on other topics because this may embarrass the master. A master should put trick questions to his students or cunningly carry out incorrect procedures in order to sharpen the wits of the students and notice whether they remember what they have been taught. It goes without saying that the master is allowed to ask them questions on topics other than the one they are studying in order to keep them on their toes.

In the great Lithuanian yeshivot and in their successors in Israel and the United States the emphasis in teaching was on the mastery of the subject in depth rather than on a wide acquaintance with the whole field of Jewish learning. There is much to the critique, frequently voiced by other scholars, that this method produced an imbalance and a one-sidedness. Yet for all its faults, and there are many, the method did encourage penetration. It succeeded in teaching the students not to be content with a superficial appraisal, to be honest with themselves, and not to indulge in groundless comparisons between subjects having no connection with one another. The celebrated head of the yeshivah at Slobodka, R. Moses Mordecai Epstein (1866–1933), advocates this method in the Introduction to his work on tractate *Bava Kama*.[1] Rabbi Epstein writes:

> *There is study and study. We find the Rabbis saying in tractate* Kiddushin *that any student who can give an adequate answer to a question put to him in a single tractate, even if it be only the small tractate* Kallah, *is called a scholar. On the other hand, the Rabbis tell us in tractate* Berakhot *that Rami bar Ḥama refused to recite Grace after meals with a person who had studied the* Sifra, *the* Sifrei *and other works. Rami bar Ḥama considered this person to be an ignoramus because he had not attended the Sages. Note the great difference! This person has studied only one tractate yet he is called a scholar while this one has studied the whole Talmud and is called an ignoramus. This is because the knowledge of the Torah does not consist mainly in an acquiantance with the bare material but with understanding the meaning and reasoning of the topics one studies. As the Rabbis say: The reward of studying is for the reasoning behind it. If a student knows a certain Halakhic rule but does not know the reasoning behind it, we cannot say that only something is lacking but that everything is lacking since the main thing is to understand what one studies. Consequently, even if one has studied the whole of the Talmud but has had no training in understanding the reasoning behind it all, he is called an ignoramus. But one who has studied no more than a single tractate yet has immersed himself in the reasoning behind it is called a scholar.*

[1] *Levush Mordekhai*, Warsaw, 1901.

Polygamy

There are in the main two reasons why polygamy was sanctioned in many ancient societies. The first is biological—a male can impregnate more than one female while a female can only be impregnated by one male. The second is social—in ancient societies the lot of a woman unprotected by a husband was far more hazardous than that of a man who was single. In any event it is true that Biblical law as well as the later Rabbinic law accepts polygamy as legitimate, though provisions are, of course, made in order to protect the interests of each of the wives. Since later Jewish law is based on the Biblical and Rabbinic systems, polygamy was only outlawed in the Ashkenazi world by a ban attributed to R. Gershom of Mainz (d. 1028) though recent research has shown that the ban was, in fact, instituted a century or two later. This is known as the *herem de-rabbenu Gershom* (*herem* = "ban"). In certain circumstances, where, for instance, the wife is incurably insane, a dispensation of the ban is sometimes granted provided the signatures of 100 Rabbis, residing in three different lands, can be obtained. Among the Sephardi communities the ban never took effect and a few Sephardi communities still practice polygamy, though it is now against the law for Sephardim as well as Ashkenazim in the State of Israel.

So much for the legal position. Morally and ideally, however, there is no doubt that Judaism upholds monogamy. It is extremely revealing that in the Adam and Eve story one man is created with one woman as his wife. When the Hebrew prophets use the illustration of a man and his wife for God's love for Israel and Israel's for God it is clear that they think of monogamy as the ideal. Hardly any of the 2,000 or so teachers mentioned in the Talmud had more than one wife and it is revealing that in discussions regarding marriage the Talmud generally refers to husband and wife, not wives. In the ideal picture of family-life presented in the last chapter of the Book of Proverbs, the "woman of worth" is the only wife in the home.

243

Pornography

Pornography is manifested in different ways in contemporary society—in books and magazines, on the stage and in the cinema. Various countries have different laws about obscene literature, blue films, and the like but the definition of pornography and obscenity is fraught with difficulties. The classic nineteenth century definition as a tendency "to deprave and corrupt" is notoriously difficult to pin down. Psychologists appear to be divided on whether reading dirty books and so forth really has a harmful effect on the character. Some have even argued that there are people whose indulgence in sexual fantasies, for example, give them release and prevent them from acting the fantasies out and harming others. Then there are the dangers of censorship, which, once given its head, is difficult to stop. For these reasons the question of legal steps against pornography is still under discussion in civilized countries, with a recent tendency to discourage too much interference by the law. In the Jewish sources pornography and obscenity are discussed mainly in the moralistic literature. There is no doubt that the Jewish teachers frown on loose or foul talk and on sexual thoughts divorced from the marital act.

On the verse: "Thou shalt keep thee from every evil thing" (Deuteronomy 23:10), the Rabbis (*Avodah Zarah* 20b) comment that this implies that one should not gaze intently at a beautiful woman, even if she is unmarried, or at a married woman, even if she is ugly, nor at a woman's gaudy garments, nor at animals when they are mating. In another Talmudic passage (*Ketubbot* 8b) there is a comment on the verse: "And every mouth speaking wantonness" (Isaiah 9:16), which runs: "Everyone knows why the bride enters the bridal chamber, but whoever disgraces his mouth and utters a word of folly—even if a decree of 70 years of happiness were sealed for him, it is turned for him into evil." At the beginning of *Pesaḥim* (3a–b) great emphasis is placed on the need to use refined speech and avoid coarse expressions.

244

It is suggested, for instance, that Scripture, where possible, avoids the term "riding" (with the legs separated) when speaking of a woman and prefers to use the term "sitting." Two disciples who studied with Rav were worn out by their exertions. One of them remarked that the discussion had made them as tired as an exhausted swine, while the other said it had made them as tired as an exhausted kid. Rav refused to speak to the first student who had used such an inelegant comparison.

According to Maimonides[1] Hebrew is called "the holy tongue" because it avoids direct references to intimate physical details and prefers to use euphemisms. Maimonides writes:

> *You know the severe prohibition that obtains among us against obscene language. This also is necessary. For speaking with the tongue is one of the properties of a human being and a benefit that is granted to him and by which he is distinguished. As it says: "Who hath made man's mouth?" (Exodus 4:11). And the prophet says: "The Lord God hath given me the tongue of them that are taught" (Isaiah 50:4). Now this benefit granted us with a view to perfection in order that we learn and teach should not be used with a view to the greatest deficiency and utter disgrace, so that one says what the ignorant and sinful Gentiles say in their songs and their stories, suitable for them but not for those to whom it has been said: "And ye shall be unto Me a kingdom of priests, and a holy nation" (Exodus 19:6). And whoever has applied his thought or his speech to some of the stories concerning that sense which is a disgrace to us, so that he thought more about drink or copulation than is needful or recited songs about these matters, has made use of the benefit granted to him, applying and utilizing it to commit an act of dis-obedience with regard to Him who has granted the benefit and to transgress His orders. He is like those of whom it is said: "And I multiplied unto her silver and gold, which they used for Baal" (Hosea 2:10), I can also give the reason why this our language is called the Holy Language. It should not be thought that this is, on our part, an empty appellation*

---

[1] *Guide*, III 8, trans. S. Pines, pp. 435–6.

> *or a mistake; in fact, it is indicative of true reality. For in this holy language no word at all has been laid down in order to designate either the male or the female organ of copulation, nor are there words designating the act itself that brings about generation, the sperm, the urine, or the excrements, no word at all designating, according to its first meaning, any of these things has been laid down in the Hebrew language, they being signified by terms used in a figurative sense and by allusions.*

Maimonides, it is known, had a more or less negative attitude to sex. His view in the above passage and elsewhere that sex is a "disgrace" is certainly unconventional in Jewish terms and has been criticized severely by other noted Jewish thinkers. Yet Maimonides speaks only about thinking of sex "more than is needful," implying that in the marriage bed a degree of frivolity is quite in order. This is implied, too, in a remarkable passage in the Talmud (*Hagigah* 5b) in which first a saying of Rav is quoted to the effect that even frivolous talk between a man and his wife is declared to him on Judgment Day. But, the passage goes on to say, a disciple of Rav, in his eagerness to study the behavior of his teacher, hid himself under Rav's bed and noted that he conversed and jested with his wife so that "his mouth was as if he had not tasted any food." There is no contradiction, the Talmud concludes. It is permitted if necessary to awaken the wife's desire. It should also be said that the Talmudic Rabbis were never guilty of the kind of prudery that rejects any talk of sex. There are many references to sexual matters in the Talmudic literature and these are discussed in the frankest way. However, these are not prurient with the exception of one strange passage in *Bava Meẓia* (84a). The nineteenth century thinker Naḥman Krochmal[1] suggests that the passage is a later interpretation from obscene tales current at the time but this has not been proven.

The Maskilim in the early nineteenth century accused Ḥasidic writers of introducing obscene references into their writings. Joseph Perl (1774–1839), in his satire on Ḥasidism, *Megalleh Temirin*,[2] gives a list of these alleged obscenities in early Ḥasidic literature. But Zweifel[3]

---

[1] *Morei Nevukhei ha-Zeman*, Chapter 13.

[2] No. 57, Ed. Lemberg, 1864, p. 40, n. 7.

[3] *Shalom al Yisrael*, Part II, pp. 99f.

has no difficulty in pointing to similar passages in the Kabbalistic literature. Erotic symbolism, of which the mystics were fond, is not pornography. Alter Druyanov (1870–1938), in his justly famed anthology of Jewish wit and humor, *Sefer ha-Bediḥah ve-ha-Ḥiddud* (1935–8), writes in the Introduction that he was of two minds whether to include in the collection doubtful jokes but finally decided against it. That off-color jokes did circulate among Jews, including scholars, is obvious. Druyanov evidently had access to a good deal of this material but thought it unprintable.

Prayer

It is typical of the Jewish approach that prayer is not left to the mood of the individual but is regulated. There are laws of prayer. As Judaism sees it there is much value in the idea of obligation and duty. Of course, spontaneity is especially significant in the life of prayer and the insertion of individual petitions in the formal prayer is encouraged, but whether or not the spirit moves him the devout Jew is expected to offer prayer to God three times each day—in the morning, in the afternoon, and at night. According to one view in the Talmud (*Berakhot* 27b), the night prayer is optional and this view is the accepted one. Nevertheless, the later codifiers argue that the Jewish community has taken it upon itself as a voluntary obligation to recite the night prayer in addition to the morning and afternoon prayers. The first tractate of the Mishnah, *Berakhot*, is devoted entirely to prayer and benedictions. Maimonides (*Yad, Tefillah* 1:1) writes:

> *It is a positive precept to pray each day, as it is said: "And ye shall serve the Lord your God" (Exodus 23:25). Tradition teaches that the service referred to here is prayer, as it is said: "And to serve Him with all your heart" (Deuteronomy 11:13). "What is service of the heart?" ask the Sages and they reply that it is prayer. But the number of the prayers and the form of prayers are not Biblical nor is a fixed time for prayers enjoined in the Bible.*

For Maimonides, then, there is a Biblical obligation for a man to pray each day, but the three prayers of the day and their form were developed later by the Rabbis. Other medieval authorities understand the Rabbinic reference to "service of the heart" to be no more than a Midrashic comment and they hold, consequently, that the duty to pray is Rabbinic. Naturally, all this concerns only the legal aspect of prayer. While normally in the traditional Jewish scale of values the study of the Torah ranks

Ḥasidim praying in a *bet midrash* by Isidor Kaufmann.

as a higher religious duty even than prayer, for man to commune with his Maker daily is his great privilege. There is a Rabbinic saying (*Berakhot* 6b) that prayer occupies the most elevated place in the whole world.

Prayers are of various kinds. The earliest and most frequent form is the prayer of petition, in which man entreats God to grant his requests. The conventional Jewish view, as found, for instance, in the Bible and the Talmud, is to believe in petitionary prayer in its literal sense. How prayer can affect God's providence is rarely discussed but that prayer can produce its results is piously accepted and never questioned, though it is not suggested that prayer is always answered. However, Jewish masters of prayer with a more mystical bent, especially among the Ḥasidim, were somewhat embarrassed, not so much by the theological difficulties of petitionary prayer as by the fact that this type of prayer calls attention to man's needs and therefore to his ego. The danger for these thinkers is that petitionary prayer causes man's attention to be focussed on his own needs and desires instead of leading him to self-transcendence in the presence of God. A typical Ḥasidic approach to petitionary prayer is that of the late Ḥasidic master Alter (1847–1905) of Ger, known, after the title of his *magnum opus*, as the *Sefat Emet*. In his commentary to Psalms[1] this teacher expresses it as follows:

> *Although it appears obvious that a man should pray when he is in need, yet the truth is that prayer's chief value is when the mind of the worshiper is on the prayer itself, not on the request to be granted. For even when a man entreats God to grant his desire, yet when he engages in prayer he should forget his needs and be affected solely by the praise of God. It may then happen that his request will be granted because it resulted in his turning to God in prayer.*

The word most frequently used for prayer in the Jewish sources is *tefillah*, from the root *palal*, meaning "to judge," "to intercede" (or possibly "to cut oneself" as in the Arabic *fella*, in which case the original meaning goes back to primitive times when worshipers lacerated their bodies). Whatever the derivation of the word it is extremely precarious to build theories about the meaning of Jewish prayer on etymology. The popular suggestion that *tefillah* means "to judge oneself" is incorrect. There have been Jewish teachers who would use their prayers as an exercise in severe self-scrutiny—for example, if I pray for wisdom am I doing all I can to attain it? If I pray for mercy do I try to show compassion in my dealings with others? and so forth. But this is a much later elaboration and does not appear to be part of the original meaning of prayer in any of the classical Jewish sources.

An important element in Jewish prayer is *kavvanah* ("concentration," "direction of the mind," "inwardness"). This means in Maimonides' definition:[2] "That a man should empty his mind of all other thoughts and regard himself as if he were standing before the Divine Presence." Baḥya Ibn Paquda[3] observes that "prayer without *kavvanah* is like a body without a soul or a husk without a kernel." The later Jewish mystics, however, understood *kavvanah* to mean that the mind of the

---

[1] London, 1952, Psalm 18:7, p. 33.

[2] *Yad, Tefillah* 6:16.

[3] *Duties of the Heart*, Gate 8, 3:9.

worshiper should not be at all on the plain intention of the words of the prayers but on the Kabbalistic mysteries it was believed are inherent in the inspired words. Prayer for the mystic is an ascent of the soul in which it soars in the "upper worlds" and dwells on all the details of their configurations as described in the Kabbalistic books.

R. Moses b. Joseph di Trani (1505–1585), known as *Mabit*, gives the following definition of prayer as understood by Judaism in his *Bet Elohim*[1]: "The act in which *man asks God for something he needs which he cannot achieve by his own efforts.*" This is explained as: *Man* and not an angel. Angels have no need to pray since God provides for all their needs without it. *Asks* and not demands. Prayer is an appeal to God to exercise His mercy. It is by God's grace that prayer is answered and not by right. *Of God* and not of the angels. It is forbidden to pray to any creature. *For something he needs* and not for luxuries. *Which he cannot achieve by his own efforts*—man should only pray when his own efforts are futile. But he should not rely on prayer to earn him a living, for example, since here God helps those who help themselves.

What is the Jewish attitude to Gentile prayer? The contemporary Halakhic authority R. Moses Feinstein[2] discusses whether, according to the teachings of the Torah, a Gentile is obliged to pray to God. The author argues that since prayer is not included in the seven Noachide laws, binding upon all men, there is no *obligation* for a Gentile to pray. If, however, he does so he performs a *mitzvah*. Does not the prophet declare: "For My house shall be called a house of prayer for all the peoples" (Isaiah 56:7)? Moreover, it can be argued that when a Gentile is in need he has as much of an obligation as a Jew to bring his need to God. That this is not counted among the seven Noachide laws should occasion no surprise, for it is surely implied in belief in God, which is similarly not included among the seven because it is the foundation of them all.

Prayer still occupies an extremely high place in Jewish religious life. Indeed, some thinkers have seen something of an imbalance in the concentration in contemporary Jewish life on the synagogue and prayer, since Judaism is intended to embrace the whole of life. The substitution of some prayers in the vernacular for prayers in Hebrew has become the

---

[1] Part I, *Sha'ar ha-Tefillah*, Chapter I, pp. 4–5.
[2] *Iggerot Mosheh*, New York, 1963. *Oraḥ Ḥayyim*, No. 24, pp. 196–198.

norm, though in varying degree, not only in Reform congregations. Among some modern Jewish thinkers there is a tendency to interpret prayer in naturalistic terms—man calling attention to the highest within him and the like—though this interpretation has not succeeded in winning many adherents.

Psychoanalysis

There are a number of aspects under which the attitude of Judaism to psychoanalysis can be discussed. One of these is the relationship between the rabbi and the psychoanalyst in seeking to help a person who is a congregant of the former and a patient of the latter. This problem also concerns other methods of treating mental disturbances or anxieties. The rabbi who is wise will not seek to usurp the functions of the trained psychiatrist. He will feel bound to acknowledge that in cases where expert knowledge is required there is no room for pseudo-methods of treatment. The competent psychoanalyst or psychiatrist, on the other hand, will not see it as his task to advise his patients how to behave when confronted with moral problems. His task is to help the patient to know himself, to uncover the hidden springs through which the patient's conduct is determined. Once this has been successfully achieved it is up to the patient to decide how to act, and in moral and religious questions he can be guided by the rabbi. To take an obvious example, it is no use at all for the rabbi to preach against stealing to a confirmed kleptomaniac, because such a person steals under compulsion. It is not a matter of consciously exercising the will but of forces deep down in his psyche over which he has no control. Jewish law recognizes that acts performed under compulsion are not culpable and if the patient is not shamming but really cannot help himself then Judaism would exonerate him, though it would urge him to be cured if this is possible. The trained physician may help him to discover, by the modern techniques available, why he feels compelled to steal, so that, with successful treatment, the compulsion to steal will vanish. Then and only then can the rabbi step in to point out how seriously Judaism views theft. The function of the psychiatrist is to heal the patient. The function of the rabbi is to encourage the patient to wish to be healed and to advise him after he has been healed. Complications will only arise where the psychiatrist urges the patient to carry out acts, as conditions of his cure, which the

253

Yeẓer ha-ra (the evil inclination) from *The Alph-
abet of Creation,* illustrated
by Ben Shahn.

rabbi, as a teacher of Judaism, has to declare forbidden. Such cases
are rare and where they do occur rabbi and psychiatrist should cooperate in finding the solution. The psychiatrist, for example, will be
called upon to see whether alternative methods of treatment are available. If they are not, the rabbi will have to determine whether the forbidden acts may be engaged in to effect a cure. He will be guided by
the general Jewish law that in order to save a life all the laws can be
set aside except the prohibition against idolatry, murder, and adultery. Most authorities argue that to cure a person who suffers from
mental illness is just as much a matter of "saving a life" as to save him
from physical death. They rule, for instance, that where no Jewish mental

home is available, such a patient can be put into a non-Jewish home even though he will be obliged to eat *terefah* food there. Furthermore, the psychoanalyst or psychiatrist will call on the rabbi to help if he is convinced that religious faith will help the patient. More and more, religion and psychiatry are discovering ways of fruitful cooperation.

A question of much interest is whether there are parallels between psychoanalytic theories on man's nature and the teachings of Judaism. David Bakan has written a book[1] in which he claims to have discovered the direct influence of the Kabbalah on Freud's thought. Bakan's thesis is very farfetched. Freud does not deny that there are indications in ancient literature that writers have been aware of the existence of something like the subconscious. Freud's claim is to have supported theory by empirical investigation. But this is a far cry from any direct influence. There is no evidence whatsoever that Freud was familiar with the Kabbalah. It is similarly futile to attempt to show the influence of other Jewish classical writings on Freud. What can be done is to show resemblances between Freudian theory and some of the positions taken in the Jewish sources, always with the proviso that the resemblances are coincidental and not at all surprising since the workings of the human mind have repeatedly exercised a strong fascination over thinkers and writers with insight into human nature. With these reservations it is not unhelpful to examine Rabbinic views on the good and evil inclination and to note their resemblance to what psychoanalysis has to say about the ego, the id, and the superego.

In psychoanalytic theory the ego is the mind of man as it is aware of itself, the conscious mind. The id is the unconscious mass of repressed impulses. From infancy we repress our impulses, pushing them out of the conscious mind into the subconscious where they continue to exist and to influence our conduct. The process starts in infancy because it is then that parents and teachers begin to teach the child to control his feelings and desires. The id, then, represents man's basic impulses and desires, many of them infantile but with later additions. These have been controlled by a censorship partly of the conscious mind, partly of the subconscious, based largely on parental discipline by which the infant is taught to behave properly. Since the infant cannot understand the meaning of parental rules this censorship is exercised in an irrational way. This controlling force is the superego. Thus man is seen as engaged

---

[1] *Sigmund Freud and the Jewish Mystical Tradition*, 2nd ed., New York, 1958.

in constant struggle within himself. His ego is in the middle, pulled downward by his id and upward by his superego. Neither of these will allow itself to be thwarted and mental disturbance is generally due to a failure to attain the correct balance. It is fatal to allow the ego to become completely dominated by either the id or the superego. Stability and harmony in life are achieved by the frank acknowledgment of man's aggressive and animal instincts as represented by the id. These man can and should control but not eradicate for they are essential if life is not to be deprived of its driving force.

Before noting the resemblances between this scheme and Rabbinic views it is necessary to appreciate that the Freudian doctrine of repression does not mean, as it is frequently and popularly misunderstood to mean, that man should always give expression to his desires and not "bottle them up." To do this would be to surrender the ego into the hands of the id. By repression, Freud means the failure to acknowledge the existence of the id's desires by pushing them out of the conscious mind, as it were, so that they form "complexes" in the subconscious. It should also be said that there is a marked tendency in present-day psychological theory to attribute mental illness far more to physical causes than Freud was prepared to do. Some forms of severe depression, for instance, are now seen by many doctors as due to something in the physical make-up of the sufferer.

The Rabbis speak frequently of man as placed, as it were, in the middle between the good inclination—*yeẓer ha-tov*—which pulls him one way and the evil inclination—*yeẓer ha-ra*—which pulls him the other. The Rabbis, like Freud, see man's internal struggle in terms of a tripartite division—the man himself, the good inclination and the evil inclination. Man *has* the two inclinations. The significant aspect of the Rabbinic doctrine is the constant demand for man to *control* the evil inclination and not to attempt to kill it, for to do this would deprive life of its driving force. The evil inclination is called "evil" because it can lead man to evil unless it is controlled, though it serves a purpose in life. Something like the Freudian doctrine of "sublimation" is anticipated in the following Rabbinic passage (*Kiddushin* 30b):

> The School of R. Ishmael taught: My son, if this repulsive creature [the evil inclination] attacks you, lead him into the House of Study. If he is stone, he will dissolve. If he is iron, he will shiver into fragments.

In another Rabbinic passage (Midrash, *Genesis Rabbah* 9:7), in a comment on the verse: "And God saw everything that He had made and behold, it was very good" (Genesis 1:31), it is said that if the verse had simply recorded "it was good" it would have referred to the good inclination. But since it says "very good" it refers to the evil inclination. For if a man did not have a *yezer ha-ra* he would not build a house, nor marry a wife, nor beget children, nor engage in commerce. Life would be "good" without the evil inclination but it would be a colorless, uncreative good. The famous Talmudic scholar R. Aryeh Leib Heller of Stry (d. 1813) adds[1] that life without the *yezer ha-ra* would be life without struggle and in such a life the "good" is bound to be weak. It is only when the "good" is tempered and refined by its need to struggle with evil that it becomes "very good." It is also possible that this is why the Rabbis refer to the *yezer ha-ra* as "the leaven in the dough" (*Berakhot* 17a). Although the leaven can be responsible for over-fermentation, without it the bread would be unpalatable. It is true that some of the mystics refer to the great saint *slaying* the *yezer ha-ra* by fasting and the like[2] but they refer only to the greatest of saints and even in this there is a departure from the basic Rabbinic doctrine.

It follows that the *yezer ha-ra* is awarded its due. Of course, Freud is right that the neurotic will find his religion catering to his neurosis, but this is not the fault of his religion. In his two Hebrew essays on the subject Alter Druyanov (1870–1938) gives a number of illustrations from his experience of how complete submission to the demands of what Freud calls the superego can produce that exaggerated and pathological guilt which is so marked a feature of many a neurosis.[3] A scribe, for instance, would repeatedly open the *tefillin* he had sewn together because of his fear that he may have placed the portions in the wrong order and so invalidate the *tefillin*. The same man would repeat every verse of the *Shema* many times out of fear that a mistake had been made in the pronunciation of the words. A rabbi refused to give decisions in ritual matters because if he decided, for instance, that a chicken brought before him was *kosher*, he was haunted by the fear that it may have been *terefah;* if *terefah* that it may have been *kosher*. Dryanov tells, too, of the case of

---

[1] Introduction to his *Shev Shema'ata*, letter *vav*.

[2] E.g., R. Shneor Zalman of Lyady, *Tanya*, Part I, Chapter 1.

[3] Druyanov's essays are to be found in the Hebrew periodical *Reshumot*, Vol. I, pp. 199–204, Odessa, 1918, Vol. II, pp. 303–357, Tel-Aviv.

a pious Jewish woman who tasted tallow in whatever she ate. When her case came before R. Joshua Leib Diskin (1818–1898) he "analyzed" her by reminding her that as a young girl she had served as a serving-maid in an observant Jewish household. Once, when milking the cow by candlelight, the candle fell into the pail of milk and, fearing the wrath of her mistress, she allowed the members of her family to drink the milk. The learned rabbi assured her that she had committed no wrong, for the small amount of tallow had become neutralized in the milk, which was therefore *kosher*. Her peace of mind was restored and the symptoms disappeared. Druyanov considers "Purim Torah" (the frivolous manipulation of Biblical texts and the parodying of Rabbinic teachers on the festival of Purim) to be an attempt by scholars, who submit to the severe discipline of the Torah during the rest of the year, to obtain relief from the otherwise oppressive demands of the superego.

There has grown up an extensive literature on the psychoanalytical interpretation of Jewish rituals, generally referring to the alleged primitive, sexual notions the rituals are said to symbolize. Most of this material is sheer guesswork, though one cannot rule out sexual associations in some of the rituals. The Kabbalists, for example, interpret the rituals in this way, i.e., as referring to the "sacred marriage" between "the Holy One, blessed be He" and His Shekhinah. Thus some of the Kabbalists see the *lulav* as a kind of phallic symbol. The literature referred to has been summarized at length and criticized by Abraham Cronbach.[1]

Finally, reference should be made to the Freudian critique of religion as an illusion fostered by the need for a "father figure" on whom man can rely in his fears once he realizes that his earthly father cannot help him. Freud's views on religion are well known: It is a collective neurosis. Moses was an Egyptian and was slain by the Israelites. Primitive man, sexually jealous of the old man of the tribe, slew and ate him and was subsequently tormented by feelings of guilt. But while Freud undoubtedly opened new windows to the human mind in his psychoanalytic work, his writings on religion are not based on scientific investigations. They consist of the brilliant speculations of an amateur philosopher and anthropologist and are viewed by experts in these fields as completely

[1] "The Psychoanalytic Study of Judaism," in *Hebrew Union College Annual*, Vols. 8–9, 1931–2, and "New Studies in the Psychology of Judaism," *Ibid.*, Vol. 19, 1945–6.

without foundation. The Freudian critique of religion as wishful thinking does, however, hit home, since religion is sometimes based on irrational desires and needs. But anti-religious attitudes can similarly be held because of irrational desires—and this applies to Freudian views as well. Judaism holds itself to be true and the truth is not affected by the means of arriving at it. This means that in a mature approach to Judaism the truth will be tested and Judaism embraced because it "makes sense" and can be supported at the bar of reason and not because it caters to infantile needs. Judaism would certainly not deny that man has need of God, but that is because the adherents of Judaism believe that God really *is*, so that He can satisfy the need of which He is the cause.

Public Relations

Public relations as a branch of social life is of comparatively recent vintage. Nowadays there are professionals whose job it is to "sell" a person and his ideas to the public. Many religious people have a built-in resistance to the whole enterprise on the grounds that it is sheer bluff. Insofar as Judaism is profoundly concerned with truth and integrity it is naturally opposed to exaggerated and untrue claims made in public relations. But, as in all other professions, there are honest and dishonest practitioners, and it would be unfair to condemn the many for the faults of the few. The more serious objection felt by some deeply religious people is that a man ought to be content with the knowledge that what he does is right in God's eyes. Why should he be concerned with what people think? If what he says and does has value and is true it will win out without any effort on his part. The Mishnah (*Eduyot* 5:7) informs us that when Akavyah b. Mahalalel was on his deathbed his son asked to be commended to Akavyah's colleagues. Akavyah replied: "Your own deeds will bring you near to them and your own deeds will keep you far from them."

But the Jewish teachers do not accept the opinion that all that matters is for a man to be right in the sight of God. He has a duty to demonstrate that what he does is right and he must refuse to do that which he knows to be right if it creates a misleading impression that he is doing wrong. In the Rabbinic literature the key text here is: "Then ye shall be clear before the Lord, and before Israel" (Numbers 32:22), which the Rabbis understand as teaching that it is not enough to clear oneself in God's eyes but it must be done in the eyes of one's fellows as well. A number of examples are given of how this principle operates. Charity collectors who had food left over after their distribution to the poor should sell the food to others and use the money for charity. But they should not buy it themselves because people may then suspect that they are obtaining the food too cheaply at the expense of charity (*Pesaḥim* 12a).

260

The family in Temple times which prepared the Temple shewbread never allowed fresh bread to be eaten in their homes so that people should not say that they were using the shewbread for their own purposes. Similarly, the family which prepared the incense never allowed the brides of the family to wear perfume because people might say that they were using the incense for their own purposes (*Yoma* 38a). The Jerusalem Talmud (*Shekalim* 3:2), on this theme of being blameless in the eyes of other people as well as of God, quotes, in addition to the verse from Numbers, two other Scriptural verses with the same implications. These are: "God, the Lord, He knoweth, and Israel He shall know" (Joshua 22:22); and: "So shalt thou find grace and good favor in the sight of God and man" (Proverbs 3:4).

Another Talmudic passage (*Nedarim* 62a) relevant to our theme is the one in which it is discussed whether or not a man should declare his worth if he is unknown. The fourth century Babylonian teacher Rava said that a man of note is permitted to reveal his identity in a place in which he is unknown. Rava's proof is from the verse: "But I thy servant fear the Lord from my youth" (I Kings 18:12). Similarly, Rava said that a scholar is permitted to inform others that he is such and thus claim the privilege scholars had in Rabbinic times. On the other hand Rava permits this only if the person concerned is unknown. Where he is known it is wrong for him to boast of his attainments because Scripture says "Let another man praise thee, and not thine own mouth" (Proverbs 27:2). A popular comment on the latter verse sums it up neatly: "Let another man praise thee; and (if) not (then) thine own mouth."

Racial Discrimination

One of the greatest passages in the whole of the Bible is the prosaic account in the Book of Genesis, Chapter 10, of the families of the nations. The remarkable feature of this passage is the description of all the known peoples of the world as descended from the three sons of Noah and forming one huge family. This is not coincidental. The belief in God as the Creator of the world and the Father of all men involves a belief in the brotherhood of man. Racial discrimination is rightly seen as opposed to the spirit of Judaism. The question has been adequately considered by Rabbi Robert Gordis in his *The Root and the Branch*.[1]

Some of the relevant Biblical passages, in addition to the above, should be examined. The Dutch Reformed Church in South Africa has relied on the story of Ham in Genesis 9:20–27 to support its view that it is the divine intention for the black peoples to be subordinate to the white. Quite apart from the fact that the identification of Ham with the black peoples is extremely questionable, modern scholarship has succeeded in uncovering the real meaning of the story. It is to be noted that it is Canaan, Ham's son, who is cursed to be "a servant of servants to his brethren" and not Ham himself. Obviously this story was told to justify the conquest of Canaan by the Israelites. The truth is, so far as Jewish interpretation is concerned, that nowhere in the whole literature is there the slightest suggestion that it is the destiny of black peoples to be slaves. The figures mentioned in the Bible as illustrations of dark-colored people are never Ham or Canaan but the Cushim, generally translated as the Ethiopians (though in Genesis 10:6 Cush is also a son of Ham). In the famous verse in Jeremiah (13:23) the prophet says: "Can the Ethiopian [*Cushi*] change his skin, or the leopard his spots?" Amos (9:7) declares:

[1] Chapter 8, pp. 115–136, Chicago, 1962.

Are ye not as the children of the
*Ethiopians (*Cushim*) unto Me,*
O children of Israel? saith the Lord.
Have I not brought up Israel out of
the land of Egypt,
And the Philistines from Caphtor,
And Aram from Kir?

For Amos God is responsible for the movements of all peoples, and if Israel has been singled out especially as His covenant people this means not privilege but greater responsibility (3:2):

You only have I known of all the
families of the earth;
Therefore I will visit upon you all
your iniquities.

Very revealing in this connection is the ruling of the Rabbis (*Berakhot* 58b) that if one sees a Negro (*Cushi*), a very red or very white person, a hunchback, a dwarf or a dropsical person, he recites the benediction: "Blessed is He who makes strange creatures." The black-skinned person was unusual in the lands of the Rabbis as were the redskins and the dwarf and the giant. The response of the Jew to the unusual sight was to be an acknowledgment that God in His wisdom has created many different kinds of people and thanks are to be given to Him for the rich variety of these creatures. It is significant that in the same passage it is said that when one sees a person with an amputated limb or a blind or lame person he recites the benediction: "Blessed be the true Judge." Here he acknowledges that he cannot see why God should have made people blind or lame but he does not question God's justice even while failing to see how it operates. It follows that the color of the skin or the unusual size of giants and dwarfs are not seen as deformities but as evidence that in His creative activity God has room in His world for the unusual as well as the usual. Of course black people would say "black is beautiful" and thank God for creating the unusual white pigmentation as He "makes strange creatures."

An important Biblical passage is the account of Miriam and Aaron's complaint against Moses for taking in marriage a Cushite woman (Numbers 12). The Rabbis, commenting on the narrative, found it hard to discover what it was they were objecting to, but a plain reading

דער דא זיכט הריזן ותגבעות והאדבדאת ואָט אן דיא ברכה ✦

בָּא֑֗אֱ֯מֶ֯רֳ֯הָ֯ עוֹשֶׂ֗֯ה מַﬠֲשֶׂ֗ה בְרֵ֯אשִׂ֗֯ית ✦

דער דא זיבט אין מחר אדר אין גיװוערג זאלט מן דיא ברבה ✦

בָּר֖וּךְ אַתָּ֨ה יֲ אֱ֯מֶֽרֳ֯הָ֯ מְשַׂנֶּ֣ה הַבְּרִי֯וֹרת ✦

Blessing (in lower panel) to be said when seeing strange creatures, in this instance — giants and dwarfs, From *Seder Birkat Hamazon,* a manuscript written and illuminated in Nicolsburg (Nikulev), 1728.

suggests that they objected to the color of the skin. The point of the narrative is that Miriam and Aaron were severely rebuked by God for their presumption. Incidentally, we learn from the narrative that Moses himself married a black woman. Of course, in Jewish teaching marriage with someone of another faith is wrong, but that is because of religious differences and would apply whatever the color of the skin of the spouse. Once conversion to Judaism has taken place there is no bar whatsoever to marriage on grounds of race. The law in Deuteronomy (23:4–7) does preclude the peoples of Ammon and Moab from "entering the assembly of the Lord," which the Rabbis understand as marriage with Jews even after conversion. But this was eventually abolished and no bar to marriage on ethnic grounds was allowed, as the following interesting Mishnah (*Yadayim,* 4:4) puts it:

> On that day came Judah, an Ammonite proselyte, and stood
> before them in the House of Study. He said to them, May I

*enter into the congregation? Rabban Gamaliel said to him:
Thou art forbidden. R. Joshua said to him: Thou art permitted.
Rabban Gamaliel said to him, Scripture says: "An Ammonite
or a Moabite shall not enter into the assembly of the Lord."
R. Joshua said to him: But are the Ammonites and the Moab-
ites still where they were?—long ago Sennacherib, king of
Assyria, came up and put all the nations in confusion, and
it is written: "I have removed the bounds of the peoples
and have robbed their treasures, and I have brought down
as a valiant man them that sit on a throne" (Isaiah 10:13).
Rabban Gamaliel answered: Scripture says: "And I will
turn again the captivity of the children of Ammon" (Jeremiah 49:6) and so they have returned. R. Joshua said to
him: Scripture says: "And I will turn against the captivity of
my people Israel and Judah, saith the Lord" (Jeremiah
30:3) and they have not yet returned. And they permitted
him to come into the congregation.*

While it is true that Judaism condemns racial discrimination it would
be unfair not to mention that a few Jewish thinkers have interpreted
the doctrine of the Chosen People in racial terms. In the writings of
Judah Halevi, Elijah of Smyrna (d. 1729), and some Ḥasidic teachers[1]
the Jewish soul is said to be qualitatively different from and superior
to the Gentile soul. But such teachings are not in the mainstream of
the Jewish tradition. Moreover, the "superiority" is understood in
terms of a special capacity for serving God and man that is the heritage
of the Patriarchs and is in no way to be compared to *Herrenvolk* theories
in which it is the destiny of the "superior" folk to be served by others.
In any event, the whole notion of "pure" races has been exploded
by modern biological science and it is obvious, in view of the numerous
conversions to Judaism, that there is no such thing as a pure Jewish
race and that every Jew has some non-Jewish blood in his veins.

[1] E.g. *Tanya*, Part I, Chapters 1 & 2.

Reincarnation

The doctrine of reincarnation is found nowhere in the Bible or the Rabbinic literature. Even though Herbert Loewe[1] has purported to discover echoes of the doctrine in one or two Rabbinic passages, he is forced to admit that there are no conscious references to the doctrine by the Rabbis. The doctrine appears to have been unknown in Judaism until the eighth century, when it began to be adopted by the Karaites (possibly, it has been suggested, under the influence of Islamic mysticism). The earliest reference we have to the doctrine is in Saadiah Gaon's *Emunot ve-Deot*.[2] Saadiah ridicules the doctrine:

> *Yet I must say that I have found certain people, who call themselves Jews, professing the doctrine of metempsychosis, which is designated by them as the theory of the "transmigration" of souls. What they mean thereby is that the spirit of Reuben is transferred to Simon and afterwards to Levi and after that to Judah. Many of them would even go so far as to assert that the spirit of a human being might enter into the body of a beast or that of a beast into the body of a human being, and other such nonsense and stupidities.*

Saadiah examines the Scriptural verses these people quote in support of their doctrine and refutes the proofs. We learn incidentally that one of the reasons these people believed in reincarnation was because of the theological difficulties in believing that God allows innocent children to suffer. That they do, it was argued, is because of sins they had committed in a previous existence. Maimonides does not refer to re-

---

[1] *A Rabbinic Anthology* by C. G. Montefiore & H. Loewe, pp. 660–663, London, 1938.

[2] *Beliefs and Opinions*, trans. Samuel Rosenblatt, New Haven, VI, 8, pp. 259–263, 1948.

incarnation at all nor does Judah Halevi. The fifteenth century philosopher Joseph Albo[1] rejects the theory. The purpose for which the soul enters the body is to become a free agent, but once a soul has become a free agent by functioning in a human body why should it return to occupy another body? Albo considers even more unlikely the opinion that human souls are transmigrated into the bodies of animals.

The Kabbalists, on the other hand, believe in the transmigration of souls. The Zohar refers to the doctrine in a number of passages (e.g. II, 94a and 99b). Naḥmanides refers to the doctrine of transmigration in a number of his writings. In his Commentary to Job[2] Naḥmanides speaks of this as a great mystery and the key to the understanding of many Biblical passages. The later Kabbalah is full of the belief in the transmigration of souls. Various sins are punished by transmigration, for example the soul of the proud man enters the body of a bee until atonement is attained. The heroes of the Bible and later Jewish history are said to be the reincarnation of earlier heroes. Thus the soul of Cain entered the body of Jethro and the soul of Abel the body of Moses. When Moses and Jethro met they rectified the sin caused by the estrangement of the two brothers. Manasseh ben Israel (d. 1657) devotes a large portion of his *Nishmat Ḥayyim*[3] to a defense of reincarnation. In Chapter 21 Manasseh observes that the doctrine was originally taught to Adam but was forgotten. It was revived by Pythagoras, who was a Jew (!) and he was taught the doctrine by the prophet Ezekiel. The Ḥasidim, as followers of the Kabbalah, believed implicitly in reincarnation. Ḥasidic penitential prayer entreated God to pardon the sins committed both in this existence and in previous existences. Ḥasidic legend tells of R. Abraham Joshua Heschel of Opatow (d. 1825) that he could remember his previous incarnations, in one of which he was the High Priest. The legend has it that when he took the services on Yom Kippur and recounted the service of the High Priest in Temple times, this master would not say: "Thus did *he* [the High Priest] say," but "Thus did *I* say."

In the Kabbalistic literature there are three types of reincarnation: (1) *gilgul*, transmigration proper, in which a soul that had previously inhabited one body is sent down again to earth to inhabit another body;

---

[1] *Ikkarim* IV, 29.

[2] Chavel, *The Writings of Naḥmanides*, Vol. I, p. 101, Jerusalem, 1963.

[3] IV, Chapters 6–24, Amst., 1651.

(2) *ibbur*, "impregnation," in which a soul comes down from Heaven in order to assist another soul in the body (this derives from the Lurianic Kabbalah and is not found before the sixteenth century); (3) *dibbuk*, a generally late concept, in which a guilt-laden soul pursued by devils enters a human body in order to find rest and has to be exorcised.

The great philosophical difficulty in the doctrine of reincarnation is what meaning can possibly be given to the identity of the soul that has been reincarnated more than once, since the experiences in the body determine the character of the soul. Scholem[1] has suggested that it was this difficulty which led the Zohar to postulate the existence of the *ẓelem* ("image"), a kind of "astral body" which does not migrate from body to body and which therefore preserves individual identity. Very few modern Jews believe in reincarnation and the doctrine is certainly not very prominent even among those who do.

[1] See Tishby, *Mishnat ha-Zohar*, Vol. II, pp. 92–93, Jerusalem, 1961.

Relativity

Einstein's theory that time is a relative concept, depending on the observer's position in space, has been worked out in great detail and received empirical verification but is intelligible in its entirety only to expert mathematicians. Insofar as relativity is a theory about the nature of the universe Judaism has nothing to say about it. The Jewish teachers have not been fond of expressing "Jewish" views on the nature of the physical universe, preferring to leave questions to experts. There is no such thing as a kosher mathematics. All we can say in this connection is that some Jewish speculations on the nature of time bear a resemblance to the theory of relativity. Here, for instance, is an account of time from the writings of the early nineteenth century Ḥasidic teacher R. Naḥman of Bratslav.[1]

> *God is higher than time, as is well known. This matter is truly marvelous and utterly incomprehensible. It is impossible for the human intellect to grasp such an idea. Know, however, that time is, in the main, the product of ignorance; that is to say, time appears real to us because our intellect is so small. The greater the intellect the smaller and more insignificant time becomes. Take a dream, for instance. Here the intellect is dormant and the imaginative faculty alone functions. In the dream it is possible for 70 years to pass by in a quarter of an hour. In the dream it seems as if a great space of time has elapsed but in reality only a very short time has passed. On awakening after a dream one sees that the whole 70 year period of the dream occupied in reality only a minute fraction of time. This is because man's intellect has been restored to him in his waking life and,*

---

[1] *Likkutei Maharan*, Part II, 61, Ostray, 1821.

> *so far as his intellect is concerned, the whole 70 year period*
> *of the dream is no more than a quarter of an hour . . . There*
> *is a Mind so elevated that the whole of time is counted as*
> *naught, for that Mind is so great that for it the whole of time*
> *is as nothing whatsoever. Just as the 70 years which pass*
> *in the dream are, so far as we are concerned, no more than*
> *a quarter of an hour in reality, as we have seen, so it is with*
> *regard to that Mind, which is so far above mind that time has*
> *no existence for it whatsoever . . .*

There is an account of Rabbinic views on time in the article "The Concept of Time in Rabbinic Literature" (Hebrew) by M. M. Kasher in *Talpiot* (Vol. V, 1952, pp. 799–827).

Einstein persistently claimed that his is a scientific theory with no implications for religion or philosophy. This has not prevented the emergence of a host of theories in which an attempt is made to apply the concept of relativity to other areas of human thought. Many propositions are said to be relative in that they depend on the viewpoint of a particular society or cultural background. Here Judaism does have something to say. The truth that there is a God and He is One is an absolute truth for Judaism and Judaism also takes issue with relativistic notions of ethics, for example that while from the point of view of the victim it was wrong for the concentration camp guard to torture him, from the point of view of the guard it was right. Judaism sees right and wrong, truth and error, as absolutes, though this is not to say, of course, that in every circumstance we can easily distinguish good from evil. Like the theory of evolution, the theory of relativity has been applied in areas where there is no evidence whatever that it operates. A scientific theory has been used in a thoroughly unscientific way. The popular cry "everything is relative" is, in fact, a nonsensical statement, for if *everything* is relative there is nothing *to* which anything can be relative.

Revenge

That it is wrong to take revenge is mentioned in the same Biblical verse in which the love of the neighbor is enjoined: "Thou shalt not take vengeance, nor bear any grudge against the children of thy people, but thou shalt love thy neighbor as thyself: I am the Lord" (Leviticus 19:18). The Jerusalem Talmud (*Nedarim* 9:4) gives the illustration of the man who cuts his hand while cutting meat. He will not be so foolish as to cut the hand which did the damage out of spite. Evidently, the Jerusalem Talmud introduces the note that revenge is wrong because of the unity of mankind. To harm the neighbor is to harm oneself. The famous Rabbinic definition of the verse (*Yoma* 23a) distinguishes between taking revenge and bearing a grudge. If a man asks his fellow to lend him his sickle and he refuses and on the morrow the second asks the first to lend him his axe and he replies: "I will not lend it to you, just as you would not lend me your sickle"—that is revenge. But if a man asks his fellow to lend him his sickle and he refuses and on the morrow the second asks the first to lend him his garment and he replies: "Here it is, I am not like you"—that is bearing a grudge. Maimonides (*Yad, Deot* 7: 7–8) adds that the wise will refuse to take revenge because worldly things are simply not worth it. To feel a sense of outrage because someone has refused to lend one a sickle is to magnify the importance of a sickle. Maimonides also understands the prohibition against bearing a grudge to be a means of avoiding the more serious offense of taking revenge. All this, concludes Maimonides, is the proper attitude to have if society is to be well established and social life possible.

Moses Ḥayyim Luzzatto (1707–1747) in his *Path of the Upright* (pp. 91–93) describes the offense in very human terms:

> Hatred and revenge. *These the human heart in its perversity, finds it hard to escape. A man is very sensitive to disgrace, and suffers keenly when subjected to it. Revenge is sweeter*

271

to him than honey; he cannot rest until he has taken his revenge. If, therefore, he has the power to relinquish that to which his nature impels him; if he can forgive; if he will forbear hating anyone who provokes him to hatred; if he will neither exact vengeance when he has the opportunity to do so, nor bear a grudge against anyone; if he can forget and obliterate from his mind a wrong done to him as though it had never been committed; then he is, indeed, strong and mighty. So to act may be a small matter to angels who have no evil traits, but not to those "that dwell in houses of clay, whose foundation is in the dust" (Job 4:19). Yet such is the sovereign decree. Scripture declares it with the utmost clearness, so that further comment is unnecessary. "Thou shalt not hate thy brother in thy heart. Thou shalt not take vengeance nor bear any grudge against the children of thy people." The difference between taking revenge and bearing a grudge is well known. To take revenge is to return evil for evil. To bear a grudge is to remind a man of the evil he has done to you though you repay him with good. The evil inclination always wants to excite us to anger, and continually attempts to have us retain at least some remembrance of the evil that our neighbor may have done to us. If the evil inclination is not able to keep alive a vivid image of the wrong done to us, he strives to have at least a faint impression of it cling to the memory. He argues that: "If you want to grant that man the favor which he refused you when you were in need, you do not have to grant it to him cheerfully. You may refuse to retaliate, but you do not have to be his benefactor or to offer him help. If you do insist upon extending considerable help to him, do so at least without his knowledge. It is not necessary for you to associate with him and again become his friend. If you have forgiven him, it is enough that you do not show yourself to him as his enemy; if you are willing to go further and associate with him once more, at least do not display as much love as formerly." With these and similar sophistries, the evil inclination endeavors to seduce men's hearts. The Torah therefore lays down a general rule which takes all these possibilities into account. "Thou shalt love thy neighbour as thyself," as thyself, without

*difference or distinction, without subterfuge and mental
reservation, literally as thyself.*

This noble passage was written by a man who suffered all his days
from persecution during a life in which he made many enemies because
of his religious ideas.

Are there any circumstances in which Jewish teaching permits the
taking of revenge? Naḥmanides in his Commentary to the Pentateuch
on the verse[1] remarks that it is obvious that where a man has a legitimate
case against his fellow it does not constitute revenge to summon him
to a court of law. In the examples given in the Talmud of the sickle
and the axe no redress is available in the courts. One is allowed to claim
compensation for wrongs done, otherwise the prohibition of taking
revenge would be an open invitation to the unscrupulous.

Furthermore, there is the curious statement in the Talmud (*Yoma*
22b–23a) that a Torah scholar who does not take revenge is no true
scholar. This is discussed in the Talmudic passage and somewhat qualified, i.e., he should not take any positive steps but should allow others
to call attention to the wrong done to him. The meaning is clearly to
advance the respect due to students of the Torah and hence to the Torah
itself. There is not, or should not be, anything personal, in the scholar's
attempt to uphold the dignity of the Torah. Otherwise the same Talmudic
passage quotes as the ideal:

> *Concerning those who are insulted but do not insult others,
> who hear themselves reproached without replying, who
> perform good deeds out of love and rejoice in their suffer-
> ings, Scripture says: "But they that love Him be as the sun
> when he goeth forth in his might" (Judges 5:31).*

[1] Ed. Chavel, *Perushei ha-Torah le-Rabbenu Moshe ben Naḥman,* Vol. II, p. 120,
Jerusalem, 1960.

Secularism

There has been a good deal of discussion among contemporary theologians about the claims of secular society on religion. Judaism has no need to be reminded of the claim. The Jew has always been expected to live in society and make his contribution to its well-being. He has never been encouraged to adopt anything like a hermit type of life, although some Jews, like others, in times of great social upheaval were tempted to shun urban life with all its problems and opportunities for enmity and strife. The synagogue, for example, is of the utmost importance in Judaism but prayer is not the be-all and end-all of Judaism. The frank and joyous acceptance of life in all its manifestations is a typical Jewish theme. Judaism certainly does not reject the secular and Jewish thinkers are not unnaturally puzzled at what all the fuss among Christian theologians is about. Judaism agrees with the sentiments expressed in Bonhoeffer's often quoted saying about "man come of age." It only disagrees in that for Judaism man has always been of age.

For all that, Judaism does not accept a secular view of human life. There is a religious dimension to life. Of course, there are Jews who speak of a "secular Judaism." By this they appear to mean an acceptance of Jewish ethical standards and the Jewish way of life without any belief in the religious teachings of Judaism. This is surely a distortion and a very serious one at that. There is no need for the religious Jew to deny that the secular man can also be doing God's will without knowing that he is doing so, without even believing in God. But at the heart of Judaism is the belief that God *is* and that all of man's activities can be sanctified by his awareness of the tremendous truth. That is why, for all of Judaism's acceptance of the secular, it is a mistake to repeat the shopworn assertion that Judaism makes no distinction between the sacred and the secular. Anyone who makes this claim has presumably never participated at the Havdalah service on Saturday night when the Jew takes leave of the Sabbath with wine, light, and aromatic spices:

274

Blessed art Thou, O Lord our God, King of the universe, who makest a distinction between the sacred and the secular, between light and darkness, between Israel and other nations, between the seventh day and the six working days. Blessed art Thou, O Lord, who makest a distinction between sacred and secular.

Solomon Schechter's remarks are perhaps a little unfair when applied to the sincere secularist Jew who really sees great value in the Jewish way, but his critique is still most relevant[1]:

Judaism, divested of every higher religious motive, is in danger of falling into gross materialism. For what else is the meaning of such declarations as "Believe what you like, but conform to this or that mode of life"; what else does it mean but "We cannot expect you to believe that the things you are bidden to do are commanded by a higher authority; there is not such a thing as belief, but you ought to do them for conventionalism or for your own convenience." But both these motives—the good opinion of our neighbors, as well as our bodily health—have nothing to do with our noble and higher sentiments, and degrade Judaism to a matter of expediency or diplomacy. Indeed, things have advanced so far that well-meaning but ill-advised writers even think to render a service to Judaism by declaring it to be a kind of enlightened Hedonism, or rather a moderate Epicureanism.

Judaism embraces secularism but cannot be identified with it. The prophet Micah (6:8) asks what it is that God wants of man and replies: "Only to do justly, and to love mercy, and to walk humbly with thy God." The secularist can practice justice and mercy and he can walk humbly. It is arrogant of the believer and untrue to experience to declare that he cannot. But the believing Jew adds to it all the dimension of the sacred. It is God who asks these things of him and when he tries falteringly to walk humbly it is with his God that he is trying to walk.

---

[1] *Studies in Judaism,* Vol. I, pp. 150–151.

Self-Expression

It can be argued that the whole idea of self-expression and self-realization is modern and was unknown to the ancient Jewish teachers. The older view appears to be that man should fulfill his obligations to God and his fellow man and realize himself in this way without thinking too much of it. There is much truth in this. Modern man's awareness of himself is partly, at least, the fruit of the Renaissance, in which a man-centered universe began to be substituted for a God-centered one. But this is not the whole truth. The rich variety of heroes and heroines in the Bible, all of them individuals, no two exactly alike, point to an appreciation that each man is a person in his own right with a particular self to realize. While in many traditional formulations, the Talmudic sages are lumped together as the "Rabbis" and are treated almost as cyphers, modern Rabbinic scholarship has succeeded in demonstrating that each of the Sages had his own approach, that what Akiva said, for instance, could only have been said by Akiva with his particular temperament and character and against the particular background of his time. Again, the great medieval Jewish teachers were not all of one mold. Some were legalists, others mystics, others philosophers, others again poets or grammarians or Biblical exegetes. The term "self-expression" is new and perhaps the emphasis as well. The concept is as old as Judaism itself.

In this connection there is a remarkable comment by the celebrated Polish Talmudist R. Samuel Edels (1555–1631) known, after the initial letters of his name, as *Maharsha* and author of a Talmudic Commentary that is printed in practically every edition of the Talmud. The comment is on the passage (*Bava Kama* 30a) in which three Rabbis give their prescriptions for attaining saintliness. One Rabbi said that the would-be saint should study *Berakhot*, dealing with prayer and worship. The second Rabbi said that he should study the portions dealing with the laws governing relations between men in order to avoid doing the slight-

276

est harm to another. The third Rabbi said that he should study *Avot* ("Ethics of the Fathers"). *Maharsha* comments that all three Rabbis are right. Saintly conduct consists in a man's having a three-fold relationship—to his God, to his neighbor, and to *himself. Ethics of the Fathers,* in this view, is seen as providing material for the highest realization of the self. This is, of course, very different from selfishness or self-centeredness. It is rather an awareness that God has distributed His gifts abundantly and that just as a man has a duty to help his neighbor do that which he can do well, he has a duty to realize his own talents and abilities. Some of the later Jewish preachers apply to this the legal definition of an imbecile (*Hagigah* 4a) as one who destroys whatever is given to him. Man's capacity for self-improvement, his particular gifts of mind and heart, are given to him freely by the Maker. It is sheer folly if he allows them to go to waste.

The Lithuanian Musar movement, founded in the nineteenth century by R. Israel Salanter, paid special attention to man's self-realization, teaching that each man must know himself and strive to give the fullest expression to his own particular spiritual and mental qualities. The critics of this movement accused it, in fact, of excessive and morbid preoccupation with the self. Introspection, the critics claimed, is not always the healthiest of religious approaches. Nonetheless, the movement did produce a number of important ideas on the way in which Judaism can help a man to find himself. The best and most comprehensive account of this provocative movement is provided by Dov Katz's comprehensive five-volume work.[1] The saying attributed to Hillel (*Avot* 1:14) is a summary of the Rabbinic attitude to this question and has often been referred to in this context: "If I am not for myself, who is for me? But if I am only for myself, what am I?"

---

[1] *Tenuat ha-Musar,* Tel-Aviv, 1958–1963.

Self-Transcendence

Self-transcendence as an aim of the religious life belongs primarily to the mystical approach to religion. The mystic believes that man's grasping ego is not his true self. Deep down in the recesses of man's psyche there is something identical with the true Reality behind the physical universe. Free from the greed of the ego man can penetrate to this Reality within himself. In English it is conventional to describe the ego as the *self*, with a small "s," and the true inner nature of man as the *Self* with a capital "S." Self-transcendence means overcoming the "self" in order to reach the "Self." The question to be considered is whether Judaism knows anything of this.

The difficulty in answering this question is due to the reticence of the Jewish mystics on their experiences. Normally the Kabbalists tell us about the "upper worlds" and the divine mysteries but hardly anything of their own spiritual techniques, and when they do speak about the latter it is in purely formal terms. The Ḥasidic masters were an exception and it is in Ḥasidism that the theme of mystical self-transcendence is profoundly explored in the doctrine of *bittul ha-yesh*, "annihilation of the self." The doctrine is found among all the Ḥasidim but is especially pronounced in the Ḥabad system. It was not unknown for instance, for Ḥabad Ḥasidim to refuse ever to use the personal pronoun "I." According to the doctrine of *bittul ha-yesh*, the only true Reality is God. God is, as it were, screened from man in order that the latter might enjoy an independent existence. But deep down in the psyche there is a "portion of God," a "divine spark" which is the true Self, though it is "clothed" (a favorite Ḥabad word) with the garments of the self. Especially in prayer man can transcend the self of his "natural soul" so that the "divine soul" within him reaches out for its source as the light of a candle moves brightly to a fire with which it is placed in close proximity.

There are numerous descriptions of *bittul ha-yesh* in Ḥasidic literature,

278

of which the following are typical. The first is from the early Ḥasidic work *Zava'at ha-Ribash*[1]:

> When a man prays he should be as if he had been stripped of his corporeality so that he is unconscious of his existence in this world. This is the meaning of: "If I am not for myself, who is for me" (Avot 1:14)? That is to say, once I attain to the stage at which I have no consciousness or awareness that I am, namely, whether or not I am in this world, then I can be sure that I will have no distracting thoughts in my prayers. For which strange thoughts can approach me in the state of being stripped of all corporeal associations? This is the meaning of "who is for me?" That is to say, which strange thought can approach near to me? But "if I am only for myself," that is to say, if I think of myself as something, as enjoying existence in this world, then, on the contrary, I am as nothing. Therefore the saying continues "What am I?" This means: What am I worth and what is my worship worth before God, since then strange thoughts will confuse me and it will then be as if I were not in this world. For the main purpose for which man was created was to worship God and I cannot worship Him because of the strange thoughts which confuse me.

It is interesting that the Rabbinic text which affirms the self is used in this text to deny it. But, of course, as has been said, the Ḥasidic emphasis on self-annihilation would naturally be suspicious of self-consciousness in prayer as a barrier between the true Self and God. However, it does not necessarily follow that the Ḥasidim have no use for the idea of self-realization. At one level of consciousness, man has to realize the best in his self. A petty, frustrated self, without ambition, dignity, or potential greatness, is scarcely worth annihilating and cannot lead to the mystical ascent of the soul. The great Ḥasidic leaders certainly battled long and unceasingly for the acceptance of their own special insights and in so doing were engaging in the task of self-realization, evidently seeing in the process no basic incompatibility with their higher mystical reaches.

Another of the many descriptions of *bittul ha-yesh* in Ḥasidic thought

[1]   p. 7a, Zolkiew, 1793.

is that of R. Ḥayyim Ḥaykel of Amdur (d. 1787) in the work *Ḥayyim va-Ḥesed*[1]:

> *The Holy One, blessed be He, fills the whole world with His glory and no space is empty of Him, just as before creation. The only division between God and man is the latter's body, just as father and son are really one essence only they have different bodies. Man only forgets this because of his pride in which he forgets the day on which body and soul will be separated (at death). Our father Abraham understood this, saying: "I am but dust and ashes" (Genesis 18:27). But Moses said: "And what are we?" (Exodus 16:8), that is to say, he did not even look upon himself as dust.*

The idea of self-transcendence is, then, not too frequent in the Jewish sources but this is, no doubt, partly at least, due to the fact noted that mystical testimonies are rare in Jewish literature.

[1] Jerusalem, 1970, from the Warsaw edition, pp. 33–4.

Sex

Our concern here is with Jewish attitudes to sex. For specific laws governing sex the best work in English is Louis M. Epstein's *Sex Laws and Customs in Judaism.*[1] There are, of course, differing attitudes to sex among Jewish teachers. A completely negative attitude was impossible since Judaism teaches that it is a religious duty to marry and celibacy was hardly ever advocated. However, especially in the Middle Ages, when the dichotomy between body and soul became pronounced, a suspicion of sexual relations did find its way into Jewish thought.

In the Bible there is not the slightest suggestion anywhere that sex inside marriage is in any way unworthy. The natural acceptance of sex is implied at the beginning of Genesis (2:21–24) in the simple yet sublime account of Eve's creation:

> *And the Lord God caused a deep sleep to fall upon the man, and he slept; and He took one of his ribs, and closed up the place with flesh instead thereof. And the rib, which the Lord God had taken from the man, made He a woman, and brought her unto the man, And the man said: "This is now bone of my bones, and flesh of my flesh; she shall be called Woman, because she was taken out of Man." Therefore shall a man leave his father and his mother, and shall cleave unto his wife, and they shall be one flesh.*

The Patriarchs, Moses, and the other Biblical heroes marry and have children. It is nowhere even remotely implied that their sex life interfered with their status as holy men and inspired teachers. Sometimes the sexual side of marriage is referred to in the frankest terms, as in the story of Jacob and Rachel (Genesis 29:20–21):

[1] New York, 1948.

281

> *And Jacob served seven years for Rachel; and they seemed*
> *unto him but a few days, for the love he had to her. And Jacob*
> *said unto Laban: "Give me my wife, for my days are ful-*
> *filled, that I may go into her."*

This last sentence was, in fact, a source of embarrassment to the Rabbis, who comment (*Genesis Rabbah* 70:7) that the commonest of the common would not use such a direct expression, but Jacob's need was to fulfill his destiny as the progenitor of the twelve tribes. The Song of Songs does not fail to sing the praises of the physical charms and relationship of the lover and his beloved. The term used for Isaac's relationship with his wife is "sporting" (Genesis 26:8), in Hebrew *meẓaḥek*, which conveys the idea of enjoyment. Physical beauty was highly admired (Genesis 29:17; 39:6; 70b 42:15).

C.G. Montefiore[1] is very critical of what he considers to be the Rabbis' excessive preoccupation with sex. Montefiore writes:

> *Social intercourse with women was usually taboo. They*
> *were the source of moral danger. They were the incitements*
> *to depravity and lust. The evil impulse—the Yeẓer ha-Ra—is*
> *especially and mainly the impulse which leads to sexual*
> *impurity. The result was not entirely healthy. The Rabbis*
> *were prevailingly chaste; there was probably much less*
> *adultery and fornication among the Rabbis than among us.*
> *But this chastity was obtained at a certain cost. The lack*
> *of healthy, simple companionship and friendship caused*
> *a constant dwelling upon sexual relations and details. In*
> *the Rabbinic literature sexual allusions are very frequent.*
> *Immense are the Halachic discussions about the details*
> *of sex life, and sexual phenomena. "Repel nature and it*
> *recurs." Repress it, and it grows up again, and not always*
> *in a healthy form. Where we should not dream of thinking*
> *that any sexual desire could be evoked, the Rabbis were*
> *always on the watch for it, dwelling on it, suggesting it.*
> *Though they were almost invariably married men, they*
> *seem to have often been oddly tormented by sexual desires;*
> *perhaps too, the very absence of natural and healthy social*

[1] C. G. Montefiore and H. Loewe, *A Rabbinical Anthology,* p. xix, London, 1938.

intercourse between men and women drove them to dwell theoretically with double frequency upon every sort of sexual details and minutiae.

In a footnote Loewe defends the Rabbis by pointing out that this tendency was characteristic of the age. Patristic literature is similarly marked. On the other hand, says Loewe, the Rabbinic writings do not eulogize virginity and monasticism. It is always a precarious thing to attempt to psychoanalyze the past, to assume that what was considered "unhealthy" in England in the Thirties was necessarily so over 1,500 years ago in Palestine and Babylon. The interests of the Rabbis in sex was not prurient. The numerous Halakhic discussions, for instance, to which Montefiore refers, are clinical in the extreme. One might just as well accuse a gynecologist of a morbid interest in sex. Sex is an important part of life. The Torah has laws concerning sex. And the Rabbis, as teachers of the Torah, had to deal with this subject as they did with all the other matters treated in the Torah. A closer look at what the Rabbis actually said about sex shows that their approach to this topic was as free, healthy, and lacking in frustration as is to be found in any work of religious literature, ancient or modern.

Detail from *Hamburg Miscellany,* Germany, c. 1427, shows a Jewess immersing herself in a *mikveh* before going to her husband.

One of the most striking features of the Rabbinic attitude to sex is their acknowledgment that a woman has strong sexual desires as well as a man. Unlike the "Victorian" attitude that it was unladylike for a wife to enjoy sex, the Rabbinic view is that a husband has a religious duty (*mitzvat onah*) to satisfy his wife. When she desires her husband she should make it obvious to him by hint, though she should not express it verbally (*Eruvin* 100b). This concept of a religious duty on the part of the husband is based on the verse (Exodus 21:10) applied by the Rabbis to every wife, in which it is stated that a husband must not withhold from his wife her "conjugal rights" (*onatah*). The Mishnah (*Ketubbot* 5:6) gives a list of the times a wife can expect her husband to be with her as an essential part of the marriage contract:

> *The duty of conjugal rights as enjoined in the Torah is: every day for those who have no occupation; twice a week for laborers; once a week for ass-drivers; once every thirty days for camel-drivers; and once every six months for sailors.*

In the Talmudic discussion (*Ketubbot* 62b) it is argued that a husband cannot change his occupation without his wife's consent if this will affect her conjugal rights—from an ass-driver to a camel-driver, for instance, since it can be assumed that a wife will prefer to have her needs satisfied even if, as a result, her husband's earnings will be less. Scholars who study the Torah during the week need fulfill their marital duties only on Friday nights (*Ketubbot* 62b). It is interesting that the Rabbis considered marital relations on the Sabbath to be especially meritorious in view of the fact that in sectarian literature the performance of the sex act on the Sabbath is strictly forbidden. A wife can demand that the sex act be performed while they are both naked and if the husband insists on the "Persian custom" of both being clothed she can petition for a divorce (*Ketubbot* 48a).

The Rabbis sternly disapprove of extramarital sex. The sex relationship between a man and an unmarried woman is called "fornication" (*beilat zenut*). If, for instance, a man and wife were divorced and they then spent the night together at an inn a new divorce is required on the grounds that people would not normally engage in fornication, so it can be assumed that they cohabited for the purpose of marriage (*Gittin* 81b). The Rabbinic sources are not too clear, however, on whether a man is allowed to take a mistress, i.e., a woman to whom he is not formally married but who lives with him alone and is not promiscuous.

The question concerns the *pilegesh* ("concubine"), which, Scripture states, is permitted to the king. Maimonides (*Yad, Ishut* 1:4) holds that the "concubine" is only permitted to the king and never to a commoner, but other medieval authorities permit it even to a commoner (see the commentaries to the passage of Maimonides). However, with the sole exception of the eighteenth century teacher R. Jacob Emden, Rabbinic authorities have frowned severely on the taking of a mistress. As for adultery, the Rabbis held this to be one of most serious of sins. Life itself must be sacrificed, according to the Rabbis, rather than an act of adultery be carried out (*Pesaḥim* 25a–b).

There are Rabbinic discussions regarding behavior in the marital bed. According to one interpretation, R. Huna advised his daughters how to practice sex techniques with the object of arousing their husband's desire (*Shabbat* 104b). Unorthodox conduct was permitted. While one Rabbi taught that children are born blind because the husband "gazes at that place," are born dumb because he "kisses that place," and are born lame because he "inverts the table," the ruling is given that all those are permitted (*Nedarim* 20a–b). The Talmud goes on to say, however, that it is forbidden for a husband to have another woman in mind during intercourse with his wife, nor must he cohabit with her if he intends to divorce her. Following the Talmudic ruling but with certain reservations R. Moses Isserles in his notes to the *Shulḥan Arukh* (*Even ha-Ezer*, 25:2) writes:

> *He can do as he wishes with his wife: he can have intercourse at any time he wishes; he can kiss any part of her body; and he can have intercourse both in the usual way and in an unusual way or on her limbs, provided that he does not spill his seed. Some are more lenient and rule that unnatural intercourse is permitted even if it involves a spilling of the seed, provided it is only done occasionally and he does not make a habit of it. Although all these are permitted, whoever sanctifies himself in that which is permitted to him is called holy.*

Among some of the medieval thinkers a less positive attitude toward sex is adopted, although other thinkers saw in any suggestion that sex is unworthy a trace of the heretical view that matter is eternal and that there is therefore permanent warfare between spirit and matter. Saadiah

Gaon[1] notes the view that sexual intercourse is the greatest of all mundane goods. Those who hold this view argue that sexual intercourse yields the most remarkable of pleasures, it increases the soul's gladness and gaiety, it drives out gloomy thoughts from the mind, and serves as an antidote against melancholy. There cannot be anything reprehensible about the sex act since God's holy men in the Bible engaged in it with His approval. Saadiah attacks this thesis for its one-sidedness. The people who advocate it as the greatest good have overlooked its deleterious results, injury to the eyes, loss of appetite, and the falling off of physical energy. "And what about the filth and defilement resulting from it, which, if a person has any sensitiveness and delicacy of feeling, will cause his very clothes to declare him filthy, even though he clean himself scrupulously?" Saadiah concludes:

> It is proper for a man to satisfy his appetite only in order to produce offspring, as Scripture also says: "And you, be ye fruitful, and multiply; swarm in the earth, and multiply therein" (Genesis 9:7). Hence he should give his impulse free rein when in the estimation of reason it seems necessary, and check it when that need has been fulfilled.

Maimonides is more extreme, stating in his esoteric *Guide for the Perplexed*,[2] though not in his Code intended for the masses of Jews, that Aristotle is right in declaring that the sense of touch is the most shameful of the senses.

The sex act is especially significant for the Kabbalists, although they insist that it must only be performed "for the sake of Heaven" and not for one's own pleasure. The sex act on earth mirrors, according to the Kabbalists, the mystical marriage of "the Holy One, blessed be He" and His Shekhinah on high. In the writings of the Kabbalists there were detailed descriptions of how husband and wife should embrace (i.e. the husband's right arm should be round the wife's neck) in order to repeat on earth the spiritual associations in the "upper worlds."

In Hasidic thought there is to be observed a tendency to deprecate any kind of pleasure in the sex act. One of the reasons for the Hasidic belief in a hereditary dynasty of *Zaddikim* is that the great *Zaddik*

---

[1] *Emunot ve-Deot*, 10:6 (*Beliefs and Opinions*, trans. Samuel Rosenblatt, pp. 371–373, New Haven, 1973).

[2] II, 36; III, 49.

has only holy thoughts at the time of intercourse and he can therefore bring down from heaven a specially lofty soul into the body of the child conceived at that time. Y. A. Kamelhaar, in his studies of Hasidic masters (*Dor Deah*, 1933), writes in his Introduction, from personal experience, how Hasidic youths recently married would be ashamed to meet their friends when their wives had children because it demonstrated that they had had sexual intercourse. True, they argued, it is a religious duty but one that can be compared to cleaning out the rubbish from the king's palace. One who does this also serves the king but there are higher ways of serving him!

An interesting study by a Hasidic master on the Hasidic attitude to sex is provided in the little work *Sur Me-Ra* (*Keter*, n.d.) by R. Zevi Hirsh of Zhydatchov (d. 1831) with notes by R. Zevi Elimelech Spira (d. 1841). After quoting (pp. 49–50) the rule for the Kabbalists drawn up by R. Hayyim Vital (Introduction to *Ez Hayyim*, Koretz, 1784), "he should sanctify himself at the time of intercourse so that he should derive no pleasure from the act," the author remarks that he had heard from his teacher, the Seer of Lublin (d. 1815), that this can only apply to the attempt to have holy thoughts before the act. "But during the act it is impossible for him not to have pleasure." The Seer quotes the saying of R. Elimelech of Lyzhansk (1717–1787) that there is no benediction before sexual intercourse (as there is before enjoying food) "because this act is impossible without an admixture of the evil inclination" (*Noam Elimelekh*, *Va-yishlah*). The author comments on this:

> However, I always instruct my disciples as follows. Although the Rabbis did not ordain that a full benediction be recited, with God's name and a reference to His sovereignty, the God-fearing man will nevertheless give praise and thanks for the pleasure God, blessed be His name, has given him. In His great mercy and goodness He has given him strength. For all that, a man should keep himself remote from having pleasure in the act so far as he is able. As I have heard it, from my master, the holy Rabbi Dov Baer (the Maggid of Mezhirech), Rabbi Judah the Prince stated on his death-bed that he had never had enjoyment from the world even with his little finger (Kettubot 104a). Rabbi Dov Baer said that this referred to the sanctification of the marital act, as the Rabbis refer

> *to "fingers" in a sexual sense* (Niddah *66a*). *However,*
> *if you do have pleasure in the act, give thanks to your Creator*
> *for it in any language you wish. By so doing you will restore*
> *the pleasure to the One who created it and you will not be*
> *guilty of using sacred things.*

R. Elimelech of Lyzhansk, quoted in the above passage, comments further on this topic (*Noam Elimelekh, Bereshit*) on the verse: "And Adam knew Eve his wife; and she conceived and bore Cain" (Genesis 4:1). Ideally a man's thought at the time of intercourse should be on the divine alone, so much so that he should be unconscious that he is engaging in the act. When Adam became conscious ("knew") of being with his wife they gave birth to Cain, the first murderer. Similarly, of Abraham it is said: "And it came to pass, when he was come near to enter into Egypt, that he said unto Sarah his wife: 'Behold *now* I know that thou art a fair woman'" (Genesis 12:11). Only when he came under the influence of the lewd Egyptians did Abraham become aware that his wife was beautiful.

In modern Jewish thought, until very recently, there have been no discussions of Jewish attitudes to sex. The reason is no doubt because of nineteenth century prudery which was reflected in Jewish writings of the time. Indeed, from the writings of Jewish thinkers writing in European languages in the nineteenth century, one would imagine that Jews had no sexual life. It is only recently, when sex has been more frankly and openly discussed, that modern Jewish thinkers have begun to consider Jewish points of view. "Jewish points of view" is the correct appellation. It can be seen from this survey that there is no single Jewish attitude except that a completely negative view of sex is not possible for thinkers in the authentic Jewish tradition.

Slander

The strongest moral disapproval is expressed in Jewish teachings of slander in all its forms. The prohibition of going up and down as a talebearer is stated in Leviticus (19:16). The prophet Jeremiah (9:2–4) castigates the people for their slanderous tongues:

> *And they bend their tongue, their*
> *bow of falsehood,*
> *And they are grown mighty in the*
> *land, but not for truth;*
> *For they proceed from evil to evil,*
> *And Me they know not,*
> *Saith the Lord.*
> *Take ye heed every one of his neighbor,*
> *And trust ye not in any brother;*
> *For every brother acteth subtly.*
> *And every neighbor goeth about*
> *with slanders.*
> *And they deceive every one his neighbor,*
> *And truth they speak not;*
> *They weary themselves to speak iniquity.*

The Psalmist (Psalms 34:13–15) declares:

> *Who is the man that desireth life,*
> *And loveth days, that he may see good*
> *therein?*
> *Keep thy tongue from evil,*
> *And thy lips from speaking guile.*
> *Depart from evil, and do good,*
> *Seek peace, and pursue it.*

It is curious, however, that Jewish law, as distinct from moral preachment, is less clear on slander as a crime punishable in the courts. The

289

Biblical law (Deuteronomy 22:13–18) rules that a man who slanderously casts doubts on the chastity of his wife is to be punished with a fine and with chastisement. Yet, according to strict Talmudic law, there is no legal redress for slanderous statement, apart from this particular case. The reason for this is the general Talmudic principle *(Bava Kama* 91a) that there is only redress if damage is done to another directly. The courts, however, had to intervene and this they eventually did on the basis of another Talmudic principle *(Sanhedrin* 46a) that a court can assume for itself powers beyond those the law normally gives it if this is for the benefit of society. Thus the celebrated German-Spanish authority, R. Asher b. Jehiel (d. 1327), remarks *(Responsa,* No. 101) that it is the custom of the courts everywhere to impose fines on "those who put others to shame with their words" and to assess the damages according to the social status of the offender and his victim. The *Shulḥan Arukh* (*Ḥoshen Mishpat* 420:38) rules:

> *If a man spits on his neighbor he is liable to pay damages but he should not pay if he only spits on his neighbor's garments or if he shames him verbally. But the courts everywhere and at all times should introduce legislation for this matter as they see fit. Some say that he is to be placed under the ban until he pacifies the victim of his insult, and some say that he is to be flogged. One who slanders his neighbor is to be treated as one who puts him to shame verbally. If a man taunts his neighbor by saying: "I am not an apostate, I am not a criminal," even if he did not add "like you" it is as if he had said "like you." If he said: "You behave like a bastard" or "You are like a bastard" it is nothing. But some authorities disagree, holding that if he said: "You are like a bastard," it is as if he had said "You are a bastard." But if he said: "You tell lies like a bastard," until the matter has been clarified and so forth, since he made it conditional, it is nothing. If a man says to his neighbor: "You are disqualified from acting as a witness in a court of law," some authorities argue that he can offer as his defense that he intended to say that he was disqualified on the grounds of near relationship and that he had no intention of insulting him. But other authorities disagree. If a man slanders those who sleep in the dust, he must take upon himself to fast and*

to repent, and he should be fined by the courts as they see fit. If they are buried nearby he should go to their graves to ask their pardon. If they are buried in a distant place he should send his agent there . . . If a man calls an informer the son of an informer, whereas he alone (and not his father) is an informer, he is not culpable. The same applies if he calls a wicked man the son of a just man or a wicked man the son of a wicked man. If a man calls his neighbor a bastard or a slave and it is true he is not culpable. But if the matter cannot be determined, even though he heard others speak in this way, he cannot be exonerated.

There is no distinction in Jewish law between written and verbal calumny (*Ḥafeẓ Ḥayyim*, 1, 4 & notes.)

Numerous are the Rabbinic teachings condemning the "evil tongue," as slander was called. A habitual slanderer was considered unworthy of meeting the Divine Countenance in the world to come. Whoever made a habit of speaking slander, say the Rabbis, acts as though he denies the existence of God (*Arakhin* 156).

In the last century the saintly scholar R. Israel Meir Kagan (1838–1933) resolved to devote his life to combating the evils of slander and malicious gossip. He decided to further his aim by publishing a work in which all the earlier teachings on slander were set out in the form of a legal code. The work was published anonymously under the title *Ḥafeẓ Ḥayyim* after the verse: "Who is the man that desireth life [*ḥafeẓ ḥayyim*] . . . Keep thy tongue from evil" (Psalms 34:13–14). The fame of the book was such that even after the discovery of the author's identity he was always referred to as "the *Ḥafeẓ Ḥayyim*." Among other things, the *Ḥafeẓ Ḥayyim* demands that the truth be told whenever withholding it would result in harm to others. The following are two examples of this principle:

If A is known as a man lacking integrity in business and B, ignorant of A's bad reputation, is about to enter into partnership with him, it is permitted to warn B of A's unscrupulousness (*Ḥafeẓ Ḥayyim*, Appendix 1). Or, where a marriage is being arranged, and it is known that one of the parties to the marriage is suffering from a disease, it is permitted to inform the other party (Appendix 7). Further points considered in the work are: the prohibition against listening to slander, making libelous statements about the merchandise of a competitor, and praising a person to his enemies, who will react by speaking ill of him. Group defamation is also considered by the *Ḥafeẓ Ḥayyim*. He quotes a Rabbinic interpretation of Isaiah 6:5. The prophet exclaimed: "Woe is me! for I am undone: because I am a man of unclean lips, and I dwell in the midst of a people of unclean lips." The Rabbis place words of condemnation of the prophet in the mouth of God: "You may speak evil of yourself but not of My children."

Slavery

Except for a very few reactionary states, civilized countries everywhere have outlawed slavery of the more obvious kind, in which one person is the property of another for all his life. (Slavery of the more subtle kind—the concept of the individual as completely subordinate to the state, for instance—is, of course, still with us.) On the grosser form of slavery Judaism has no longer any need to speak, but that is because it has already spoken and its message has been heeded. Campaigners against slavery—Wilberforce is one example among many—were indirectly inspired by the teachings of Judaism. A religion which teaches that every man is created in God's image and is, therefore, a person in his own right and not a thing to be used; a religion with freedom from bondage in the Exodus as one of its central themes; a religion which stresses compassion and justice as God's demands on man—such a religion is bound to protest vehemently against slavery.

The historical problem is, however, that both Biblical and Rabbinic law recognize the validity of slavery as an institution, though slavery is never enjoined. During the great struggle over the slavery issue in America in the last century, there were Jews as well as Christians on both sides of the debate. While Rabbi David Einhorn, who risked his life to oppose slavery, declared it to be "the greatest possible crime against God," Rabbi Morris J. Raphall pointed to the Biblical law in support of the institution. Raphall must have been aware that even in the Biblical law a marked tendency can clearly be observed to limit slavery and to demand that slaves be treated humanely. In the Code of Hammurabi, the slave who escapes from his owner has to have his ear cut off. It can hardly be other than a reaction to the law of the time that the law in Exodus rules that a slave who wishes to *remain* a slave when he can go free has to have his ear pierced (Exodus 21:2–6). And the Deuteronomic law states (Deuteronomy 23:15–16):

293

Thou shalt not deliver unto his master the slave who escapes from his master unto thee: he shall dwell with thee, even among you, in that place which he shall choose in one of thy gates, where it liketh him best: thou shalt not oppress him.

But Raphall argued, as many have done before and since, that the Bible does not condemn slavery outright; therefore, what was good enough for Moses is good enough for us. It is hard for some people to give up the attitude expressed in the song of the fundamentalist:

Gimme that old time religion,
Gimme that old time religion,
Gimme that old time religion,
It's good enough for me.
It was good for old Moses,
It was good for old Moses,
It was good for old Moses,
And it's good enough for me.

To have such an approach to the Bible is to be completely unhistorical. The Bible has been described as "eternity expressing itself in time." This means that the eternal values expressed in Biblical teachings, for them to be expressed at all in human language, had to be conveyed, as it were, against the background of a particular period in human history. For Biblical legislation to have outlawed slavery entirely would have been to overthrow society. Institutions such as slavery and polygamy were part of the fabric of ancient society and, it must be appreciated, had sound social and economic reasons to support them at that time but not for all time. Something of this sort is behind the Jewish doctrine of the Oral Law, which constantly sifts and refines and reinterprets the written law so as to make the latter viable in changed circumstances. The Oral Law, as expressed in and through the historical experiences of Israel as the covenant people, states that such commands as "Thou shalt love thy neighbor" are binding for all time and that the command to stone criminals to death was not to be applied in practice. Nowhere in the whole of the Jewish tradition is there a command for men to own slaves. Jews everywhere rejoiced when slavery was eventually abolished and they rejoiced, moreover, not in any spirit of a reluctant acceptance of the forces of social progress, but because abolition of this foul practice accorded fully with the whole tenor of Judaism.

The emphasis on humane treatment of slaves is nowhere seen more clearly, even at a time when the institution was accepted, than in Maimonides' statement at the end of the laws on slavery in his great Code (*Yad, Avadim* 9:8):

> *It is permitted to make a Canaanite slave work with rigor. However, though this is permitted according to the strict letter of the law, it belongs to the trait of saintliness and to the ways of wisdom that a man should be compassionate and fair so that he should not make his yoke rest heavy on his slave and he should not torment him. Rather he should give him to eat of all the food he eats and to drink all that he drinks. The Sages of old used to give their slaves something of every dish they enjoyed themselves. They would see that their animals and slaves were fed before they ate themselves. Behold Scripture says: "As the eyes of slaves unto the hands of their master, as the eyes of a female slave unto the hand of her mistress" (Psalms 123:2). So, too, a man should not insult his slave either by raising his hand to him or by means of words. Scripture gave slaves for service, not that they be shamed. He should not shout at the slave too much and should not be angry with him but should speak gently to him and listen to his complaints. So it is stated explicitly in regard to the good ways of which Job boasted: "If I did despise the cause of my slave, or of my female slave when they contended with me . . . . Did not He that made me in the womb make him" (Job 13:13, 15). Cruelty and tyranny are only to be found among the idolatrous heathen. But as for the seed of Abraham, namely, the people of Israel, upon whom the Holy One, blessed be He, has bestowed the good that is the Torah and whom He commanded just laws and statutes, they are compassionate to all. And so, too, with regard to the qualities of the Holy One, blessed be He, which He commanded us to imitate, it is said: "And His tender mercies are over all His works" (Psalms 145:9). Whoever is himself compassionate will be treated compassionately as it is said: "And He will give thee compassion and have compassion upon thee" (Deuteronomy 13:18).*

When it is realized that Maimonides wrote the above in medieval Egypt and that it was not possible for the sage to get out of his skin, as it were, to anticipate the much later total abolition of slavery, the humaneness of his approach shines through his acceptance of slavery itself. Can there be any doubt which side Maimonides would have taken on the slavery issue if he had been alive in the nineteenth century?

Space Travel

The ability of man to travel to the moon has fired the imagination of men everywhere and there is now much talk of further explorations into space. On the technical aspects of space travel there is, of course, no specifically Jewish point of view. How a spaceship is to be built, launched and monitored is a matter for the experts. But there are wider implications of a religious and ethical nature for which Judaism should be consulted.

First, reference might be made to the religious problems which an observant Jewish astronaut will face. Of purely theoretical interest at the moment, there is nonetheless an Halakhic treatment of this theme by Rabbi David Slush.[1] Is an astronaut bound to recite the *Shema*, wear *tefillin* and the like, and if so, when? (Everyone by now knows the joke about the Jewish astronaut who emerged from the capsule worn out by having to recite the three daily prayers within the ninety minutes it took to circle the world.) Some of Slush's conclusions are doubtful. For instance, he is of the opinion that the astronaut should recite the *Shema* when he goes to sleep and when he rises irrespective of what time it is in the zone of the earth over which he passes. But from the Talmudic discussion at the beginning of *Berakhot* it appears that the "time when men go to sleep" is a definition of time and not of state.

The more serious question is whether space exploration is ethically sound in view of man's failure to solve the problems of war, poverty, and the like which he faces here on earth. Should not the vast amounts of money spent on space travel be better expended on helping the unfortunates of this planet? On the other hand, it is doubtful, to say

[1] "Sabbath and Festival Observance for an Astronaut," in *Torah she-be-al Peh,* pp. 85–94, Jerusalem, 1965, reviewed under the heading "Mitzvah observance for Space Travellers," in *Tradition*, Vol. 8, No. 2, pp. 83–85, Summer, 1966, by Rabbi Immunel Jakabovits.

the least, whether the money would have been made available for these other projects and, it might be argued, God's blessing to man to conquer the "earth" (Genesis 1:28) can be applied to space, since, presumably, whatever man can reach is implied in the word "earth" in this context. In other words, it is possible to see a religious motivation in space travel as in other aspects of man's cultural and intellectual endeavors. Again, in the words of C. S. Lewis, it might be argued that "Great powers might be more usefully but are seldom less dangerously employed than in fabricating costly objects and flinging them, you might say, overboard. Good luck to it! It is an excellent way of letting off steam." Jewish thinkers like A. J. Heschel[1] are, nonetheless, dubious of the whole enterprise from the religious angle. But judging by the enthusiasm with which the majority of Jews hailed the landing on the moon, the prevailing view among Jews seems to be that of acceptance of space travel. Indeed, Rabbi M. M. Kasher[2] somewhat fancifully argues that the fact that the moon landings coincide with the age which saw the emergence of the State of Israel is a fulfillment of the prophecy: "Then the moon shall be confounded, and the sun ashamed; For the Lord of hosts will reign in mount Zion, and in Jerusalem, And before His elders shall be Glory" (Isaiah 24:23).

A question without present-day significance but one that may become acute in the future is what, if any, readjustments in our thinking will be required if it is discovered that there are intelligent, moral creatures on planets other than earth? There are so far only two discussions in English of this question: Rabbi W. Gunther Plaut's consideration of the problem in his *Judaism and the Scientific Spirit*[3] and Rabbi Norman Lamm's *"The Religious Implications of Extraterrestrial Life."*[4] Basically, there is no reason why Jewish faith should be disturbed if it is discovered that God has created other recipients for His love and care than man, although the view held by some medieval Jewish thinkers that the universe was created solely for man's sake will have to be abandoned. For the rest, we can safely leave issues of this kind to the Creator together with other problems concerning the mystery of His creative activities.

---

[1] *New York Post*, May 8, 1958, p. 2.

[2] *Noam*, Vol. 13, 1970.

[3] New York, 1962, pp. 36–39.

[4] *Tradition*, Vol. 7, No. 4; Vol. 8, No. 1, pp. 5–56, Winter 1965–Spring 1966.

Spiritualism

Insofar as Spiritualism is a religion, with hymns, Christian references, and the like, it is obviously at variance with Judaism and it is obvious that no Jew can be at the same time a Spiritualist. But what of attending seances and other attempts at contacting the dead and psychical research?

On the face of it there is a direct Biblical injunction against any attempt at contacting the dead (Deuteronomy 18:10–12):

> *There shall not be found among you any one that maketh his son or his daughter to pass through the fire, one that useth divination, a soothsayer, or an enchanter, or a sorcerer, or a charmer, or one that consulteth a ghost or a familiar spirit, or a necromancer. For whosoever doeth these things is an abomination unto the Lord . . .*

The story of the Witch of En-dor (I Samuel 28) is also relevant. Some of the medieval Jewish thinkers, puzzled by the ability of the woman to raise the spirit of Samuel, declared that she did not really do so but engaged in fraud pure and simple, as many mediums do in modern times.

However, the Rabbinic interpretation of the acts forbidden in Deuteronomy is that these are magical practices in which the wizard spends the night in a cemetery and the like in order to "cause an unclean spirit to rest upon him" (*Sanhedrin* 65b). The matter is further complicated by the curious tale (*Berakhot* 18b) of a "saint" (*Ḥasid*) who spent the night in a cemetery and overheard the ghosts of the dead conversing with one another. In the tale there is no suggestion that the *Ḥasid* acted illegally or sinfully. Maimonides (*Yad, Avodat Koḥavim*, 11:13) is nonetheless quite uncompromising:

> *What is the meaning of necromancy? It refers to one who starves himself and then stays overnight in the cemetery*

299

> *in order that a dead person should visit him in a dream to give him some information he requires. Some say that they [the necromancers] don special garments, utter incantations, burn a special kind of incense, and then sleep alone—in order that a certain dead person should visit him and converse with him in a dream. The principle is as follows: Whoever carries out any act the purpose of which is for a dead person to visit him and impart information, is to be flogged, as it is said: "There shall not be found among you . . . or a necromancer."*

On the other hand in the Commentary to Maimonides' Code (on this passage), known as *Hagahot Maimoni*, by a pupil of R. Meir of Rothenburg (d. 1293) there is a curious distinction made by R. Eleazer of Metz (d. 1198). This is that the prohibition applies only when one inquires of the corpse itself but not of the spirits of the dead. Consequently, in this view, it is permitted for two friends to make a pact to the effect that the one who dies first will return in spirit to the one who remains alive. The *Shulḥan Arukh* (*Yoreh Deah* 179:14) states the position in this way:

> *It is permitted to make a dying person swear to return after his death in order to convey some information he will be asked. And some permit an attempt to do this even after the person has died provided that he does not conjure the actual corpse but the ghost of the dead man.*

The point here is that in the first instance there is no offense since when the promise is made the man is still alive. The second opinion goes further and understands the whole prohibition as referring only to an attempt somehow to conjure up the actual corpse and not the spirit or ghost of the dead. Rabbi Ẓevi Hirsh Spira of Munkacs (d. 1913), in his *Darkhei Teshuvah* (*Yoreh Deah* 179, Note 6), quotes recent authorities who have considered the question of table-rapping and holds that this is strictly forbidden under the heading of magical practices.

The question of whether spiritualistic activities are permitted was asked of Rabbi A. I. Kook in a letter dated 1912.[1] The questioner evidently was of the opinion that if attempts to contact the spirits of

---

[1] *Da'at Kohen*, 2nd edition, No. 69, pp. 165–168, Jerusalem, 1969.

the dead were shown to be successful it would deal a blow to any materialistic philosophy and would be a cause of strengthening religious faith. After quoting the views mentioned above, Rabbi Kook concludes:

> *It does not seem worth it in my humble opinion to strengthen faith by means of such dubious methods which can easily lead to forbidden practices. It is far better to obey the injunction: "Thou shalt be whole-hearted with the Lord thy God" (Deuteronomy 18:13)* . . . *All this I see fit to reply to you in brief as it appears to me. But it is obvious that it is impossible for me to express any* definite *opinion before I know certain details of this deep and mysterious business.*
> [Author's emphasis.]

In a postscript Rabbi Kook adds: "It is proper for the holy nation to cleave only to the Lord God of life."

In other words, it is not clearly stated that attendance at a seance for purposes of psychical research or even sheer curiosity is forbidden. But, as Rabbi Kook says, this is by the strict letter of the law. The Jew who believes in "the Lord God of life" should have no desire to pierce the veil and should be concerned with the duties to God and man on this side of the grave.

Sport

There are not many references to sport in the classical sources but this is in all probability purely coincidental and not due to lack of interest. Archery was practiced as a sport in ancient Israel, as can be seen from the story of David and Jonathan (I Samuel 20:21–22). Jeremiah's reference to "contending with horses" (12:5) has been understood as meaning a kind of athletic contest, but this is very uncertain. The Psalmist's reference to the strong man running his course (Psalms 19:6) is much clearer, though even here the reference may not necessarily be to sport. The Mishnah (*Sukkah* 5:4) and the Talmudic comments to it refer to pious men in Temple times on the festival of Tabernacles dancing and juggling lighted torches. Ball games were played in Talmudic times. The Midrash (*Lamentations Rabbah* 2:4) gives as a reason for the destruction of Jerusalem that ball games were played on the Sabbath. However, in medieval France ball games were permitted on the Sabbath in private, though not in public (Tosafists *Bezah* 12a). The *Shulḥan Arukh* (*Oraḥ Ḥayyim* 308:45) records two opinions on the permissibility of playing ball games on the Sabbath. Details of Jewish sports and pastimes among medieval Jews are to be found in Israel Abraham's *Jewish Life in the Middle Ages*.[1] In more recent times in Eastern Europe horseback riding was enjoyed by many Jews. There are even tales of some of the Ḥasidic masters being fond of this sport.

The values promoted by sporting activities—health, the team spirit, refreshment of mind and body—are acceptable to Judaism. But it can be argued that sports such as boxing and wrestling, in which violence is consciously done to the person, are hardly in keeping with the spirit of Judaism. One of the Talmudic Rabbis said (*Sanhedrin* 58b) that whoever lifts up his hand against his neighbor is called "wicked" and

[1] pp. 373–378, Philadelphia, 1911.

Doron Mordechai, aged 97, with his grandson, in the Israel Four-Day March, April 1963.

he quotes in support the verse: "And he said to the wicked one: 'Wherefore smitest thou thy fellow?'" (Exodus 2:13). Although both contestants in a boxing match agree to participate and therefore allow one another to inflict any injuries they can, Jewish law forbids a man to allow another to harm him physically. In the *Shulḥan Arukh* of R. Shneor Zalman of Lyady (Part V, *Nizkei Guf va-Nefesh*, 5) he formulates it in this way: "It is forbidden for a man to hit his neighbor even if the latter authorizes him to do so since a man has no right to harm his own body." This is based on the idea that a man's body is not his own to destroy or to harm since he belongs to God. In an interesting study of the Shylock trial according to Jewish law, Rabbi S. Zevin[1] puts this forward as one of the reasons why a Shylock contract, in which a man promises to give a pound of flesh if he does not pay his debts, would be null and void in Jewish law. Even cruelty to animals is strictly forbidden in Judaism, and it goes without saying that cruelty to human beings is forbidden. Consequently, cruel sports should be anathema

[1] *Le-Or ha-Halakhah*, pp. 181–196, Jerusalem, 1946.

to the Jewish conscience. It is also obvious that Judaism would frown on the practice of "throwing" games for financial and other gain on the general grounds of the strongest disapproval of dishonest practices.

Sterilization

A useful summary of the treatment of this question in the Responsa literature of recent years is provided by Rabbi I. Jakobovits in *Essays Presented to Chief Rabbi Israel Brodie on the Occasion of his Seventieth Birthday*.[1] The background is as follows.

The Biblical law has it that a priest who "hath his stones crushed" must not serve in the Sanctuary (Leviticus 21:20) because he has a "blemish" compared in the verse to other persons with blemishes such as a hunchback or a dwarf. The Deuteronomic law (Deuteronomy 23:2) rules: "He that is crushed or maimed in his privy parts shall not enter into the assembly of the Lord." The Rabbis understand this to mean that he must not marry. The Mishnah (*Shabbat* 14:3) rules that since it is forbidden to drink medicine on the Sabbath it is forbidden to drink a certain "cup of roots" (*kos ikkarim*) which is a cure for jaundice. The Talmud (*Shabbat* 110a) comments on this that the mixture while efficacious for jaundice causes the sufferer to become impotent and from the subsequent discussion (*Shabbat* 110b–111a) it emerges that it is forbidden for a man to drink this potion because it falls under the heading of castration, which prohibition the Rabbis derive from the verse: "Neither shall ye do thus in your land" (Leviticus 22:24), i.e., you shall not do thus to yourselves. The passage concludes that the full prohibition of "Neither shall ye do . . ." does not apply to a woman but that a woman, too, is forbidden to drink such a potion because she, too, is obliged to have children. However, in another Talmudic passage (*Yevamot* 85b) it is said that the obligation to have children does not devolve on a woman and that, therefore, the wife of R. Ḥiyya, who had severe pain in giving birth to two sets of twins, resolved to drink the "cup of roots" in order to prevent further pregnancies. On the basis of this the ruling is that any interference with the organs of generation

---

[1] pp. 193–4, London, 1967.

by a direct act is forbidden but that a woman may drink the "cup of roots" (according to some authorities only if she has severe pains in childbirth, according to others even if she has not). We are no longer in possession of the facts about the "cup of roots" (does modern medicine recognize any such thing?) but, of course, this does not affect the principles laid down.

The *Shulḥan Arukh* (*Even ha-Ezer* 5:11–12) rules (and the ruling is accepted by all Orthodox authorities) that any act which prevents the organs of generation from functioning is forbidden whether performed on a man or woman or even an animal. A woman is, however, permitted to sterilize herself by means of the "cup of roots." That is why some Orthodox authorities, incidentally, tend to permit women to use the pill, a modern form, in fact, of the Talmudic "cup of roots," and even better, since it appears that the "cup of roots" was irreversible.

Stoicism

The stoic attitude to life involves a refusal to yield to sorrow, anguish or pain or even to be greatly affected by them. Stoicism is today more of a mood than a philosophy, so that it is somewhat pointless to discuss what Judaism has to say about it. No doubt there have been Jews who faced life stoically as there have been Jews with the opposite approach. A good deal here depends on individual temperament. Nevertheless, Judaism does not normally encourage its adherents to be impervious to suffering. Of course, there are Rabbinic teachings about the acceptance of suffering in love, but that is a very different thing from indifference to pain. The Jewish laws of mourning are relevant. Mourning customs are enjoined when one of the near relatives dies—father, mother, husband, wife, sister, brother, son, and daughter. The purpose of it all is to give expression to the natural grief one feels and there is no suggestion anywhere in the Jewish sources that there is something unworthy about mourning or weeping when a loss is sustained. In the Bible, for example, there are many references to people being moved to tears when confronted by death or suffering. The idea that it is unbecoming for a grown-up man to shed tears is completely foreign to the Biblical record. On the contrary, a man's emotions are as much a part of him as his intellect and it is more a sign of nobility than otherwise when a man is deeply moved. The third century Palestinian teacher R. Eleazar said (*Berakhot* 32b) that after the destruction of the Temple the gates of prayer are closed but the gates of tears are still open. The great Jewish masters of prayer were often observed pouring out their hearts in tearful supplication for the sufferings of Israel and of humanity as a whole. Maimonides, who can hardly be accused of a too emotional approach, expresses the Jewish attitude effectively when he says (*Yad, Evel* 13:11–12) that to mourn too much when a near relative dies is foolish since one cannot do other than accept the inevitable. But, Maimonides goes on to say, anyone who does not mourn is cruel.

307

The meaning is that far from a failure to be moved being evidence of a lofty soul, it demonstrates that a man has no real feelings. He is hard-hearted and cruel. The loss of his near ones fails to move him because his love was weak in the first place.

Strikes

One cannot expect any direct reference to the problem of strikes in the classical sources because, before the industrial age, the economic forms of society were quite different. Among other differences is that in Biblical and Rabbinic times, workmen did not hire themselves out as more or less permanent employees of a particular employer, nor was there much organized labor. Nevertheless, there are important principles laid down governing the rights of workmen and those can be applied to our situation. In the State of Israel attempts have been made to find some guidance in the ancient Jewish sources. Among Responsa on the subject there is a full-scale treatment, upon which the following relies heavily, by Rabbi K.P. Tkursh.[1]

In Biblical law (Leviticus 19:13; Deuteronomy 24:14–15) there are stern injunctions against keeping back the wages of a workman. The *Sifrei* (Deuteronomy 279) comments:

> *Why does this workman ascend the highest scaffolding and risk his life if you do not pay him his wages as soon as they are due?*

Among other Rabbinic rulings regarding the rights of workmen is the rule that a workman hired for a day can break the contract in the middle of the day if he so wishes (*Bava Meẓia* 10a) though in the Talmudic discussion this right is somewhat qualified. In a ruling based on the Talmud (*Ketubbot* 105a), Maimonides (*Yad, Shekalim* 4:7) records:

> *Those who kept the scrolls in order in Jerusalem and the judges who decided in cases of robbery in Jerusalem received their wages from the Temple treasury. How much did they receive?*

[1] *Keter Efrayim,* No. 19, pp. 260–271, Tel Aviv, 1967; oddly enough, not listed in the table of contents.

309

> *Ninety manehs a year. If this amount was insufficient, the wages should be increased, even if they objected to the increase, so as to be adequate for their own provisions and for those of their wives and families.*

A workman's right to eat some of the food he produces is discussed at length in *Bava Meẓia* (Ch. 7–8) and codified in detail in the *Shulḥan Arukh* (*Ḥoshen Mishpat* 337). The Talmud (*Sukkah* 51b; *Bava Kama* 116b) speaks with approval of craftsmen organizing themselves in guilds for their own protection. Similarly, the Talmud (*Bava Batra* 8b–9a) rules that the people of each locality are entitled to determine democratically such matters as prices and wages.

The following Talmudic passage (*Yoma* 38a) is also relevant:

> *Our Rabbis taught: The house of Garmu was expert in preparing the shewbread, but would not teach it. The Sages sent for specialists from Alexandria of Egypt, who knew how to bake as well as they, but did not know how to take the loaves down from the oven as well . . . When the Sages heard this, they quoted: "Everyone that is called by My name I have created for My glory" (Isaiah 43:7) and they said: Let the house of Garmu return to their office. The Sages sent for them, but they would not come. Then they doubled their wages and they came. Before this they used to get 12 manehs for the day. After this, 24 manehs . . . The Sages said to them: What reason did you have for refusing to teach your skills? They replied: In our father's house they know that this House [the Temple] will be destroyed, and perhaps an unworthy man would learn the art and then serve an idol with it.*

In the same passage a similar story is repeated about the house of Avtinas, who was expert in preparing the incense but would not teach the art.

None of this amounts to a clear statement about strikes in the modern sense but there can be no doubt that the sentiments expressed are those which would justify the organization of workers into trade unions with the perfectly legitimate right to strike. Naturally, Judaism encourages its adherents to avoid industrial as well as other forms of strife. The ideal social order is where fair wages and conditions of employment can be negotiated favorably without recourse to strikes and lockouts.

Sturm und Drang

It is extremely hard to judge but it would seem that some Jewish teachers never experienced religious doubts, never passed through a period of crisis, always were composed and serene in their beliefs. Maimonides and the Gaon of Vilna are perhaps the best examples of such religious stability. If one reads the early writings of Maimonides and compares them with the works written in his maturity and old age, one notices hardly any change of view, all the more remarkable in that this great thinker's works were all largely concerned with the philosophical problems of faith. Maimonides wrote his *Guide for the Perplexed,* but he himself never appears to have had anything about which to be perplexed. There were, however, among Jewish teachers more turbulent souls for whom faith was won only with difficulty. Some of these can be noted here.

In the first half of the second century there flourished in Palestine a group of great teachers, the most prominent of which was Rabbi Akiva. A member of the group was Elisha b. Abuyah, the teacher of R. Meir. Elisha eventually became estranged from Judaism and there are differing reports on how his hostility expressed itself. They all agree that he was a renowned student of the Torah and some of his sayings are, in fact, quoted in the Rabbinic literature. In a well known but very cryptic passage (*Hagigah* 14b) Elisha is said to have been one of the four who "entered Paradise." This no doubt refers to some kind of mystical contemplation and the result was, according to the sources, that Elisha became an apostate unlike Akiva who "entered and returned in peace." There are differing opinions as to whether Elisha repented before he died. Milton Steinberg's novel on Elisha's life has the revealing title of *As a Driven Leaf.*

Other much more recent teachers who appear to have gone through a *Sturm and Drang* period to emerge, however, successfully were R. Moses Hayyim Luzzatto (1707–1747) and the two famous Hasidic

311

masters, R. Naḥman of Bratslav (d. 1810), great-grandson of the Ba'al Shem Tov, and R. Menahem Mendel of Kotsk (d. 1859). In a fine study *(Ha-Kushya be-Torat R. Naḥman mi-Bratslav)*,[1] J. G. Weiss has analyzed the complex thought of R. Naḥman. His was a soul in which faith and doubt struggled unceasingly so that the only way in which he could find relief was to adopt a complete and even to some extent irrational acceptance of faith and to embrace the paradox as an essential ingredient in faith. R. Naḥman, in fact, resembles very strongly his near contemporary Søren Kierkegaard. A particularly striking formulation of R. Naḥman (*Likutei Maharan, Tinyana*, 52) is:

> *It is entirely proper that objections be found to God. It is right and suitable that this should be so because of God's greatness and exaltedness. Since in His exaltedness He is so elevated above our minds there are bound to be objections to Him.*

A saying in similar vein attributed to R. Naḥman is in the form of a comment to the verse: "And the people stood afar off; but Moses drew near unto the thick darkness where God was" (Exodus 20:18). The ordinary people are afraid of the darkness but Moses draws near to it and discovers God in the very darkness of doubt. As for R. Menahem Mendel of Kotsk, it is still a mystery what exactly happened on the ill-fated Friday night of which the Ḥasidim speak with bated breath. It is certain, however, that afterwards the Rabbi lived the life of a recluse, abandoned by some of his followers, venerated all the more by others.

A Ḥasidic tale relates that a man came to R. Ḥayyim of Zans (d. 1876) and complained that he failed to understand what he was doing when he recited the *Ani Ma'amin* ("I believe with perfect faith . . ."), the Jewish confession of faith. "If I do not believe, why do I say that I do? And if I do believe, why do I sin?" R. Ḥayyim is reported as replying that *Ani Ma'amin* was not so much a declaration of faith as a prayer to believe!

---

[1] In the Salman Schocken Jubilee Volume, *Ale Ayin*, pp. 245–291, Jerusalem, 1952.

Theater

Although there is no evidence of theatrical performances in ancient Israel, some of the Biblical literature gives the impression of being composed for public recitation in dramatic form. The Book of Job, for instance, is a great dramatic poem in which each speaker has his part in the development of the argument. In the Hellenistic world the Jews were certainly aware of the cultural institutions of that world and some of them must have participated in them. But in the Rabbinic literature, when theaters are mentioned it is to express strong disapproval. A typical comment is that of the *Sifra* (to Leviticus 15:3) on the verse: "Neither shall ye walk in their statutes" (Leviticus 18:3). The *Sifra* understands this as a prohibition against attending "theaters, circuses and race-courses." The intention was clearly to keep Jews far away from pagan gatherings. The Rabbis viewed with horror the spectacle of gladiators pitted against one another and against wild beasts and there is evidence that in the theater of that time it was not unusual for comedians to mock the Jews and their religion. During the Middle Ages, Jewish communities occasionally staged theatrical performances of a kind, especially on the festival of Purim.

The theater in modern times is a major art medium with an appeal to anyone interested in the riches of language, the communication of human emotions and the problems and conflicts of the human scene. As with the cinema and television, the Jew, influenced by his religion, will not necessarily approve of every theatrical performance. But the need to exercise discrimination is no excuse for any wholesale condemnation of the theater, which, in any event, very few Jews would make nowadays. Judaism sees nothing wrong with harmless entertainment, but the contemporary theater involves more. Insofar as the theater makes people more conscious of life's complexities and heightens their awareness of themselves and others, it can make a contribution to a broadening of mind and sympathy that Judaism can only view with approval.

Tobacco

When tobacco first began to be used in Europe there was considerable prejudice against. it. Israel Abrahams[1] claims that the objections were only raised by the Church but that "Jewish Rabbis, on the other hand, hailed the use of tobacco as an aid to sobriety." Abrahams also noted that, so far as its use in Europe is concerned, tobacco was discovered by a Jew, Luis de Torres, a companion of Columbus.

The use of tobacco was discussed by the legal authorities from a number of points of view. One of the questions was whether a benediction should be recited over tobacco. The Talmudic Rabbis coined benedictions for eating and drinking in obedience to the principle that God should be praised and thanked when man enjoys His gifts. The Rabbis had no knowledge of tobacco but now that this new means of enjoyment was available the question was whether a benediction should be recited over it? The question was considered by the celebrated commentator to the *Shulḥan Arukh*, R. Abraham Gombiner (d. 1683), in his *Magen Avraham*.[2] Gombiner remarks:

> *Further thought has to be given to the question of those who place the herb known as tobacco into a pipe which they light and inhale the smoke and then exhale it. The problem is whether this is to be compared to one who tastes food but does not swallow it, in which case no benediction is required. Or whether it should rather be compared to smelling sweet spices over which a benediction is required, and this would apply here* a fortiori *since there is bodily pleasure in that some people are as sated from smoking as if they had enjoyed food and drink. Further thought is required.*

[1] *Jewish Life in the Middle Ages,* pp. 138–9, Philadelphia, 1911.
[2] *Oraḥ Ḥayyim,* 210, note 9.

314

The custom, however, is not to recite a benediction over tobacco.

Other legal questions connected with tobacco are:

Is it permitted to smoke on a festival? The prevailing opinion is in the affirmative (except when it coincides with the Sabbath). Is it permitted to smoke on the Fast of Av? Most authorities permit it after midday. Is it permitted to take snuff on Yom Kippur? The authorities permit it on the grounds that the definition of "fasting" embraces only abstention from food and drink and not from tobacco. Is it permitted to smoke in the synagogue? Rabbi David Hoffmann (1843–1921) in his *Melammed le-Ho'il*[1] quotes the authorities for and against and concludes that it is forbidden. Since Christians do not smoke in their churches it would be a profanation of God's name (*ḥillul ha-shem*) if Jews gave the impression that they behaved with less reverence in their houses of worship.

Among the Ḥasidim tobacco occupied an important role. There are many references to the subject in Ḥasidic writings and Ḥasidic lore. Some of these are mentioned in A.I. Sperling's *Ta'amei ha-Minhagim*,[2] A. Wertheim's *Halakhot ve-Halikhot ba-Ḥasidut*,[3] and M. Wilensky's *Ḥasidim u-Mitnaggedim*.[4] Some of the Ḥasidic masters looked upon tobacco as the modern equivalent of incense in Temple times and would smoke a pipe before they offered their prayers. In the Lurianic Kabbalah there are "holy sparks" in all things to be released and reclaimed for the holy by the deeds of man. It was said that tobacco was discovered and brought to Europe so that the especially subtle "sparks" found in the herb might be elevated by the *Ẓaddikim*. One of the later Hasidic masters said that tobacco was used by pagan savages before it was brought to Europe. Its use by the Ḥasidim raises the weed from the profane to the holy in that no one is ashamed to accept from another a peck of snuff or a pipeful of tobacco and so acts of benevolence are carried out through it all the time.[5] The smoking of a pipe by the Ḥasidim must have been an early practice. In the polemics against the early Ḥasidim published by Wilensky there are repeated accusations that the Ḥasidim waste hours in smoking. The Ba'al Shem Tov's *lulke* fre-

[1] Vol. I, No. 15, p. 11, Frankfort, 1926.

[2] p. 102, Jerusalem edition, 1957.

[3] pp. 224–5, Jerusalem, 1960.

[4] Index: *ishun be-mikteret*, Jerusalem, 1970.

[5] R. David Moses of Tchortkow, *Divrei David*, p. 66, Husiatin, 1904.

quently turns up in Ḥasidic legend. It is even reported that the Ba'al Shem Tov used to recite a benediction before smoking his pipe.

Rabbi S. Zevin[1] reports a curious episode about smoking in the life of the famous yeshivah head R. Baruch Ber Leibovitz (1866–1939). R. Baruch Ber had an original way of "smoking" cigarettes. He would place a cigarette in his mouth and chew and suck it without ever lighting it, deriving a certain amount of satisfaction in this way. The reason for it was that his father once gave him a cigarette but his teacher, seeing him smoking, said: "Why should you smoke?" Anxious to satisfy the demands of both his father and his teacher, he decided to take cigarettes into his mouth without lighting them.

In recent years cigarette smoking has been severely criticized by the medical profession on the grounds that it can lead to heart disease, emphysema, and especially lung cancer. In an interesting article, which seems nonetheless to have been ignored, Moses Aberbach[2] has argued that, in view of the risks, cigarette smoking should be held to be forbidden. According to all the Halakhic sources a Jew is not allowed to take risks when health is at stake.

[1] *Ishim ve-Shittot,* Tel Aviv, 1952, pp. 278–9.
[2] "Smoking and the Halakhah," in *Tradition,* Vol. 10, No. 3, Spring 1969, pp. 49–60.

Tolerance

It has to be appreciated that religious tolerance is in the main a modern notion advanced by thinkers like Spinoza, John Locke, and John Stuart Mill, who broke consciously with tradition in this matter. There are certain ideas of value to men today which are simply not found in earlier writings. The majority of Jews today have accepted this position as the only one possible and desirable in a pluralistic society. This means, however, that we shall look in vain for anything like the modern ideal in the classical sources of Judaism, but no one with a sense of history will expect it to be otherwise.

The most striking fact which emerges from the Biblical writings in the matter of tolerance is that the prophets of ancient Israel were totally uncompromising with apostasy and idolatry among their own people but tolerant of the idolatry of their pagan neighbors who had no opportunity to know the God of Israel. The prophets do castigate the neighboring peoples for the atrocities they commit in the furtherance of their cult—Moloch worship is a case in point—but nowhere do we find in the Bible that the worship of the pagan gods by the nations is condemned in itself. So far as the internal life of the people was concerned, the Hebrew prophets had to be ruthless if the long struggle against idolatry was to have been successful. The cry of Elijah was echoed by all the prophets (I Kings 18:21):

> How long halt ye between two opinions? if the Lord be God, follow Him; but if Baal, follow him.

Similarly, while the Deuteronomist declares that the gods of the nations were "allotted" to them by God Himself (Deuteronomy 4:19), he is altogether ruthless when it comes to Israel worshiping strange gods (13:13–19):

> If thou shalt hear tell concerning one of thy cities, which the Lord thy God giveth thee to dwell there, saying: "Certain

317

> *base fellows are gone out from the midst of thee, and have*
> *drawn away the inhabitants of their city, saying: Let us go*
> *and serve other gods, which ye have not known; then shalt thou*
> *inquire, and make search, and ask diligently; and behold*
> *if it be truth, and the thing certain, that such abomination*
> *is wrought in the midst of thee; thou shalt surely smite the*
> *inhabitants of that city with the edge of the sword, destroying*
> *it utterly, and all that is therein and the cattle thereof, with*
> *the edge of the sword. And thou shalt gather all the spoil*
> *of it into the midst of the broad place thereof, and shalt*
> *burn with fire the city, and all the spoil thereof every whit,*
> *unto the Lord thy God; and it shall be a heap for ever; it*
> *shall not be built again. And there shall cleave nought of*
> *the devoted thing to thy hand, that the Lord may turn from*
> *the fierceness of His anger, and show thee mercy, and have*
> *compassion upon thee, and multiply thee, as He hath sworn*
> *unto thy fathers; when those shalt hearken to the voice of*
> *the Lord thy God, to keep all His commandments which*
> *I command thee this day, to do that which is right in the eyes*
> *of the Lord thy God.*

It should nonetheless be noted that, as the Rabbis remark, this passage is academic. There is no record of this kind of procedure ever having been carried out in the history of Judaism.

Among the Rabbis, too, there appears the distinction between tolerance to those outside and those within. The Rabbis teach everywhere that converts to Judaism can only be accepted if they come of their own free will. But there are numerous instances in Rabbinic literature of coercion in matters of belief and practice so far as Jews are concerned. Maimonides (*Yad, Edut* 11:10) observes that unbelievers (*epikorsim*) have to be destroyed and have no share in the world to come. Twentieth century Orthodox thinkers declare that these rules no longer apply. According to Rabbi A. I. Kook, present-day unbelievers are quite different from the defiant *epikoros* of whom the Rabbis speak, while the famous Talmudist R. Abraham Isaiah Karelitz (1878–1953), known as the "Ḥazon Ish," declares that nowadays we must try so far as we can to bring them back to the truth by means of the cords of love and to help them to see the light."[1]

---

[1] For these two opinions, see *Encyclopedia Talmudit*, Vol. 2, p. 137.

Torture

Torture for the purpose of extracting confessions is prevalent in many parts of the world. Together with brutal elements of punishment it has, however, been banished in civilized countries. There can be no doubt that Judaism with its stress on compassion, its hatred of violence, and its respect for human dignity, approves of the abolition of torture.

The Talmudic Rabbis were fully aware of the limited capacity of man to withstand pain. In a remarkable passage (*Ketubbot* 33b) it is said that a severe flogging is worse than death and that if Hananiah, Mishael and Azariah had been flogged they would have worshiped the golden image. For all that there are many instances in the history of Jewish martyrdom of men and women suffering the most horrible torture rather than being false to the faith of their ancestors.

It is worthy of note that in Jewish law a man can never be punished as a result of his own confession of guilt. Witnesses to his guilt are required by the court and his own testimony has no validity (*Yevamot* 25b). The reason is in all probability that a man may condemn himself in a fit of temper or under duress, confessing to a crime that he did not commit. Nowhere, in fact, in the whole range of discussion in Jewish law regarding penal methods, is there any suggestion that the courts are entitled to resort to torture as a means of extracting confessions.

319

Tradition

Tevye in *Fiddler on the Roof* speaks of his people's loyalty to "Tradition" where the original Yiddish version of the story has "Torah." The change may have been unconscious but is revealing. The idea of Jewish observances being carried out because such is the Jewish way of life or the tradition is comparatively new. The classical sources prefer to speak of the Torah, which has to be followed because it is true and not because it is a way that others have tried. For the religious mind there is even a kind of betrayal in the appeal to tradition in that it might pander to ancestor worship and act as a barrier between the individual and his God. Kierkegaard, for instance, protested against the notion that he should obey the demands of his religion because millions of others had obeyed in the past. For Kierkegaard, the fact that others had obeyed was a reason for him not to obey. The religious man wishes to know what God would have him do, not what the tradition would have him do, even when he sees the demands of God conveyed to him through the tradition. Rabbi S. Zevin has acutely said that in modern times some Jewish thinkers have inverted the old saying that the *minhag* ("custom") of Israel is Torah, so that it reads: the Torah of Israel is *minhag*. That is why in the later development of Jewish law not every custom of the past has to be followed and one frequently comes across such sayings as: "This is a foolish custom"; "This custom is unfounded"; "The Hebrew word for custom (*minhag*) has the same letters as those of the word for Hell" (*gehinnom*).

The classical Jewish view in this matter is that tradition is of great value but only insofar as it serves as a means of worshiping God. Judaism as a historical religion naturally gives considerable binding force to the ways of the past because it is in these that God's will becomes revealed. There is an appeal to tradition in Moses' song (Deuteronomy 32:7):

> *Remember the days of old,*
> *Consider the years of many generations,*

Ask thy father, and he will
declare unto thee,
Thine elders, and they will
tell thee.

David Gans (1541–1613), the author of *Zemah David*, one of the earliest works on Jewish history, quotes this verse as Biblical support for the study of Jewish history. A Talmudic interpretation (*Berakhot* 35b) understands the "father" in the verse: "Hear my son, the instruction of thy father, and forsake not the teaching of thy mother" (Proverbs 1:8) to be God and the "mother" the Community of Israel. Solomon Schechter's idea of "Catholic Israel" as the source of Jewish teaching and its deciding factor is based on Rabbinic views of this kind. The verse in Proverbs is also applied by the Rabbis (*Pesahim* 50b) to local and parental customs which are binding upon those affected by them.

In short, the Jewish tradition itself is that of Jewish tradition deriving its authority not from and in itself but from God. Tradition is helpful as a guide. It is not a god to be worshiped.

Transplants

A summary of contemporary Rabbinic discussions on the ethics of organic transplants is given by Rabbi Immanuel Jakobovits in *Essays Presented to Chief Rabbi Israel Brodie on the Occasion of his Seventieth Birthday*.[1] Some of the decisions quoted by Rabbi Jakobovits seem most reasonable. Others are bizarre in the extreme. Most authorities permit a man to donate his eyes to be used after his death for the purpose of corneal transplanting. Indeed, there are views that it is meritorious to do so. But what are we to make of the following? "One rabbi also urges informing the donor that the gift of his eyes, however meritorious, may compromise his atonement after death by reason of the deliberate mutilation of his body. Another rabbi, however, insisting on the inviolability of any Jewish body after death, is prepared to sanction *post-mortem* transplants to the living only if taken from non-Jews" (*sic*). The truth is that discussions by Jewish teachers on organic transplants are as recent as the new methods themselves and the whole subject still awaits careful study. It is possible here to state only the general principles involved.

No Jewish thinker has objected to surgical transplants on the grounds that this is to interfere with nature. The Jewish view is that the doctor is obliged to save lives if he can and the preservation of life comes first. Although it is forbidden to benefit from a corpse or its organs and it is also forbidden to mutilate a corpse these prohibitions can be set aside in order to save a life. These principles would also cover the right to perform heart transplants if life can be prolonged thereby. Naturally, it is essential to make sure that the man from whom the organ is being removed for the transplant is really dead. The heart is a physical organ and a transplant does not affect any change in the patient's character. If one day, though it is extremely unlikely that this will ever happen,

[1] pp. 188–189, London, 1967.

322

brain transplants will become possible, serious moral questions will have to be answered since the brain does influence the character.

Rabbi Solomon B. Freehof[1] discusses whether the transplanting of a pig's heart into a human body would be permitted according to the Jewish legal tradition. Freehof remarks that the saving of life takes precedence and the operation may be performed. In this he is undoubtedly right but not when he refers to the prohibition against benefit from a pig being set aside. In fact, there is no need to "set it aside" since there is no prohibition. In Jewish law the pig is forbidden as food but one may benefit from it.

[1] *Modern Reform Responsa*, No. 37, pp. 217–222, Cincinnati, 1971.

Truth

"The seal of the Holy One, blessed be He, is truth" (*Shabbat*, 55a). This Rabbinic saying is typical of Jewish regard for truth. God is to be found where there is truth. His absence is felt where there is falsehood.

All the Jewish moralists are eloquent in advocating truthfulness. As an example we may quote from Rabbi Isaac Aboab's *Menorat ha-Ma'or* ("Candelabrum of Light"—fourteenth century). In the section dealing with the virtue of truthfulness (Part II, 2:2) Aboab refers to the verses: "The Lord God is truth" (Jeremiah 10:10) and "Thy Torah is truth" (Psalms 119:142). Telling lies in order to mislead others, says Aboab, is a serious offense but even the telling of comparatively harmless lies is forbidden. "They have taught their tongue to speak lies, they weary themselves to commit iniquity" (Jeremiah 9:4). The verse: "And speaketh the truth in his heart" (Psalms 15:2) means that a God-fearing person should keep a promise even if he only made it in his heart. This is based on the Talmudic tale of R. Safra, who was approached to sell something he had and was offered a price which suited him but was unable at the time to signify his consent because he was reciting his prayers and was unable to interrupt them. The buyer, under the impression that R. Safra had rejected his bid, kept on increasing the price but R. Safra insisted on selling for the original price to which he had consented "in his heart." Aboab continues:

> There are other matters which fall under the heading of falsehood; for example, when a man praises himself for having virtues he does not really possess. It sometimes happens that a man may persuade his friend into believing that he has spoken well of him or done him a good turn when, in fact, he has done nothing of the kind. In this connection our Rabbis teach that it is forbidden to mislead others even

324

if they are heathens. Another example is one who promises to do something for his neighbor and fails to carry out his promise. All this is to fulfill the verse: "The remnant of Israel shall not do iniquity, nor speak lies, neither shall a deceitful tongue be found in their mouth" (Zechariah 3:13). The meaning is that even where nothing iniquitous is involved, they shall not have a deceitful tongue in their mouth but all their words should be truthful. Some liars mislead their neighbors into believing that they are friends, who have their welfare at heart, but their real purpose is only to win their neighbor's confidence so as to be able to harm him. Of those it is said: "One speaketh peaceably to his neighbor with his mouth, but in his heart he layeth wait for him" (Jeremiah 9:7). The verse goes on to say: "Shall I not punish them for these things? saith the Lord; shall not My soul be avenged on such a nation as this?" (Jeremiah 9:8). Other liars have their eyes on future benefits and tell lies in order to persuade their neighbors to give them gifts. Other liars mislead their neighbors by telling lies so as to obtain something of value from them or from others so that they can steal it for themselves. The Rabbis compare this to idolatry for this is precisely what the idolators do when they pretend that their gods have power.

In addition to truthfulness in the moral and ethical sphere, the Jewish teachers stress the need for intellectual honesty. All the Talmudic debates are founded on the need to arrive at the truth, to refuse to be cowed by the brilliance of an argument if it is unfounded, to examine the evidence and follow wherever it leads. In the Middle Ages, the great Jewish thinkers' attempts at reconciling the rival claims of reason and revelation, and the bold steps they were prepared to take in order to realize their aim, were based on a determination to see the truth and nothing but the truth. The fact that many of their solutions are outdated should not blind us to the courage and integrity of their endeavors. The similar attempts by modern Jewish thinkers to face the challenges provided by new knowledge, including the new and more scientific picture of how the Bible, for instance, came to be composed, were also motivated by the belief that truth is one and must be upheld even if it involves the surrender of cherished, traditional positions. The protest by numerous profound Talmudists against the excesses of *pilpul* (literally "pepper"), the far-fetched though scintillating dialectics and schemes of association of diverse concepts, in which some students indulged themselves, was based on their conviction that the truth was to be discovered by patient analysis rather than by intellectual fireworks and that the craving for novelty was likely to lead away from the truth. The stern admonitions to the judges against accepting gifts from one of the parties to a dispute were made because once the judge had placed himself in the debt of one of the disputants he would be biased in his favor and would be unable to see the truth as it is (Deuteronomy 16 :19):

> *Thou shalt not wrest judgment; thou shalt not respect persons; neither shalt thou take a gift; for a gift doth blind the eyes of the wise, and pervert the words of the righteous.*

In a remarkable Talmudic passage (*Yoma* 69b) the prophets are declared to have refused to utter praises to God which seemed contrary to their experience because "they knew that the Holy One, blessed be He, is the God of truth and they could not ascribe false things to Him." The Hasidic master R. Menahem Mendel of Kotsk (d. 1859) was called the "pillar of truth" because he battled for this quality all his life. He is reported to have said: "Everything in the world can be imitated except truth. For truth that is imitated is no longer truth!"

The Rabbis believed, on the other hand, that occasionally a "white lie" is permissible, for instance, where the intention is to promote peace and harmony (*Yevamot* 65b). The Talmud (*Bava Mezia* 23b–24a) observes that a scholar will never tell a lie except in the three instances of "tractate," "bed," and "hospitality." The commentators explain "tractate" to mean that a modest scholar is permitted to declare that he is unfamiliar with a tractate of the Mishnah in order not to flaunt his learning. "Bed" is understood to mean by Rashi that if a man is asked intimate questions regarding his marital life he need not answer truthfully. "Hospitality" is understood to mean that a man who has been generously treated by his host may decide not to tell the truth about his reception if he fears that as a result the host will be embarrassed by unwelcome guests.

Vegetarianism

Some have read into Biblical passages the ideal of vegetarianism as a way of life. In the Creation narrative (Genesis 29:30), for instance, both man and the animals are given the herbs of the field for their food and they were not to prey on one another. In Isaiah's vision, too, the "lion shall eat straw like the ox" (Isaiah 11:7). But at the most these passages express an ideal which obtained only at the beginning of Creation and which will obtain at the end of days. It is nowhere suggested in the Bible that vegetarianism is an ideal for men before human history culminates in the Messianic age. When Noah and his sons emerge from the ark the animals are given to them as food (Genesis 9:3).

Judaism is firmly opposed to cruelty to animals but it does allow man to use animals for his needs—to work for him and provide him with wool and milk, for instance—and it even permits him to kill them for food, though it insists that the pain caused to the animals in the process be reduced to the minimum. In the Talmud (*Pesaḥim* 109a) it is said that meat and wine are the means by which man "rejoices" and on this basis it has long been customary for Jews to eat meat and drink wine on the festivals.

The Kabbalists have the idea that when man eats the meat of animals and then worships his Creator with renewed strength he "elevates" the animal by using the strength it has given him in God's service. This is the Kabbalistic interpretation of why the *am ha-arez*, the man who does not study the Torah, may not eat meat (*Pesaḥim* 49b).

There is, of course, no obligation for Jews to eat meat and there are even some Jewish vegetarian societies. But it can be argued that for a Jew to adopt vegetarianism because he objects to killing animals for food is to introduce a moral and theological idea which suggests that Judaism has, in fact, been wrong all the time in not advocating vegetarianism. That is why many traditional Jews tend to look askance at the advocacy of vegetarianism as a way of life superior to the traditional Jewish way.

Welfare State

The principle of care for those unable to care adequately for themselves is stressed in many Pentateuchal regulations. Even if some of the legislation is theoretical it is still indicative of the principle (Leviticus 23:22):

> *And when ye reap the harvest of your land, thou shalt not wholly reap the corner of thy field, neither shalt thou gather the gleaning of thy harvest; thou shalt leave them for the poor, and for the stranger: I am the Lord your God.*

The Deuteronomic rule (Deuteronomy 15:1–11) stresses the duty of the more affluent to care for the needy as well as for creditors to release debts on the seventh year, the "year of release." Similarly, the Deuteronomic legislation has it (Deuteronomy 14:28–29):

> *At the end of every three years, even in the same year, thou shalt bring forth all the tithe of thine increase, and shalt lay it up within thy gates. And the Levite, because he hath no portion nor inheritance with thee, and the stranger, and the fatherless, and the widow, that are within thy gates shall come, and shall eat and be satisfied, that the Lord thy God may bless thee in all the work of thy hand which thou doest.*

Again in Leviticus (19:9) the law is clearly stated:

> *And when ye reap the harvest of your land, thou shalt not wholly reap the corner of thy field, neither shalt thou gather the fallen fruit of thy vineyard; thou shalt leave them for the poor and for the stranger: I am the Lord your God.*

The Biblical principles were put into practice in Jewish communities. As an example the passage in the Babylonian Talmud (*Bava Batra* 8a–11a) can be referred to in which the actual details of communal legislation in the Jewish communities of Babylon are described in full. From the passage it follows that the Babylonian communities, who had a considerable degree of autonomy, made it compulsory for all the inhabitants of a town to contribute toward the digging of new wells, town walls and gates, charitable purposes, the home guard, the supervision of the town armory, and other social purposes. The townspeople were also entitled to fix weights and measures and prices and wages, and to inflict penalties for the infringements of their rules.

Jewish communities everywhere had a pattern of social welfare. The details are fully described in Salo W. Baron's *Jewish Community*.[1] In Rome, Frankfort, Cracow, and other large Jewish communities there were both paid and honorary officials in charge of such matters as public safety and sanitation. There were rules protecting the rights of tenants and controlling rents. Communal support of the poor and provision for the education of poor children were the norm in most Jewish communities. Many Jewish communities maintained hospitals. The leaders of the London community in 1678 declared:

> *It is a general virtue of all the congregations of Israel, in all the places where they dwell, to establish and form a Hebra, which shall practice the meritorious and urgent charity which is due to the sick and dead.*

Many medieval rabbis ruled that one might divert a gift or legacy destined for the building of a synagogue to the erection of a hospital or to any other form of aid for the sick. Widows and orphans were the special care of the community. Baron records that every provincial rabbi of Hesse-Cassel had to take the following oath on assuming office:

> *I wish to take faithful care of the Jews' widows and orphans in all matters under my jurisdiction, and see to it that they be placed by the authorities under capable and reliable guardians, that they be raised in the observance of the Jewish law and ceremonies, and that their property be administered faithfully and suffer from no embezzlement.*

Some communities established special orphan asylums. The community provided poor brides with dowries and trousseaus. Of course, these regulations were not uninfluenced by economic fluctuations and the

---

[1] Vol. 2, Chapter 16, pp. 290–350, Philadelphia, 1945.

particular circumstances of the community concerned. The state of social welfare was not always of the highest, but the spirit of justice, fairness, and compassion advocated by the Bible and Talmud was always an impetus toward the emergence of a more just society in which the strong and powerful help the weak and defenseless.

In the light of all this, and recognizing that the problems after the Industrial Revolution and the rise of capitalism are far more complex than, for instance, in the ghetto period, there is little doubt that the Jewish teachings are strongly in favor of communal care for the sick, of education for all, of adequate provisions, undertaken by the state, for all its citizens. In a word Judaism would approve of the Welfare State.

Women's Liberation

There are many different movements sponsored in modern society with the aim of improving the social position of woman, of granting women a greater degree of freedom, better opportunities, and equality with men. How far Judaism would approve of these movements depends on what exactly they wish to achieve. It can, however, be stated without qualification that Judaism is on the side of justice and would wish injustices against women to be removed.

It cannot be denied that women have suffered certain disabilities under Jewish law. Some of these have been removed by the determined efforts of the Jewish teachers, others still await their solution. On the whole it is true that in theory the Jewish woman is held in the highest regard, but law proceeds and develops slowly so that theory and practice did not always coincide. In the Rabbinic literature, compiled, it must not be overlooked, by men, there are a few sayings uncomplimentary to women such as "Women are unstable" (*Shabbat* 33b); "Women do not take kindly to guests" (*Bava Meẓia* 87a). But these are more than balanced by sayings in praise of women and their virtues: "Women have greater powers of discernment than men" (*Niddah* 45b); "Women have greater powers of faith than men" (*Sifrei* to Numbers 27:6); "Women are compassionate" (*Megillah* 14b); "A man's wife is his home" (*Yoma* 2a); "A man should love his wife as much as himself and respect her more than himself" (*Yevamot* 62b). This last saying and numerous similar Rabbinic teachings would certainly support the demand of women's liberation movements that men should treat women as persons and not as sexual objects. On the question of the career woman it is interesting that, according to the Rabbis, a woman has no obligation to marry (*Yevamot* 65b). She commits no offense if she prefers to carve out a career for herself and compete with men. It is even more interesting that there is no objection in Jewish law to a woman serving as a Rabbi. The Rabbi is not a priest. He is a teacher

331

Prime Minister Golda Meir inspects a guard of honor of the Women's Corps ("Ḥen") of the Israel Defense Forces, at Lydda, 1969.

of the Torah and there is no reason why a woman knowledgeable in the Torah should not act as a teacher. However, so far at least, the idea of a congregation having a woman Rabbi has not caught on (although the first woman Reform rabbi was recently ordained in the U.S.).

The medieval authorities discussed whether a woman could be appointed as a judge. There is no definite Rabbinic statement on this question. In the Bible Deborah was a judge (Judges 4:4). Nonetheless, the majority of teachers hold that a woman cannot be appointed as a judge and that Deborah was in a different category either because she was a prophetess or because the term "judge" meant in her case a leader and not one who gives decisions in a court of law (Tosafists to *Bava Kama* 15a and *Niddah* 50a). Maimonides (*Yad, Melakhim* 1:4) rules that a woman cannot be appointed to any communal office. The commentators find it hard to discover any Rabbinic warrant for Maimonides' ruling. Nevertheless, it is the practice in most Orthodox synagogues to appoint only men to positions of leadership. This problem became particularly acute once the democratically governed State of Israel emerged. With few exceptions, Orthodox Jews in Israel recognized Mrs. Golda Meir as Israel's Prime Minister.

Great strides have, in fact, been made in the State of Israel in the matter of women's rights. An example is the Equal Pay for Equal Work Law of 1964. But in matters of personal status there are still some inequities. For instance, while the consent of both husband and wife is required for a divorce to be valid there are certain circumstances in which a bill of divorce can be delivered to a wife against her will or where the husband is permitted to remarry without a divorce from his first wife. True, these are few and far between and coercion can be exercised against a recalcitrant husband, but some inequality does remain. There are problems, too, regarding the laws of inheritance. On the other hand, in Orthodox Jewish law, it is the religion of the mother which determines whether or not a child is a Jew. The child of a Jewish father and non-Jewish mother is not a Jew while the child of a non-Jewish father and a Jewish mother is a Jew.

In considering this question of women's rights in Judaism reference should also be made to the Mishnah (*Horayot* 3:7), in which it is stated that in some respects a woman takes precedence over a man and in others a man over a woman. If both a man and a woman are in danger and only one can be saved the man's life comes first. (There are other interpretations of this clause in the Mishnah but the one given seems to be correct.) Similarly, if both a man and a woman lose some property and it is only possible to restore the property of one of them, that of the man comes first. On the other hand, a woman must be provided with clothing from the charity chest before a man because she suffers greater embarrassment and for the same reasons if both are captured by bandits the woman must be ransomed first. If both a man and woman stand in danger of defilement by bandits the man must be freed before the woman because his defilement (by other men) is unnatural.

From the above it can be seen that there is considerable tension in this whole matter but that a marked tendency can be discerned in the Jewish sources towards fairness and equity. There are still, however, problems to be faced and solutions to be found.

Work

One of the earliest sayings recorded in *Ethics of the Fathers* (1:10) is that of Shemaiah: "Love work; hate lordship; and seek no intimacy with the ruling power." Dr. J. H. Hertz[1] comments on this:

> *Far from looking upon manual labor as a curse, the Rabbis extolled it as an important factor in man's moral education; and many of the most eminent scholars were manual laborers. The slowness among Western nations to recognize the dignity of labor is no doubt due to the fact that, till quite recent times, classical literature monopolized the education of the governing classes among European peoples. As with the Greeks and Romans, idleness was for ages the mark of nobility.*

Hertz's observation regarding the Greeks and Romans is probably far too much of a generalization. One can no doubt find work extolled in Greek and Roman writings as well as among the Rabbis. But Hertz is right that in much of Jewish teaching work is held to be of great value. A helpful collection of Jewish teachings on this theme has been assembled by Israel H. Levinthal.[2]

A panegyric to work is found in the Rabbinic elaborations to *Ethics of the Fathers,* known as *The Fathers According to Rabbi Nathan.*[3] Among the teachings recorded here are: "A man should love work and no man should hate work." "Even Adam tasted nothing before he worked, as it is said: 'And He put him into the Garden of Eden to dress and to keep it; [only then] of every tree of the garden thou mayest freely eat' (Genesis 2:15f.)." "The Holy One, blessed be He, did not cause His Divine Presence to rest upon Israel before they did work,

---

[1] *Authorized Daily Prayer Book,* p. 621, London, 1947.

[2] *Judaism: An Analysis and Interpretation,* pp. 209–242, New York, 1935.

[3] Trans. Judah Goldin, Chapter 11, pp. 60–61, New Haven, 1955.

as it is said: 'And let them make Me a sanctuary, then shall I dwell among them' (Exodus 25:8).'' "If a man has no work to do, what should he do? If he has a run-down yard or run-down field let him go and occupy himself with it."

Remarkable is a Rabbinic interpretation (*Pesaḥim* 118a) of Adam's curse (Genesis 3:17–19):

> *Cursed is the ground for thy sake; in toil shalt thou eat of it all the days of thy life. Thorns also and thistles shall it bring forth to thee; and thou shalt eat the herb of the field. In the sweat of thy face shalt thou eat bread . . .*

Adam was disturbed, according to this comment, when he heard that he was to eat the herb of the field, for this would make him no different from his ass whose food is ready to hand. When, however, Adam heard that he was to toil for his daily bread his mind was set at rest. The dignity of man is seen in the effort he has to make in order to earn a living. It is in this that he is elevated above the animal. It is part of what the Rabbis refer to when they speak of man as a co-partner with God in the work of creation (*Shabbat* 119b). Another famous Rabbinic saying in praise of work runs (*Berakhot* 8a):

> *A man who lives from the labor of his hands is greater than the one who fears heaven. For with regard to the one who fears heaven it is written: "Happy is the man that feareth the Lord" (Psalms 112:1) while with regard to the man who lives from his own work it is written: "When thou eatest the labor of thy hands, happy shalt thou be, and it shall be well with thee" (Psalms 128:2). This means: "Happy shalt thou be" in this world, "and it shall be well with thee" in the world to come. But of the man that fears heaven it is not written: "and it shall be well with thee."*

The great Babylonian teacher Rav urged his disciple R. Kahana: "Rather skin a carcass for a fee in the market than be supported by charity. Do not say: 'I am a priest' or 'I am a great man' and it is beneath my dignity" (*Pesaḥim* 113a).

Levinthal concludes his summary of the Jewish teachings on the dignity of labor with a plea that this aspect of Judaism be adequately recognized:

> *Suffice it at this time to say, in answer to the indictment of modern labor against Religion and the Church, that the Jew*

can, with a clear conscience, plead: Not Guilty! Of all the religions, of all the cultures and civilizations of ancient and modern times, Judaism can truly claim that she has always recognized the dignity, the nobility, the sacredness of labor; that she has always known how to evaluate its true worth and essential need in the life of man, and that she still has a living, vital message to the modern man and to a modern world!

Reference must be made to A. D. Gordon's (1856–1922) "religion of labor," which has had the greatest influence on the kibbutz movement in Israel. At the age of 48 Gordon settled in Palestine to till the soil with his own hands and to preach that modern man can rediscover God by working close to nature in the fields.

For all that, in our world, the ideal of work must not be made into a fetish. Most of the modern problem is that so many men are doomed to perform routine and boring tasks. If the machine can help man to achieve far greater opportunities for leisure there is no valid reason for opposing this on the grounds of the sanctity of work. Something of this idea is contained in the old Jewish teachings about the need for every man to set aside time each day for the study of the Torah. The problem increasingly to be faced is not so much that of work as of leisure. The Jewish ideal of work as dignified, in that through it man becomes self-supporting and is able to look after his family, is far removed from any ideal of work for work's sake. The Rabbis (*Berakhot* 32b) tell of the "saints of old" whose work was "blessed" so that they were able to earn their living without too much effort and so devote more time to prayer. There are obvious disadvantages in the machine age, but one of its advantages, and it should not be resisted through any spurious assessment of the total demands of labor and effort, is that it makes it possible for man's work to be "blessed" and so releases him to spend his time as he wishes.

Zen

From one point of view it is absurd to ask what Judaism has to say about Zen. As a branch of Buddhism and the discipline of a particular culture, the Japanese Zen is a totally different way of life from Judaism. The two are quite incompatible, so that no person can consistently embrace both Judaism and Zen at the same time. Zen in its "pop" or "hippie" form has sometimes won adherents in the Western world but such a manifestation is hardly authentic Zen in any event. Added to this is the notorious difficulty of grasping the Zen philosophy, which prides itself in being neither a philosophy nor something to be grasped. The elusiveness of Zen is another reason why it is futile to engage in any serious discussion of what Judaism has to say about it. The most that can be attempted is to see whether here and there in Judaism teachings are to be found which seem to parallel what some of the Zen masters appear to be saying.

The Zen masters, for example, frequently suggest that the way to grasp reality is to relinquish the quest for meaning and yield to life. A favorite illustration is that of the bough covered with snow. If the bough, bending under the weight of the snow, is sufficiently pliant it will yield under the pressure so that when the snow melts the bough will still be firm on the tree. If the bough is too rigid the weight of the snow will cause it to snap. Japanese wrestling and archery seem to be based on the same principle. The opponent is vanquished, the target reached, by not struggling too much against the resistance offered. This idea is not unknown in the Jewish sources. A famous Talmudic passage (*Eruvin* 13b) discussed why a "heavenly voice" decided in favor of the School of Hillel against the School of Shammai, though both were "the words of the living God." The reason given for this decision is that the School of Hillel was less concerned with fame, less bothered by the desire that its views should be adopted. The passage continues:

> *This teaches you that him who humbles himself the Holy One,*
> *blessed be He, raises up, and him who exalts himself the*
> *Holy One, blessed be He, humbles; from him who seeks fame,*
> *fame flees but him who flees from fame, fame follows; he who*
> *forces the hour is pushed back by the hour but he who allows*
> *himself to be pushed back by the hour finds the hour pushed*
> *back on his behalf.*

But even in passages such as this one, it is God's will that is stressed. Man should not be too eager, too grasping, too avid for experience, not because, paradoxically, this will enable him to know more of life but because ultimately it is God's will that he wishes to be done and not his own. The Zen masters speak of the ideal of living as if one were already dead. Something similar is said by the early Ḥasidic master, R. Elimelech of Lyzhansk, but, again, with the emphasis on self-abandonment in service of the divine. R. Elimelech remarks (*Noam Elimelekh, Ḥayei Sarah* beg.) that the *Ẓaddik* who brings down the divine flow of grace from above should have no thought for himself at all "as if he were not in this world."

In fact, an attempt has been made by Martin Buber, in an essay entitled "The Place of Ḥasidism in the History of Religion," to point out resemblances between Ḥasidism and Zen. The essay impressed people with an interest in Zen sufficiently to have it reprinted in the *Anthology of Zen.*[1] For instance, both in Ḥasidism and Zen (and, for that matter, in other mystical traditions), there are tales of a master refusing to open the door to a disciple who declared "I am here" because the disciple, aware of his "I," is still remote from enlightenment. But Buber's treatment here and elsewhere suffers from his contention that Ḥasidism does not seek to abolish the "I" but insists on the "I-Thou" relationship. It is highly questionable whether this view of Ḥasidism is correct. The main difference in this matter which emerges from any comparison of Ḥasidism with Zen is that in Zen the "I" is left behind in order to attain enlightenment; in Ḥasidism it is left behind in order to discover God.

---

[1] Ed. William Briggs, pp. 225–237, New York, 1961.

GLOSSARY

Amora (pl. **amoraim**), title given to the Jewish scholars in Ereẓ Israel and Babylonia in the third to sixth centuries who were responsible for the *Gemara*.

Ashkenazi (pl. **Ashkenazim**), German or West-, Central-, or East-European Jew(s), as contrasted with Sephardi(m).

Badḥan, jester, particularly at traditional Jewish weddings in Eastern Europe.

Bar, "son of . . ."; frequently appearing in personal names.

Baraita (pl. **beraitot**), statement of *tanna* not found in Mishnah.

Bar mitzvah, initiation of a boy of 13 into the Jewish religious community.

Ben, "son of . . ."; frequently appearing in personal names.

Bet din, Rabbinic court of law.

Bet ha-midrash, school for higher Rabbinic learning; often attached to or serving as a synagogue.

Conservative Judaism, trend in Judaism developed in the U. S. in the 20th cent. which, while opposing extreme changes in traditional observances, permits certain modifications of *halakhah* in response to modern demands.

Diaspora, Jews living in the area of Jewish settlement outside Ereẓ Israel.

Ereẓ Israel, Land of Israel; Palestine.

Exilarch, lay head of Jewish community in Babylonia and elsewhere.

Gemara, traditions, discussions, and rulings of the *amoraim*, commenting on the Mishnah, and part of the Babylonian and Palestinian Talmuds.

Get, bill of divorce.

Ḥabad, initials of *ḥokhmah, binah, da'at*: "wisdom, understanding, knowledge"; ḥasidic movement founded in White Russia by Shneor Zalman of Lyady.

Haggadah, ritual recited in the home on Passover eve at *seder* table.

Ḥanukkah, eight-day celebration marking victory of Judah Maccabee over Syrian king Antiochus Epiphanes and rededication of the Temple.

Ḥasid, adherent of Ḥasidism.

Ḥasidei Ashkenaz, medieval pietist movement among the Jews of Germany.

Ḥasidism, (1) religious revivalist movement of popular mysticism among Jews of Western Germany in the Middle Ages; (2) religious movement founded by Israel ben Eliezer Ba'al Shem Tov in the first half of the 18th century.

Haskalah, "Enlightenment"; movement for spreading modern European culture among Jews c. 1750–1880. An adherent was termed *maskil*.

Havdalah, ceremony marking the end of Sabbath.

Ḥazzan, leader of prayers in synagogue; previously a synagogue official.

Kabbalah, the Jewish mystical tradition.

Karaite, member of a Jewish sect originating in the eighth century which rejected Rabbinic (Rabbanite) Judaism and accepted only Scripture as authoritative.

Ketubbah, marriage contract, stipulating husband's obligations to wife.

Kiddush, sanctification prayer over wine or bread on Sabbaths and festivals.

339

Kohen (pl. **Kohanim**), Jew(s) of priestly (Aaronide) descent.

Kosher, ritually permissible food.

Lulav, palm branch; one of the "four species" used on Sukkot together with the *etrog* (citron), *hadas* (myrtle), and *aravah* (willow).

Maggid, popular preacher.

Mahzor (pl. **mahzorim**), festival prayer book.

Maskil (pl. **maskilim**), adherent of Haskalah ("Enlightenment") movement.

Menorah, candelabrum; seven-branched oil lamp used in the Tabernacle and Temple; also eight-branched candelabrum used on Hanukkah.

Midrash, interpreting Scripture to elucidate legal points *(Midrash Halakhah)* or to bring out lessons by stories or homiletics *(Midrash Aggadah)*.

Mikveh, ritual bath.

Mishnah, earliest codification of Jewish Oral Law.

Mitnagged (pl. **Mitnaggedim**), opponents of Hasidism in Eastern Europe.

Mitzvah, biblical or rabbinic injunction; applied also to good deeds.

Musar movement, ethical movement developing in the latter part of the 19th century among Orthodox Jewish groups in Lithuania; founded by R. Israel Lipkin (Salanter).

Nazirite, a person who vows (sometimes for a specific period) to abstain from grapes or their products, cutting the hair, and touching a corpse.

Neturei Karta, group of ultrareligious extremists, who do not recognize the establishment of a secular Jewish state in Erez Israel.

Orthodoxy (Orthodox Judaism), modern term for the strictly traditional sector of Jewry.

Passover, a spring festival commemorating the Exodus from Egypt.

Purim, festival held on Adar 14 or 15 in commemoration of the deliverance of the Jews of Persia in the time of Esther.

Rabban, honorific title higher than that of rabbi, applied to heads of the Sanhedrin in Mishnaic times.

Rabbi, a Talmudic sage (strictly speaking, one who had been ordained in Erez Israel, a Babylonian sage being referred to as *rav*); from the Middle Ages, the spiritual leader of the Jewish congregation or community.

Reb, rebbe, Yiddish for rabbi, applied generally to a teacher or Hasidic rabbi.

Reform Judaism, trend in Judaism advocating modification of Orthodoxy in conformity with the exigencies of contemporary life and thought.

Responsum (pl. **responsa**), written opinion given to question on aspects of Jewish law by qualified authorities; pl. collection of such queries and opinions in book form.

Rosh Ha-Shanah, two-day New Year holiday (one day in biblical and early mishnaic times) at the beginning of the month of Tishri.

Sanhedrin, the assembly of ordained scholars which functioned both as a supreme court and as a legislature before 70 C.E. In modern times the name was given to the body of representative Jews convoked by Napoleon in 1807.

Seder, ceremony observed in the Jewish home on the first night of Passover (outside Erez Israel first two nights), when the *Haggadah* is recited.

Sefer Torah, manuscript scroll of the Pentateuch for public reading in synagogue.

Sephardi (pl. **Sephardim**), Jew(s) of Spain and Portugal and their descendants, wherever resident, as contrasted with Ashkenazi(m).

Shavuot, Pentecost; Festival of Weeks; second of the three annual pilgrim festivals commemorating the receiving of the Torah at Mt. Sinai.

Shekhinah, Divine Presence.

Shema (*Yisrael*; . . . "hear (O Israel)," Deut. 6:4), Judaism's confession of faith, proclaiming the absolute unity of God.

Shofar, horn of the ram (or any other ritually clean animal excepting the cow) sounded for the memorial blowing on Rosh Ha-Shanah, and other occasions.

Shulḥan Arukh, Joseph Caro's code of Jewish law (1564–65) in four parts: *Oraḥ Ḥayyim*, laws relating to prayers, Sabbath, festivals, and fasts; *Yoreh Deah*, dietary laws, etc; *Even ha-Ezer*, laws dealing with women, marriage, etc; *Ḥoshen Mishpat*, civil, criminal law, court procedure, etc.

Sifra, a Halakhic Midrash to the Book of Leviticus.

Sifrei, a Halakhic Midrash to the books of Numbers and Deuteronomy.

Sukkah, booth or tabernacle erected for Sukkot when, for seven days, religious Jews "dwell" or at least eat in the *sukkah* (Lev. 23:42).

Talmud, "teaching"; compendium of discussions on the Mishnah by generations of scholars and jurists in many academies over a period of several centuries. The Jerusalem (or Palestinian) Talmud mainly contains the discussions of the Palestinian sages. The Babylonian Talmud incorporates the parallel discussions in the Babylonian academies.

Tefillin, phylacteries, small leather cases containing passages from Scripture and affixed on the forehead and arm by male Jews during morning prayers.

Terefah, food that is not *kosher*, owing to a defect in the animal.

Torah, Pentateuch or the Pentateuchal scroll for reading in synagogue; entire body of traditional Jewish teaching and literature.

Tosafist, talmudic glossator, mainly French (12th–14th centuries), bringing additions to the commentary by Rashi.

Yeshivah (pl. **Yeshivot**), Jewish traditional academy devoted primarily to study of the Talmud and rabbinic literature.

Yom Kippur, Day of Atonement, solemn fast day observed on the 10th of Tishri.

Zaddik, person outstanding for his piety; especially a Ḥasidic rabbi or leader.

Zizit, fringes attached to the *tallit* (prayer shawl) and *tallit katan* (garment worn beneath clothing by observant male Jews).

Zohar, mystical commentary on the Pentateuch; main textbook of Kabbalah.

INDEX OF SCHOLARS QUOTED

ILLUSTRATION CREDITS

London, British Museum, Add. 27210, fol. 3r, p. 15

New York, Jewish Theological Seminary, Ms. Mic. 4817, page 15b, p. 26

Courtesy: Hauptampt fuer Hochbauwesen, Photo Ferd, Schmidt, Nuremberg, p. 31

Photo Alinari, Florence, p. 32

Photo courtesy: Union of American Hebrew Congregations, p. 33

Jerusalem, Israel Museum, p. 37

Photo David Harris, Jerusalem, p. 37, 80

New York, Jewish Theological Seminary, p. 39

London, British Museum, Add. 11639, fol. 516v, p. 49

Tel Aviv, Israel Government Press Office, p. 56, 205, 303, 332

Jerusalem, Israel Department of Antiquities and Museums, p. 61

London, British Museum, Or. 1067, p. 73

Cecil Roth Collection, p. 80, 112, 152

Jerusalem, J. N. U. L., p. 99

Courtesy T. Schrire, Capetown, p. 131

London, British Museum, Add. 23162, fol. 6v, p. 146

Prague, State Jewish Museum, p. 149

Milan, Ambrosian Library Ms. B. 32 inf. fol. 136, p. 160

Jerusalem, Israel Museum Reproduction Archives, p. 180

Dublin, Chester Beatty Library, Ms. 414 fol. 68v, p. 193

Jerusalem, J. N. U. L., Ms. Heb. 4°1193, fol. 32, p. 208

Photo M. Ninio, Jerusalem, p. 215

Photo R. Cleave, Jerusalem, p. 220

Leipzig University Library, Ms. V. 1102 Vol. I, fol. 131, p. 238

New York, Oscar Gruss Collection, p. 249

Photo Frank J. Darmstaedter, New York, p. 249

Courtesy Schocken Books, New York, p. 254

Copenhagen, Royal Library, Cod. Heb. 32, fol. 10v, p. 264

Hamburg, Staats- und Universitaetsbibliothek, Cod. Heb. 37, fol. 79v, p. 283